Media Law in Kuwait

Media Law in Kuwait

Mariam Alkazemi
Ali A. Dashti
Ildiko Kaposi
Matt J. Duffy†

This book was originally published as a monograph in the International Encyclopaedia of Laws/Media Law.

Founding Editor: Roger Blanpain
General Editor: Frank Hendrickx
Volume Editors: Peggy Valcke & Eva Lievens

Wolters Kluwer

Published by:
Kluwer Law International B.V.
PO Box 316
2400 AH Alphen aan den Rijn
The Netherlands
E-mail: international-sales@wolterskluwer.com
Website: lrus.wolterskluwer.com

Sold and distributed in North, Central and South America by:
Wolters Kluwer Legal & Regulatory U.S.
7201 McKinney Circle
Frederick, MD 21704
United States of America
Email: customer.service@wolterskluwer.com

Sold and distributed in all other countries by:
Air Business Subscriptions
Rockwood House
Haywards Heath
West Sussex
RH16 3DH
United Kingdom
Email: international-customerservice@wolterskluwer.com

Printed on acid-free paper

ISBN 978-94-035-0311-0

e-Book: ISBN 978-94-035-0192-5
web-PDF: ISBN 978-94-035-0245-8

Printed in the United Kingdom.

The Authors

Mariam Alkazemi (PhD, 2014, University of Florida) is Assistant Professor of mass communication at the Gulf University for Science and Technology in Kuwait, where she teaches courses in research methods, public relations, and advertising. Her research appears in *Communication Law & Policy*, *International Communication Gazette*, *Journal of Media and Religion*, and *Journalism: Theory, Practice & Criticism* among others. Dr. Alkazemi has been a recipient of several awards for teaching and research. Further, she has served as a research fellow at the London School of Economics and a Carnegie fellow in support of the Arab social sciences at the University of North Carolina in Chapel Hill. Dr. Alkazemi holds degrees from George Washington University (BA, 2007, Journalism) and Michigan State University (MA, 2009, Advertising/Public Relations). Dr. Alkazemi plans on joining Virginia Commonwealth University in the fall 2018 semester.

The Authors

Ali A. Dashti is an Associate Professor in the Mass Communication department at Gulf University for Science & Technology. Dashti has worked in numerous fields, ranging from being a staff writer for school newspapers to TV reporting, public relations, and political campaigns. He has published numerous papers related to media studies, women studies, social media, and political communication. His doctoral dissertation is titled "The Effect of Online Journalism on the freedom of the Press: The Case of Kuwait" from the University of Stirling in Scotland. He earned his BA in Journalism and Political Science from Eastern Illinois University and his MS in mass communication from Kansas State University. Dashti has taught introductory and advanced courses in Mass Communication and served in various committees. In 1990, he served in the US Army during Operation Desert Shield and Desert Storm as a translator for the 66th Military Intelligence. He is the author of "*Sergeant over One Week*" & "*How 0.01 Can Change Your Life.*"

The Authors

Ildiko Kaposi is a social scientist whose work focuses on issues of democracy from the perspective of media and communication. She has studied the roles of the press and Internet in fostering participation in emerging or transitioning democracies in post-communist Europe and the Middle East. Employing mainly qualitative but also quantitative methods she specializes in in-depth explorations of the intersections of democratic principles and their interpretations in specific social, legal, political, and cultural contexts. She is Assistant Professor at the Mass Communication and Media department of the Gulf University of Science and Technology, Kuwait, where she teaches Media Law.

The Authors

Dr. Matt J. Duffy taught journalism, international media law, and ethics. He specializes on Middle Eastern journalism and media law, and his book "Media Laws of the United Arab Emirates" was published in 2014 by Wolters Kluwer. His peer-reviewed publications appear in *Journal of Middle East Media, Journal of Mass Media Ethics, Newspaper Research Journal,* and *Communication Law & Policy*. He earned his Ph.D. in Public Communication from Georgia State University He currently serves as an Assistant Professor at Kennesaw State University in Kennesaw, Georgia. Dr. Duffy also serves on the board of the Arab-United States Association for Communication Educators, an organization that aims to improve journalism in the Middle East. Dr. Duffy, who encouraged his coauthors to write this book when he was invited to a social media conference by the Kuwaiti Ministry of Information, died on January 17, 2018.

Table of Contents

Table of Contents

Table of Contents

Preface

On a global level, this year has been an extremely interesting time to write a book about media law. The Committee to Protect Journalists (CPJ) reported several threats against journalists in the United States following articles about a suicide[1] as well as for their coverage of political affairs.[2] Similarly, security concerns have threatened the protections journalists provide to their sources in the United Kingdom.[3] Thus, media freedoms and privacy have been salient issues in developed nations.

In the developing world, and particularly in the Middle East and North Africa, this year has seen even more developments influencing the advancement or withdrawal of media freedoms. Some of the activities that have been reported by the CPJ include nations such as Morocco, Yemen, Bahrain, Qatar, Saudi Arabia, and Jordan.[4] In June 2017, CPJ reported that some members of the Arab Gulf States wanted to restrict one nation's media ability to criticize "the leadership of other member states."[5]

These regional and global events shed light on the importance of understanding the media laws in the Gulf States and place them within context of the legal system, as well as the cultural and social practices that affect them. The idea of this book was born at a conference in which Dr. Matt J. Duffy was flown out to Kuwait thanks to the State of Kuwait's Ministry of Information's International Press Office as well as the Kuwaiti Ministry of Foreign Affairs. There, he met with Kuwaiti scholars who agreed about the absence of literature on Kuwaiti media law. This book was written for scholars, communication and legal practitioners, and students of Kuwait. The authors hope that it would help develop an understanding of Kuwaiti media law that could also serve as a comprehensive starting point for assessment of future developments. As the book idea developed and the health conditions of the authors changed, the inclusion of a fourth author with experience teaching media law at a university in Kuwait was invaluable.

In developing this project, the authors received inputs from legal and media institutions, lawyers, professors, journalists, librarians, businessmen, and more. We would like to acknowledge and thank these professionals for their supportive services. Further, we would like to give a special acknowledgement to the families of the authors

1. Committee to Protect Journalists (CPJ), *Noose left at U.S. newspaper's office door at* https://cpj.org/2017/04/noose-left-at-us-newspapers-office-door.php (accessed Jan. 17, 2018).
2. Alexandra Ellerbeck, *Security risk for sources as U.S. border agents stop and search journalists CPJ* at https://cpj.org/blog/2016/12/security-risk-for-sources-as-us-border-agents-stop.php (accessed Jul. 29, 2017).
3. CPJ, *Expanded surveillance powers could threaten work of journalists in UK*, https://cpj.org/2017/05/expanded-surveillance-powers-could-threaten-work-o.php (accessed Jan. 17, 2018).
4. CPJ, *Middle East and North Africa*, https://cpj.org/mideast/ (accessed Jul. 29, 2017).
5. Justin Shilad. *Amid Gulf Tensions, Press Is Used as a Political Pawn.* PJ at https://cpj.org/blog/2017/06/amid-gulf-tensions-press-is-used-as-a-political-pa.php (accessed Jan. 17, 2018).

who offered support and encouragement throughout the completion of this project, which coincided with less than ideal health circumstances for some of the authors. The time and effort we spent collecting laws, translating them, contextualizing them, and making them accessible is worthwhile when it can be of service to our profession and society. We hope that our work can be used for the sake of improving the understanding, practices, and policies of the Kuwaiti media.

General Introduction

§1. General Background of Kuwait

I. Political and Legal System of the State of Kuwait

A. *Introduction*

1. Freedom House is an organization that measures freedom of the press around the globe by considering the legal, political, and economic environment in their evaluations. Some of the legal indicators examine constitutional provisions for freedom of the press, the judiciary's support of such freedoms, and any obstructions to the implementation of such laws pertaining to them.[6] Further, the indicators examine protections provided to public officials, threats to journalists, and procedures put into place for handling such threats. The laws are examined for their ease of establishing media firms and their ease of obtaining public information in addition to other concerns. As for political indicators, attention is paid to pressure applied to journalists from public officials and media corporations to influence media content. Among the political factors the Freedom House[7] examines the degree to which news is partisan, the professional trajectories of journalists, the degree to which journalists can access unofficial sources, the presence of censorship bodies, the practice of self-censorship, the diversity of news content, and the diversity of media personnel. Finally, economic factors that are examined in relation to press freedom include the degrees to which private and state-owned media operate in a given country as well as the independence of the media from the editorial stances of the state or of the company. Transparency of ownership for private media enterprises, the political affiliation of these owners, the influences of ownership on media content, and the application of fees or provisions of funding to media organizations are also put into consideration in Freedom House's evaluations.[8]

2. Examinations of the validity of Freedom House's data have been considered credible due to studies, such as that of Becker, Vlad and Nusser[9] that demonstrate fluctuations in media freedoms after changes in political systems in Eastern Europe.

6. Freedom House (FH). *Freedom of the Press 2016 Methodology*. https://freedomhouse.org/report/freedom-press-2016-methodology (accessed Jan. 17, 2018).
7. *Ibid.*
8. *Ibid.*
9. Lee B. Becker, Tudor Vlad & Nancy Nusser. *An Evaluation of Press Freedom Indicators*. 69 International Communication Gazette. 5, 28. (2007).

In the Middle East, such changes were reflected in media freedom scores in 2012 when Tunisia rose in rankings after significant legal reform in the aftermath of the Arab uprisings that had taken place in the early 2010.[10] In the case of Kuwait, the media freedom ranking has been "partly free" since 2002, the earliest date available on their websites, despite fluctuations in the regional rankings over time[11]. Similarly, *Reporters without Borders'* website shows that no journalists, citizens, or media assistants were killed in Kuwait in the given calendar year by April 2017.[12]

3. A constitutional emirate, the Kuwaiti government consists of both appointed and elected officials.[13] The head of state is a hereditary Amir, who appoints a Prime Minister and his cabinet of ministers.[14] Elected officials consist of members of the parliament, who sit on the meetings of the National Assembly along with the cabinet of ministers.[15]

4. Conflict often arises between the elected and appointed members of the National Assembly, and the Emir has the power to dissolve parliament when the two groups cannot get along.[16] When the National Assembly is dissolved, Kuwait's freedom of speech and press are limited and censorship occurs.[17] This sentiment is reiterated by the Middle Eastern Law professor, Chibli Mallat, who stated that one must view the Middle Eastern court systems within the political system in which they exist. According to Mallat,[18] Kuwait is one of the least repressive countries in the Middle East despite its occasional censorship. Therefore, Chapter 1 provides information about the organization of the political system and the court system in Kuwait.

5. As Kuwaiti democracy developed, political changes have reflected changes in the demographics of Kuwait's population.[19] For example, four liberal candidates became the first female members of parliament in the May 2009 elections after women were enfranchised in 2005.[20]

10. FH. *Tunisia.* https://freedomhouse.org/report/freedom-press/2012/tunisia (accessed Jan. 17, 2018).
11. FH. *Kuwait.* https://freedomhouse.org/report/freedom-press/2016/kuwait (accessed Jan. 17, 2018).
12. Reporters without Borders (RSF). *Kuwait.* https://rsf.org/en/taxonomy/term/163 (accessed Jan. 17, 2018).
13. Rania Al-Nakib *Human Rights, Education for Democratic Citizenship and International Organisations: Findings from a Kuwaiti UNESCO ASPnet School.* 42 Cambridge Journal of Education. 97,112. (2012).
14. *Ibid.*
15. *Ibid.*
16. *Ibid.*
17. Nabeel A. Jurdi & Ali A Dashti. *Communication Policies in the State of Kuwait.* 96 Annals of The Faculty of Arts XIV (1994).
18. Chibli Mallat. *Introduction to Middle Eastern Law.* (Kindle ed., Oxford University Press on Demand, 2007).
19. Rania Al-Nakib *Human Rights, Education for Democratic Citizenship and International Organisations: Findings from a Kuwaiti UNESCO ASPnet School.* 42 Cambridge Journal of Education. 97,112. (2012).
20. *Ibid.*

B. The Constitutional Emirate State Structure

6. Although the first elections in Kuwait can be traced to the 1930s, they preceded Kuwait's independence from the British colonial administrators.[21] Upon its independence in 1961, Kuwait's Constitution established an electoral system that borrowed from the British electoral system.[22] Ratified in 1962, the Kuwaiti Constitution allows for a democratic system.[23] Its provisions establish several branches of government that share power in Kuwait, including the monarchy, executive, legislative, judiciary, military, and administrative proceedings by which financial decisions regarding the state budget are made.

7. The Kuwaiti Constitution establishes a monarchy between Articles 54 and 78.[24] The monarch, called an Amir, has the power to appoint ministers to National Assembly; however, two-thirds of the members of the National Assembly must be elected by the people.[25] In Article 56, the Constitution provides the monarch the power to appoint and dismiss prime ministers, and Article 57 specifies that the entire Cabinet of Ministers must be reconstituted in every new legislative term of the National Assembly.[26] The Constitution also includes provisions for a Deputy Head of State that is expected to exercise power in the state while the monarch is traveling.[27] For a law to be passed in Kuwait, two-thirds of the National Assembly must vote for it, and then the Amir has thirty days from the day it was submitted to him in order to put it into effect.[28] Article 65 explains that national holidays do not count as part of the thirty-day period, and this time period can be reduced to seven days in urgent matters.[29] Article 68 of the Kuwaiti Constitution gives the Amir the power to declare defensive war and outlaws offensive war.[30]

8. The executive power in Kuwait, established in Articles 123–133 of the Constitution, consists of the Prime Minister and the Cabinet of Ministers.[31] The Prime Minister's role is to supervise and coordinate between the various ministries, according to Article 127.[32] The Constitution makes the deliberations of the Cabinet of Ministers private and secretive in Article 128, which also commits the ministers with a minority opinion to the decisions made.[33] In case there are equal votes, the Constitution awards the Prime Minister's side more power to make decisions.[34]

---

21. Abdullah Al-Remaidhi & Bob Watt. *Electoral Constituencies and Political Parties in Kuwait: An Assessment.* 11 Election Law Journal. 518,528 (2012).
22. *Ibid.*
23. *Ibid.*
24. *Ibid.*
25. Kuwait National Assembly. *Aldistour Alkuwaiti* http://www.kna.kw/clt-html5/run.asp?id=2024 (accessed Jan. 17, 2018).
26. *Ibid.*
27. *Ibid.*
28. *Ibid.*
29. *Ibid.*
30. *Ibid.*
31. *Ibid.*
32. *Ibid.*
33. *Ibid.*
34. *Ibid.*

9. In Article 55, the Constitution clearly states, "the Amir exercises his powers through his Ministers."[35] Article 123 lays out the functions of the Council of Ministers in the government. The Council "has control over the departments of the state. It formulates the general policy of the government, pursues its execution, and supervises the conduct of work in government departments."[36] Furthermore, Article 130 explains the job of the minister which is "to supervise the affairs of his ministry and shall carry out the general government policy concerning it. He shall also determine the ministry's policies and supervise their execution."[37]

10. The National Assembly was dissolved eleven times since its first elections in 1963. Article 102 of the Constitution states that if the prime minister is not cooperating with the National Assembly, the matter can be upheld to the Amir who will decide either to dissolve the Council of Ministers or the National Assembly.[38]

11. Kuwait's legislative power, the National Assembly, is established in Articles 79–122 of the Constitution. Article 79 states that the National Assembly has the power to pass laws, as long as they are made effective by the Amir.[39] Article 80 states that the National Assembly is made up of fifty elected members that are decided upon through a confidential and direct elections process that is described by the electoral law.[40] Ministers are considered members of the National Assembly, although they are appointed.[41] Article 81 states that the districts of constituents are decided upon by a law. Article 82 sets the requirements for a Member of the National Assembly: Kuwaiti citizenship, meeting criteria set by electoral laws, exceeding the age of 30, and Arabic literacy. Article 83 states that the National Assembly's term is four years after its first meeting.[42] In its first session, Article 92 states that the National Assembly must decide upon a president, often referred to as a Speaker of the House, in addition to a vice president.[43] Article 94 makes the sessions of the National Assembly public, with exceptions for sessions that are called upon by the Speaker of the House, the Cabinet of Ministers, or requested by a group of ten members of the National Assembly.[44]

12. The Kuwaiti judiciary power is established in Articles 162–173.[45] Article 164 provides several courts with varying levels of power and types of jurisdictions. Article 165 states that court hearings are public, with exceptions established by law. Article 167 gives the General Prosecutor's Office the right to enforce criminal law and enforce sentences. The Constitution establishes that laws will regulate the administrative needs, decision-making processes, and conflict resolution processes within the judicial branch of the Kuwaiti government.

---

35. Constitute. *Kuwait's Constitution of 1962 Reinstated in 1992.* https://www.constituteproject.org/constitution/Kuwait_1992.pdf?lang=en (accessed May 15, 2017).
36. *Ibid.*
37. *Ibid.*
38. *Ibid.*
39. Kuwait National Assembly. *Aldistour Alkuwaiti* http://www.kna.kw/clt-html5/run.asp?id=2024 (accessed Jan. 17, 2018).
40. *Ibid.*
41. *Ibid.*
42. *Ibid.*
43. *Ibid.*
44. *Ibid.*
45. *Ibid.*

13. According to the Kuwaiti Constitution, the military is regulated by law.[46] Articles 157–161 state that the goal of Kuwait's military affairs is to ensure peace and security of every citizen.[47] Administrative proceedings by which financial decisions regarding the state budget are made are also regulated by provisions in the Constitution.[48] For example, Article 134 says that the establishment of taxes can only be implemented through law.[49]

14. Kuwait distinguishes itself from other Arab Gulf states with its "extensive experience" with its parliament, which has convened "most years since 1963."[50] Parliamentary elections matter in Kuwait for several reasons, including the influence of the National Assembly in "setting the public agenda."[51] The degree to which democracy has developed in Kuwait can be influenced by both internal and external pressures. External pressures include foreign relations, particularly in the aftermath of the Iraqi invasion of Kuwait. Internal pressures include the inclusion of women in public life, a relatively independent press, and a unique national character of the Kuwaiti people.

15. An examination of external pressures can be helpful in emphasizing the importance of the internal dynamics of democracy in Kuwait. Yetiv[52] wrote about complaints by U.S. leaders after the liberation of Kuwait from the Iraqi invasion that the United States was not protecting a democracy, but a monarchy. According to Yetiv,[53] leadership from Kuwait understood the importance of hiring public relations practitioners to improve the perceptions of Kuwait as a nation that treats women as second-hand citizens and lacks democracy. Even scholars, like Yetiv,[54] who understand the international context in which Kuwait's democracy developed, acknowledge that the "internal dynamics are central in explaining" advances in democratization as well as improvements to the status of women—which was often opposed by Islamists elected to parliament.[55] Yetiv[56] cites the U.S. ambassador applauding the October 1992 elections as facilitating grassroots political movements. Thus, it is extremely important to examine the role of internal factors that lead to democratic developments in Kuwait.

16. The monarchy in Kuwait "shapes the likely path of any further democratization."[57] Women, who make up approximately half of the Kuwaiti population, received the right to vote and hold public offices in May 2005.[58] According to Thuroczy,[59] the Amir

---

46. *Ibid.*
47. *Ibid.*
48. *Ibid.*
49. *Ibid.*
50. Michael Herb. *Emirs and Parliaments in the Gulf.* 13 Journal of Democracy. 41. (2002).
51. *Ibid.*
52. Steve Yetiv. *Kuwait's Democratic Experiment in Its Broader International Context.* The Middle East Journal. 247,271. (2002).
53. *Ibid.*
54. *Ibid.*
55. *Ibid., 260.*
56. *Ibid., 247,271.*
57. Michael Herb. *Emirs and Parliaments in the Gulf.* 13 Journal of Democracy. 43. (2002).
58. Ferencz Attila Thuroczy. *Kuwait: Democratization in Process: Five Factors of Democratization and Their State in Kuwait.* (Lund University, 2010).
59. *Ibid.*

first published a decree to include women in the public sphere in 1999 but withdrew it due to opposition. Herb[60] claims that the "Kuwaiti National Assembly is best known in the West for its 1999 rejection of the Amir's proposal to allow women to vote."[61] At that time, thirty members voted for the inclusion of women in the public sphere, but thirty-two voted against it.[62] Then, in 2005, thirty-five members of parliament voted to include women in the public sphere while twenty-three voted against the measure. Thuroczy[63] credits the inclusion of women in politics as one of the factors that has allowed democracy to further develop in Kuwait.

17. Another fact that has led to further democratization in Kuwait is the relative press freedom it enjoys.[64] This freedom has been described as "a degree of diversity, competition and outspokenness."[65] Newspapers in Kuwait are owned by Kuwaiti families, but ownership does not necessarily predict the editorial stance of the newspaper.[66] Arab media scholar William A. Rugh[67] explains that the editorial stance of newspapers changes overtime and depending on the issue. These press freedoms are provided in the Constitution, and the provisions will be described in more depth in "Chapter 3: Freedom of Speech."

18. These freedoms protect the right to criticize many elements of Kuwaiti democracy. Despite criticisms of Kuwait's democracy, Herb[68] explains that the results of Kuwaiti elections reflect the intention of voters, demonstrating a freedom unusual in most Arab states. Herb[69] explains several factors that make Kuwait's democracy unique—including the ability of elected members to the National Assembly to engage in a parliamentary procedure that can remove appointed members of the National Assembly from power. Further, the character of people in Kuwait has historically enriched their democracy because of their negotiation of power with various elites.[70]

19. Herb[71] has written extensively on how the Kuwaiti Constitution is more liberal than that of other Arab Gulf states. The previously mentioned summary of the constitutional provisions of power describe the various branches of power and the checks and balances among them. However, it can be helpful to understand less fundamental elements of Kuwait's Constitution. For example, within the first five articles, the Constitution clearly states that Arabic is the official language of the State

60. Michael Herb. *Parliaments in the Gulf.* Journal of Democracy 13, 41–47. (2002).
61. Michael Herb. *Emirs and Parliaments in the Gulf.* 13 Journal of Democracy. 42. (2002).
62. Ferencz Attila Thuroczy. *Kuwait: Democratization in Process: Five Factors of Democratization and Their State in Kuwait.* (Lund University, 2010).
63. *Ibid.*
64. *Ibid.*
65. William A. Rugh. *Arab mass media: Newspapers, radio, and television in Arab politics.* 99. (Greenwood publishing group, 2004.).
66. *Ibid.*
67. *Ibid.*
68. Michael Herb. *Emirs and Parliaments in the Gulf.* 13 Journal of Democracy. 41,47. (2002).
69. Michael Herb. *The Origins of Kuwait's National Assembly.* (2016, London School of Economics and Political Science, http://eprints.lse.ac.uk/65693/1/39_MichaelHerb.pdf).
70. *Ibid.*
71. *Ibid.*

of Kuwait.[72] The second article of the Kuwaiti Constitution states that Islam is one of the main sources from which laws can emerge.[73] Yet, the sources from which Kuwaiti law is made up vary. The next section will examine the different sources of Kuwaiti law.

C. *Civil Law versus Common Law Jurisdiction of the State of Kuwait*

20. According to several sources,[74] the State of Kuwait employs a mixture of civil, common, and Islamic Sharia law in its legal system. In order to examine how these different components work, it is important to think about the history of the development of Kuwait's legal system.

21. In the eighteenth and nineteenth centuries, the legal systems of GCC nations relied on *Majellat al-Ahkam al-Adliya*, a system developed by the Ottoman Empire, which translates to the catalogue of just laws. The Hanafi School of Islamic thought was employed to create a system of civil law during the Ottoman Empire.[75] Prior to the establishment of nation states in the Middle East, Islamic law was extremely important because "the languages of Muslim peoples possessed no word for secularism."[76]

22. Many of the GCC states were also subjects to the British Government through various treaties toward the end of the nineteenth century.[77] In the late 1940s, Islamist thinkers, including Hasan Al-Banna of the Egyptian Muslim Brotherhood, began to write about how the separation of religious institutions from state institutions is a model to avoid.[78] By the end of the Second World War, the Arab Gulf states were no longer dependent on pearl diving economically and were able to export oil.[79] This new economic resource allowed the Arab Gulf states to urbanize and establish political systems. In June 1961, Kuwait declared its independence of Great Britain and adopted the parliamentary system within five months.[80]

23. Starting in the mid-1970s, the Arab Gulf states saw a renewed cultural and intellectual interest in Islamic law. The idea of merging Islamic institutions and state institutions, which Khomeini had called upon,[81] became more salient in the Arab Gulf states by the 1980s. Organizations, both governmental and nongovernmental, emerged to integrate Islam with banking systems and legal codes. By the time Kramer[82] wrote

72. Kuwait National Assembly. Aldistour Alkuwaiti http://www.kna.kw/clt-html5/run.asp?id=2024 (accessed Jan. 17, 2018).
73. *Ibid.*
74. Central Intelligence Agency's (CIA) World Factbook. *Kuwait.* https://www.cia.gov/library/publications/the-world-factbook/geos/ku.html. (accessed May 17, 2017).
75. Mohammad Al-Moqatei. *Introducing Islamic Law in the Arab Gulf States: A Case Study of Kuwait.* 4 Arab Law Quarterly. 138–148. (1989).
76. Martin Kramer. *The Ideals of an Islamic Order.* 3 The Washington Quarterly. 3. (1980).
77. Mohammad Al-Moqatei,. *Introducing Islamic Law in the Arab Gulf States: A Case Study of Kuwait.* 4 Arab Law Quarterly. 138–148. (1989).
78. Martin Kramer. *The Ideals of an Islamic Order.* 3 The Washington Quarterly. 3,13. (1980).
79. Mohammad Al-Moqatei,. *Introducing Islamic Law in the Arab Gulf States: A Case Study of Kuwait.* 4 Arab Law Quarterly. 138–148s. (1989).
80. *Ibid.*
81. Martin Kramer. *The Ideals of an Islamic Order.* 3 The Washington Quarterly. 3, 13. (1980).
82. *Ibid.*

about the development of law in nations with predominantly Muslim populations, most of these nations had an article in the Constitution that expressed Islam as the state religion. So coveted was this provision that "the omission of such an article in 1973 from a new draft Constitution for Syria served as the pretext for rioting."[83] Islamic legal codes—including "the death penalty for apostasy to Islam"[84] began to become common in various Arab Gulf states, including Kuwait, along with other punishments for adultery and defamation—an offense relevant to communication industries.

24. Kuwait saw attempts to amend the second article of the Kuwaiti Constitution such that it states that Islamic law, also known as Sharia, is the main source of Kuwaiti legislation.[85] These efforts, which were seen as populist, did not pass in 1973 because the proposal was not submitted to the Amir to be promulgated before the end of the parliamentary session.[86] In 1975 again, the law was not passed because the government stated that National Assembly had the right to employ Islamic law without it.[87] In 1981, a vote resulted in that it was difficult to implement such a law due to the legal questions it raised. Islamists continued to raise the question in 1984, as they did not feel that Islamic law being only one source of legislation in Kuwait was acceptable.[88] The inclusion of such an article in the Constitution was not without its dissenters, especially because it would essentially create "lawlessness in the country" by violating the modified Constitution.[89]

25. Instead of amending the Constitution, other measures were taken to Islamicize law in Kuwait.[90] Thus, institutions like the House of Zakat were created to distribute 2.5% of savings of Muslims from the wealthy to alleviate poverty.[91] Similarly, Islamic economic models were adopted to disallow interests and replace them with similar models that are endorsed by Islam.[92] The sale of alcohol was also prohibited, and the Citizenship Law was amended so that only Muslims could become Kuwaiti.[93] Further, Family Law was altered such that all aspects of family law were regulated by Islamic Law.[94] These laws, called Personal Status Laws, deal with issues such as marriage, divorce, custody of children, and inheritance laws, in which Islam gives men double the portions of women.[95]

26. Thus, Sharia law is used in some aspects of life in Kuwait. It is notable to consider the opinion of some scholars that the desire to establish Islamic legal codes

83. Martin Kramer. *The Ideals of an Islamic Order.* 3 The Washington Quarterly. 5. (1980).
84. *Ibid., 6.*
85. Mohammad Al-Moqatei. *Introducing Islamic Law in the Arab Gulf States: A Case Study of Kuwait.* 4 Arab Law Quarterly. 138–148. (1989).
86. *Ibid.*
87. *Ibid.*
88. *Ibid.*
89. Mohammad Al-Moqatei. *Introducing Islamic Law in the Arab Gulf States: A Case Study of Kuwait.* 4 Arab Law Quarterly. 142. (1989).
90. *Ibid.*
91. Mohammad Al-Moqatei. *Introducing Islamic Law in the Arab Gulf States: A Case Study of Kuwait.* 4 Arab Law Quarterly. 138–148. (1989).
92. *Ibid.*
93. *Ibid.*
94. *Ibid.*
95. *Ibid.*

in the Arab world is rooted in a rejection of Western ideologies, whether it be Marxism, liberalism, or capitalism.[96][97] Those who study Kuwait sometimes give additional reasons as a "revival of interest in indigenous cultural roots."[98] However, the Kuwaiti legal system is also very much influenced by the common law system of Great Britain as a result of the agreement signed in 1899 to make Kuwait a Protectorate of Great Britain, in part to avoid being a part of the Ottoman Empire.[99]

27. In his comparison between various legal systems, Siems[100] explains that both courts and statutes coexist in legal systems. In civil legal systems, lawyers place a greater emphasis on factors, such as formal codes that are structured logically, than the prior decisions of courts which is the focal point of common law. Yet, Siems[101] also suggests that these methods of classifying legal structures are not enough to examine the extent to which legal systems can work with various indigenous cultures, such as Islamic customs and laws. Although the Kuwaiti legal system may be influenced by Great Britain, its legal system does not rely on precedent. Instead, there are legal codes that must be followed and applied—a system known as French Civil Law. Civil Law is considered more rigid, and the emphasis in the civil law system is on legal codes, or statutes, rather than the courts.[102]

28. Legal and anthropological scholars use the term legal pluralism to refer to this type of overlap between various legal systems. Among the topics studied when examining legal pluralism are analyses of the origins of the various coexisting legal sources—including official law, customary law, religious law, commercial law, functional law, and communal law, the degree to which various legal systems harmonize or conflict with one another, and the differences of power assigned to each.[103] Under some conditions, including when the legal professionals are inadequately trained, when there is an inadequate body of legal knowledge or when the law is perceived to be manipulated by the elite or perceived to be foreign, corrupt, inefficient, or relating to the needs of a particular group of the population, then "a substantial proportion of the populace will not identify with state law—they will not see it as their law, serving their needs."[104] In these circumstances, people rely on religion, tradition, or other normative ways of resolving disputes that are accepted in that subculture but independent of the state's

96. *Ibid.*
97. Sayyid Qutbs. *Social Justice in Islam.*Trans. John B. Hardie and Hamid Algar, Rev. Ed.(Islamic Publications International, 2000).
98. Mohammad Al-Moqatei. Introducing Islamic Law in the Arab Gulf States: A Case Study of Kuwait. 4 Arab Law Quarterly. 148. (1989).
99. Peter C. Valenti & B.J. Slot. *Mubarak Al-Sabah: Founder of Modern Kuwait, 1896–1915.* International Journal of Middle East Studies, 40. 522. (2008).
100. Mathias M. Siems. *Legal Origins: Reconciling Law & Finance and Comparative Law.* 52 McGill Law Journal. (2007).
101. *Ibid.*
102. *Ibid.*
103. Brian Z. Tamanha. *Understanding Legal Pluralism: Past to Present, Local to Global.* 30 Sydney Law Review. 375. (2008).
104. Brian Z. Tamanha. *Understanding Legal Pluralism: Past to Present, Local to Global.* 30 Sydney Law Review. 378. (2008).

legal system.[105] In other words, social practice is extremely relevant when studying developing countries.[106] While the concept of legal pluralism is even found in places like the U.S. as various normative ideas from various legal sources are selected, examined, utilized, or denied,[107] it is more important in a developing country. Particularly in Kuwait, the overlap of legal systems can be seen through this lens because of the variety of cultural, religious, and historical factors.

D. The Organization of Kuwaiti Courts

29. The hierarchy of the courts is important to understand in any legal system, and the Kuwait Institute for Judicial and Legal Studies summarized the organization of the Kuwaiti judiciary in a handbook that has been further paraphrased and translated into the English language. Since Arabic is the official language of the court system, the names of various courts have been transliterated.

30. Kuwait's legal system is organized into two components.[108] The first component is called *qanun alejra'at*, procedural law, which serves the purposes of explaining how to apply the law. The second component is called *almahamat aljaza'iya*, or criminal law, which relates to punishment assigned to a legal system. Punishments cannot be enforced in Kuwait except after the courts engage in the due process of law, according to the first article of Law No. 17 of 1960.

31. There are two kinds of criminal courts in Kuwait: *almahakim aladiyah*, ordinary courts, and *almahakim alkhasa*, specialized courts.[109] Specialized courts include military courts, martial courts, and ministerial courts. Ordinary courts explain the organization of the judiciary for public law.

32. Within ordinary criminal courts, there are two levels.[110] The first level includes the courts for misdemeanors, called *mahkamat aljonah*, and the courts for felonies, called *makhamat aljinayat*. However, there are cases where misdemeanors are not filed as other courts specialize in them; for example, the traffic court, juvenile court, and the court of felonies. Article 3 of 2006 of the press and publications law is among the laws that are categorized as felonies as there are sections that relate to Article 5 of the penal code. Interviews with former Member of Parliament, Dr. Hassan Johar,[111] on March 12, 2017, revealed that attempts to pass the original legislation for the publication law of 2006 were complicated by the penal code. To reconcile the conflict, a clause was included to express that the new publication law would respect

105. Brian Z. Tamanha. *A Non-Essentialist Version of Legal Pluralism*. 27 Journal of Law and Society. 296,321. (2000).
106. *Ibid.*
107. Carol J. Greenhouse. *Legal Pluralism and Cultural Difference: What Is the Difference? A Response to Professor Woodman.* 30 The Journal of Legal Pluralism and Unofficial Law. 61, 72. (1998).
108. Kuwait Institute for Judicial and Legal Studies. *Altantheem Alqadhaey Fe Nitaq Alqanun Alaam.* (Ministry of Justice, 2012).
109. *Ibid.*
110. *Ibid.*
111. *Ibid.*

the criminalization of communication crimes in the penal code and should not violate the rest of Kuwaiti laws.

33. The two kinds of courts on the first level are different in several ways.[112] For example, three types of judiciary officials must be present in sessions of the court for misdemeanors: a judge, an investigator, and a writer for the session. However, there are three judges in the court of felonies in addition to the public prosecution and writers of the session. On the second level are two courts of appeal: the court of misdemeanor appeals, *mahkamat aljonah almosta'nafa*, and the higher Court of Appeals, *mahkamat alesti'naf alolya*.

34. There are some disputes that are not criminal in nature, such as civil, commercial, labor, administrative, and personal.[113] These courts are categorized into two levels. On the first level are the courts for urgent situations *mahkamat alomoor almosta'jela*, the courts for execution of law *makhamat altanfeeth*, the international courts *almahkama alalamiyah*, the personal status court *mahkamat alahkam alshakhsiyah*, the Court of First Instance *almahkama alkoliyah*, administrative courts *almahkamah aledariyah*, the rent court *mahkamat alejarat* with a rent circuit *da'irat aleyjarat*, the sales court *mahkamat abeyoo'*, and the high appeals court *mahkamat alesti'naf alolyah*, which includes circuits for civil *da'irah madaniyah* and commercial affairs *da'irah tejariyah*. On the second level is the Court of Appeals with a committee of judges—more figuratively translating to the Western concept of a judge's bench—sitting on cases, *almahkamah alkoliyah bi haya'a ist'inafiya* and a higher Court of Appeals *mahkamat alesti'naf alolyah*, which includes a civil circuit, *da'irah madaniyah*.

Finally, the highest level of court in Kuwait is called the Court of Cassation. This court includes circuits that are civil, commercial, international, administrative, and of personal status.

35. In 2016, the prosecution received 3,143 cases of which 2,865 were media crimes violating the Kuwaiti electronic media law in which 251 cases related to press misdemeanors and 27 audio-visual misdemeanors.[114] Out of these cases, 2,924 were dealt with of which 1,339 were referred to the court, 1,585 were reserved, and 219 cases are still under investigation. Moreover, 80% of the crimes are committed through social media (WhatsApp, Twitter, and Instagram) allegedly harming the dignity and reputation of the complainants.[115]

E. The National Assembly

36. Kuwait's National Assembly is deep-rooted in Kuwaiti culture and history. In 1938, a group of traders assembled to show interest in participating in Kuwait's political system in what they called *alkutla alwataniya*, or the National Block. Supported by the ruler, the bloc developed a draft of a democratic system that afforded them civil and political rights. This assembly was stopped due to interference with the ruler's

112. *Ibid.*
113. *Ibid.*
114. Hussain Abdullah. *Alqimlas Liljareeda: 3143 Qadia Talaqatha Niyabat Alelam Alam Almadi Minhal 2865 Jarima Elektroniya* http://www.mohamoon-kw.com/default.aspx?action=DisplayNews&type=2&id=37783&Year=20170131 (accessed May 15, 2017).
115. *Ibid.*

power, and efforts to revive it failed until 1962. A new assembly was established in 1962 when *almajless alta'aseesi*, the Constituent Assembly, was formed. In 1963, the first convention of Kuwait's National Assembly allowed it to share power to enact legislation with the Amir. Laws drafted by the legislative body would have to be signed by the Amir within a month to be validated.[116]

37. The National Assembly consists of fifty members, and a maximum of a third of these and fifteen ministers are appointed by the Amir. These norms are set by the Constitution whose Article 56 states that "the entire number of Ministers shall not exceed one third the number of the members of the National Assembly." Elected officials serve for four-year terms and are not exempt from being appointed as ministers. Until 2005, women were not allowed equal rights to run and vote for the National Assembly.[117] Among the functions of the National Assembly are the ability of its members to debate government programs, pass laws, policies, question ministers, or take vote of no confidence regarding ministers' performance.[118] The National Assembly mainly consists of three major political and social groups: businessmen, Bedouins, and middle-class citizens.[119]

38. The first administrative body called Establishment Council *majles alinshaa* was established in 1952, and in 1954, the Supreme Executive Committee was established to regulate government departments and agencies. Through a series of reformations, the current system was developed. Articles 51 and 79 of the Constitution gave the legislation power to the Amir and the National Assembly. Today, the National Assembly ratifies laws and the Amir sanctions it.

39. In his book on political systems in Kuwait, Asiri[120] writes about four reform movements in Kuwait. The first reform movement started in Kuwait in 1921 when the ruling family and business class people agreed to give more power to business people to manage the country, leading to the establishment of an advisory board that consisted of twelve appointed members functioning as advisory authority only.[121] Regardless of having only advisory power, it formed the first base for public participation in the government, but it only lasted two months.[122] It drafted the first written Constitution with only five articles.[123]

---

116. Ahmed Aly Khedr. *Kuwait's Legal System and Legal Research*. Hauser Global Law School Program, New York University School of Law, http://www.nyulawglobal.org/globalex/Kuwait.html (accessed Mar. 15, 2017).
117. Muhamad S. Olimat. *Women and the Kuwaiti National Assembly*. 12 Journal of International Women's Studies.76,95. (2013).
118. Ahmed Aly Khedr. *Kuwait's Legal System and Legal Research*. Hauser Global Law School Program, New York University School of Law, http://www.nyulawglobal.org/globalex/Kuwait.html (accessed Mar. 15, 2017).
119. Kamal Osman Salih. *Kuwait: Political Consequences of Modernization, 1750–1986*. 27 Middle Eastern Studies. 46,66. (1991).
120. Abdulridha Asiri, *Political System in Kuwait Alnitham Asiyasi Fel Kuwait* [in Arabic]. 9th ed. Kuwait: (Alwatan Press, 2007).
121. *Ibid.*
122. *Ibid.*
123. *Ibid.*

40. In 1938, a second reformation was made to improve management in the government.[124] The National Block, *alkutla alwataniya*, was supported by some members of the royal family.[125] The royal family decided to make limited elections among 150 elite families to establish a legislature board consisting of fourteen members, but it lasted only six months.[126] It composed a more developed Constitution from the previous one. Six days after the dissolution of this legislature, a second one was established in 1938. Four hundred people participated in the elections to elect twenty members.[127] This board gave the ruler more power compared to the previous board and became advisory rather than legislative in character. In 1939, after less than three months, the board was dissolved and many members were arrested, executed, or escaped to Iraq.[128]

41. Asiri[129] explains that the third reform was conducted to absorb public anger. In 1939, the ruling family decided to establish a Consultative, or known in Arabic as *Shura,* Council with fourteen members, four of whom were from the ruling family. The Council had no power, which made the members withdraw one after another.[130] Finally in 1961, the ruler of Kuwait issued a decree to form an elected Constituent Council to draft the country's Constitution. Twenty members were elected, and in 1962, the Constituent Council adopted the Constitution unanimously. The Constitution was then ratified by the late Amir Sheikh Abdullah Al-Salem Al-Sabah.[131]

42. Culturally, the explanatory note of the Constitution provides insight that demonstrates the kind of system adopted in Kuwait. It sets the premise that the Constitution is congruent with the Islamic principle of consultation in public affairs.[132] The concept of consultation or what is called in Arabic *shura*, which is defined as the process of decision-making by consultation and deliberation is adopted from Islam to be the base for the political system in Kuwait setting guidance of the relations between the ruler and the people. This cooperation is put in practice through the National Assembly. Despite similar terminologies and underlying cultural justifications, it is worth noting that Kuwait's national assembly is not analogous to any of the consultative bodies in other GCC states because of its "substantial legislative powers"[133] as well as the power granted to parliamentarians to grill ministers.[134] In fact, Ottaway[135] even goes as far to call Kuwait's National Assembly "cantankerous" from the perspective of neighboring states.

124. *Ibid.*
125. *Ibid.*
126. *Ibid.*
127. *Ibid.*
128. *Ibid.*
129. *Ibid.*
130. *Ibid.*
131. *Ibid.*
132. Kuwait NationalAssembly. *Distour Dawlat Alkuwait: Almothakara Altafseriyah.* http://www.kna.kw/clt-html5/run.asp?id=51# (accessed May 17, 2017).
133. Michael Herb. *Emirs and Parliaments in the Gulf.* 13 Journal of Democracy. 41. (2002).
134. Michael Herb. *Emirs and Parliaments in the Gulf.* 13 Journal of Democracy. 41,47. (2002).
135. Marina Ottaway. *Bahrain: Between the United States and Saudi Arabia.* Carnegie Endowment for International Peace 2011.

II. Geography and Population

43. Historically a port city where pearl diving and trade generated revenues,[136] Kuwait is a small country between Iraq and Saudi Arabia that lies on the Persian Gulf. Having been a protectorate of Great Britain until it gained its independence in 1961, its borders were challenged by Saddam Hussein when Iraqi troops invaded it in 1990.[137] Kuwait was freed in February 1991 by an international coalition of allies.[138] Consisting of 17,818 square kilometers, it is approximately the size of New Jersey.[139] There are also 9 Kuwaiti islands, including one—Failaka—that has artifacts dating back to 3,000 B.C.[140] Kuwait broke the record for the highest recorded temperature on Earth in July 2016, which was 54 degrees Celsius—approximately 129.3 degrees Fahrenheit.[141]

44. According to Kuwait's Central Statistical Bureau, the population of Kuwait was approximately 3.9 million by June 2015.[142] Approximately 69.2% of the population is non–Kuwaiti, and 30.7% are Kuwaiti nationals. Consistent with the trend in most Arab nations,[143] the largest demographic segment in Kuwait is below the age of 35—about 53.3% of the overall population. On the surface, it would appear that there are more males (60.8%) in Kuwait than females (39.1%); however, this difference is due to a disproportionate amount of male expatriates working in Kuwait. The percent of Kuwaiti males and Kuwaiti females that make up the overall population is approximately 15% for each group.

III. Social and Cultural Values

45. Kuwait has one of the highest per capita incomes in the world, and the Kuwaiti Dinar is equivalent to more than USD 3 by June 2017. Aladwani[144] states that it "consistently scores very high on the Human Development Index" due to the high educational attainment its citizens possess. As a result, several theorists have empirically

136. Jill Crystal. *Oil and Politics in the Gulf: Rulers and Merchants in Kuwait and Qatar.* Cambridge University Press. (1995).
137. Dawlat Ahmed Sadek, Jill Ann Crystal, John Duke Anthony & William L. Ochsenwald. *Kuwait.* (Encyclopædia Britannica, Inc., 2016).
138. *Ibid.*
139. Central Intelligence Agency's (CIA) World Factbook. *Kuwait.* https://www.cia.gov/library/publications/the-world-factbook/geos/ku.html. (accessed May 17, 2017).
140. Kuwait Times. *Failaka Island Contender for Unesco Recognition* (Jun. 23, 2013).
141. Shaikh, Thair. Kuwait Swelters in 54c Heat—What Could Be the Highest Temperature Ever Recorded on Earth. (The Independent, Jul. 23, 2016). http://www.independent.co.uk/news/world/middle-east/kuwait-swelters-record-breaking-54c-heatwave-weather-7152911.html (accessed Mar. 12, 2017).
142. The State of Kuwait's Central Statistical Bureau. *Alihsa'at alsikaniya: taqderat alsikan fe montasaf al'am.*" (2013., accessed Mar. 12, 2017, https://www.csb.gov.kw/Socan_Statistic.aspx?ID=67).
143. LeVine M (2008) *Heavy metal Islam: rock, resistance, and the struggle for the soul of Islam*: Crown.
144. Adel M Aladwani. *Facilitators, Characteristics, and Impacts of Twitter Use: Theoretical Analysis and Empirical Illustration.* 35 International Journal of Information Management. 18. (2015).

demonstrated that Kuwaitis tend to be technologically savvy.[145] Various scholars have interpreted this trend differently. While Al Nashmi et al.[146] interpret it as a way to demonstrate "social status by being the first to own the latest trend," others view it as a foundational component of the Kuwaiti national identity, characterized by an "openness to globalization."[147]

46. This openness is partially driven by the availability of foreign media to Kuwaiti people.[148] While electronic colonialism theory might suggest that such circumstances would lead to the development of loss of a national identity,[149] Wheeler[150] demonstrates that the "compulsion to have the latest technologies and global media texts immediately available"[151] actually develops the national consciousness of the Kuwaiti people.

47. One way Kuwaiti culture is preserved is through religion. For example, Kuwaitis are supportive of some kinds of censorship, such as the censorship of pornography.[152] This religious ethos is reflected in the Kuwaiti Constitution, which clearly states that Islam is the official religion of the State of Kuwait. While no statistics accurately estimate the size of the followers of various sects, Kuwaiti Muslims are— and have historically been— composed of a Sunni majority and a Shi'a minority. The degree to which Islam permeates public life can be felt in daily life, with calls to prayer publicly broadcast from the minarets of mosques. Here, it is worth noting that Islam is different from Islamism. Cagaptay[153] suggests that followers of Islam as a religion often have tension with Islamists, who are defined by their antagonistic attitudes toward Jews, Christians, capitalism, and communism by distorting religious texts to justify this antagonism.[154] In Kuwait, Brown[155] suggests that Islamism is a movement that combines both what is constitutional and is consistent with Sharia, or Islamic law. The

145. Eisa Al Nashmi, Johanna Cleary, Juan-Carlos Molleda & Melinda McAdams. *Internet Political Discussions in the Arab World: A Look at Online Forums from Kuwait, Saudi Arabia, Egypt and Jordan*. 72 International Communication Gazette. 723. (2010).
146. *Ibid.*
147. Deborah Wheeler. *New Media, Globalization and Kuwaiti National Identity*. The Middle East Journal 444 (2000).
148. Deborah Wheeler. *New Media, Globalization and Kuwaiti National Identity*. The Middle East Journal 432, 444 (2000).
149. Thomas L. McPhail. *Global Communication: Theories, Stakeholders, and Trends*. (John Wiley & Sons, 2010).
150. Deborah Wheeler. *New Media, Globalization and Kuwaiti National Identity*. The Middle East Journal 432, 444 (2000).
151. Deborah Wheeler. *New Media, Globalization and Kuwaiti National Identity*. The Middle East Journal 444 (2000).
152. Ildiko Kaposi. *The Culture and Politics of Internet Use among Young People in Kuwait*. 8 Cyberpsychology: Journal of Psychosocial Research on Cyberspace. (2015).
153. Soner Cagaptay. *Muslims vs. Islamists*. The Washington Institute. http://www.washingtoninstitute.org/policy-analysis/view/muslims-vs.-islamists (accessed May 14, 2017).
154. *Ibid.*
155. Nathan Brown. *Pushing toward Party Politics? Kuwait's Islamic Constitutional Movement*. Carnegie Endowment for International Peace, http://carnegieendowment.org/files/cp79_brown_kuwait_final.pdf (accessed May 14, 2017).

effects of such a vision, Brown[156] explains, is the protection of a conservative culture and a push toward making Sharia a more prominent source of legislation.

48. An Islamist-led parliament passed legislation that required institutions of higher education to be segregated by sex so that male and female students can lead a more modest, moral life from a fundamentalist perspective.[157] Although this rule was challenged in the constitutional courts in the mid-2010s, the ruling remains in place and gives power to university administrations to decide the extent to which gender integration should occur.[158] More recently, a Kuwaiti parliamentarian demanded that Christmas be declared a national holiday to honor Kuwaiti Christians in response to the Minister of Social Affairs and Labor's order to remove a Christmas tree from a commercial part of a residential area, Aldasma.[159] Izzak[160] reported that there are 200 Kuwaiti Christians and thousands of other Christians living in Kuwait.

49. While Kuwait is proud of the multicultural fabric of its society, there is often tension between different groups of Kuwaitis. For example, there is a tribal conflict between urban (i.e., hadhar) and rural (i.e., edouin) populations that leaves nonurban Kuwaitis feeling they have to defend the degree to which they belong in Kuwait.[161] Similarly, there is sectarian conflict between the majority (i.e., Sunni) and minority (i.e., Shi'a) sects of Islam that leaves Shi'as feeling a similar pressure to defend the degree to which they belong to Kuwait.[162] Therefore, cultural conflicts emerge when the various threads of the interwoven sections of Kuwaiti society are scrutinized.

50. These conflicts are described by Tétreault[163] as being rooted in conflicts which have "characterized Kuwaiti domestic politics for nearly a hundred years."[164] Tétreault[165] refers to this conflict as a negotiation of national identity that exists to include or exclude various populations that benefit from material privileges that come with citizenship. Most interesting is Tétreault's tracing the roots of this struggle as one that "predate[s] the oil era" and is indigenous to the Kuwaiti population.[166] In fact, Tétreault recounts various myths used in this struggle, including one that explains that Kuwaiti democracy is a result of the influence of Great Britain—one that is described

---

156. *Ibid.*
157. Habib Toumi. *Kuwaiti MPs Push for Reinstating Co-Education*. Gulf News, Jun. 3, 2013.
158. *Case against Gender Segregation Rejected. Arab Times.* Dec. 17, 2015.
159. B. Izzak. *MP Fadhl Demands Holiday on Christmas, Erect Large Ree on Safat Square; 200 Kuwaiti Christians Living in Kuwait.* Kuwait Times http://news.kuwaittimes.net/website/mp-fadhl-demands-holiday-christmas-erect-large-tree-safat-square-200-kuwaiti-christians-living-kuwait (accessed May 14, 2017).
160. *Ibid.*
161. Rania Al-Nakib *Human Rights, Education for Democratic Citizenship and International Organisations: Findings from a Kuwaiti UNESCO ASPnet School.* 42 Cambridge Journal of Education. 97,112. (2012).
162. *Ibid.*
163. Mary Ann Tétreault. *Stories of Democracy: Politics and Society in Contemporary Kuwait.* (Columbia University Press, 2000).
164. *Ibid.*, 33.
165. *Ibid.*
166. *Ibid., 33.*

as part of "vigorous propaganda campaigns" to "insist on the foreignness of democracy and its unsuitability to local traditions and values."[167]

51. Regardless of how these conflicts are viewed, it is important to pay attention to the evolution of marginalized groups over time. Although the types of vulnerabilities facing these groups vary, three groups of people are vulnerable from a human rights perspective: women, children, and expatriates. First, women are not afforded the same rights afforded to men in Kuwait. For example, a woman who marries a non-Kuwaiti national cannot pass on her citizenship to her children or husband.[168] Further, she and her family would automatically be excluded from a host of social and economic privileges available to Kuwaitis, including housing subsidies.[169] Second, children are technically not citizens until they have reached 18 years of age, which poses challenges as the youth are increasingly active in political movements.[170] Finally, expatriates have limited rights despite making up a majority of the population of Kuwait.[171] Additionally, the Bidoon are a group of "completely disenfranchised" individuals who "have restricted access to services."[172] Thus, a focus on marginalized groups demonstrates the cultural issues faced by members of Kuwaiti society.

52. Despite such challenges, actions that promote human rights of these marginalized groups—including the improvements of rights afforded to children, women and the children of Kuwaiti women with expatriate spouses—are noteworthy. When a man had refused to permit his wife and three children their passports so they could travel, Kuwait's Constitutional Court ruled that women can travel without the permission of their husbands. The move gave women the freedom of movement without obtaining the signature of a husband to obtain a passport. Even at this victory, news reports cited activists who expressed a greater desire to move toward gender equality in the eyes of the law.[173] This is consistent with the opinion of Political Scientist Michael Herb[174] in which he affirms that Kuwait is the Arab Gulf State most uniquely equipped for the development of democracy, partly due to a cultural tendency to negotiate power with elites that Kuwaitis exhibit.

167. *Ibid., 65.*
168. Rania Al-Nakib. *Human Rights, Education for Democratic Citizenship and International Organisations: Findings from a Kuwaiti UNESCO ASPnet School.* 42 Cambridge Journal of Education. 100. (2012).
169. *Ibid., 101.*
170. *Ibid., 97, 112.*
171. *Ibid.*
172. *Ibid., 101.*
173. *Kuwaiti Women Win Right to Obtain Passport without Husband's Approval.* The Telegraph, Oct. 22, 2009.
174. Michael Herb. *The Origins of Kuwait's National Assembly.* (2016, London School of Economics and Political Science, http://eprints.lse.ac.uk/65693/1/39_MichaelHerb.pdf).

§2. THE MEDIA LANDSCAPE

I. Overview of Kuwait Media

A. Introduction

53. Kuwait's media landscape is quite robust. There are many newspapers, radio stations, and televisions that operate in Kuwait. There are both public and private media outlets. In this chapter, we will outline the operating of traditional media outlets and provide some information about the ownership model of Kuwaiti media.

54. To contextualize the use of media in Kuwait, the current chapter will provide some social scientific works that will explain how the ownership of Kuwaiti media affects editorial content. Further, this chapter will explain the work of ethnographers who explain that Kuwaiti culture is unique in its adoption of new technologies, including for media consumption.

55. Finally, Kuwaitis are adept at using social media and the global trend of media convergence is witnessed in Kuwait. As Kuwait develops its communication technologies infrastructure, changes are made to the regulatory authorities overseeing them. This chapter will provide definitions of engineering technologies often used in telecommunications before providing statistics on the penetration of these technologies in Kuwait.

B. Radio

56. Radio was an important medium across the globe for several reasons that resonate across the Arab world. Early in the development of radio in the Arab world, the medium was seen as a way to appeal to the masses, both urban and rural, who might be illiterate. The way radio was utilized as a form of political communication varied according to the historical eras with which it overlapped—including colonization, post-colonization, and eventually globalization.[175]

57. Colonial powers across the Arab world used radio to further the interests of their government.[176] Much of the Arab world was colonized by British, French, or Italian powers. Ayish[177] cites radio as beginning in Egypt, Morocco, and Tunisia in the 1920s, Lebanon and Algeria in 1937, and Syria in 1946. Throughout these decades, German and Italian governments directed messages to Arab audiences, which resulted in the establishment of BBC Arabic in London in January 1938. Although not everyone could afford a radio receiver, it would not be uncommon for restaurants, coffee shops, and other public spaces in urban areas to have radios for people to enjoy.

175. Muhammad Ayish. "Radio Broadcasting in the Arab World." Chap. 4 In Arab Media: Globalization and Emerging Media Industries edited by Muhammad Ayish Noha Mellor, Nabil Dajani, Khalil Rinawi, 67–84. Cambridge, UK: Polity Press, 2011.

176. *Ibid.*

177. *Ibid.*

58. The post-colonial era marked the time that most Arab nations gained independence from their colonizers.[178] At this time, the radio was an equally important tool for political communication.[179] It was often operated by the government to advocate for state policies. As illiteracy was combatted, radio became an important medium that resonated with the cultural familiarity of the oral tradition in the Arab world.[180] Ayish[181] explains that Kuwait, Lebanon, and Morocco were unusual in that their political systems were not authoritarian, leading to the development of content for broadcasts in these three countries that were more likely to include subjects relating to the political and ethnic diversity of these nations.

59. In the 1990s, the globalization era of radio began. Across much of the Arab world, private radio stations were established.[182] The content of radio programming would contain more entertainment than in previous decades. As new technologies emerged, a greater number of people would have access to Arab radio stations across the world.[183] Despite such changes, government-to-people initiatives continued to take place through Arab radio. For example, Ayish[184] points to Radio Sawa: a radio station operated by the U.S. State Department that includes music, talk shows, and newscasts in a combination of Arabic and English.

60. In Kuwait, 1951 was the start of radio broadcast. Today, the government controls the radio waves and most radio stations. The Kuwaiti Ministry of Information began granting licenses for private radio and television stations in 2003.[185] The government radio stations provide twenty-four hours of programs on various subjects besides music. They are mainly in Arabic, but have hours for broadcasting in English, Persian, and Urdu. According to the Ministry of Information's website,[186] there are nine radio stations on FM worth noting. Although some other sources state that there are more radio stations,[187] twenty-two stations were verified and are included in the table below.

Radio

#	*TV*	*Public or Private*
1	Kuwait FM	Government
2	AlQuran Alkarem	Government
3	Super Station FM	Government

178. *Ibid.*
179. *Ibid.*
180. *Ibid.*
181. *Ibid.*
182. *Ibid.*
183. *Ibid.*
184. *Ibid.*
185. *Ibid.*
186. State of Kuwait's Ministry of Information. *Radio Live Broadcast*. http://www.media.gov.kw/LiveRadio1.aspx (accessed Jun. 7, 2017).
187. World Radio Maps. *Radio Stations in Kuwait City*. http://worldradiomap.com/kw/kuwait (accessed Jun. 7, 2017).

4	Kuwait Radio One	Government
5	Alshabab OFM	Government
6	Traditional Station	Government
7	The Old Arabic Singing	Government
8	Easy & Sports	Government
9	Kuwait Radio Two	Government
10	Kuwait FM	Government
11	AlQuran Alkarem	Government
12	Super Station FM	Government
13	Old Arabic Music	Government
14	BBC Arabic	British
15	Marina FM	Private
16	BBC World Service	British
17	Radio Kuwait Int'l	Government
18	Sawa Radio	American
19	VOA News	American
21	Radio France International	French
22	Monte Carlo	French

C. Broadcasting

61. To contextualize the environment of Kuwaiti broadcast media, it is important to trace back the roots of its emergence in the Arab world. Media scholars explain the historical developments of television in the Arab world in three time periods: the mid-1950s through the 1970s, the 1970s to the 1990s, and 1991 and beyond.[188] Prior to explaining the development of Kuwaiti television, a description of the three phases provides useful insights to understand regional trends.

62. The first time period, which Ayish[189] estimates to begin in 1954 and end in 1976, is the formative phase for the development of broadcast media in the Arab world. While most states in the Arab world controlled television due to their perception of the medium as a potent tool for mobilizing the masses, Kuwait is among a handful of Arab nations, including Morocco, Iraq, and Lebanon, where the private sector developed television in order to seek profits.[190] In Kuwait, television started as a private enterprise in 1957, six years after the establishment of the radio. Television then came under the

188. Muhammad Ayish. "Television Broadcasting in the Arab World: Political Democratization and Cultural Revivalism." Chap. 5, In Arab Media: Globalization and Emerging Media Industries, edited by Muhammad Ayish Noha Mellor, Nabil Dajani, Khalil Rinawi, 85–102. Cambridge, UK: Polity Press, 2011.

189. *Ibid.*

190. *Ibid.*

control of the Ministry of Information after independence from Britain in 1961.[191] Ayish[192] explains this trend among Arab nations is due to three factors: familiarity with British and French models of public service television, lack of familiarity with commercial models of broadcasting popular in the United States, and heightened political tensions in the region during this time period.

63. Following the formative phase, the national expansion phase begins in 1976–1990.[193] At this point, the Arab world saw more cooperation in order to produce material that would then be transmitted from one country to another. In this phase of the development of television, governments in larger Arab nations ensured that rural regions would secure access to programming.[194] One of the most important nations from which television programming was imported was Egypt, causing Egyptian dramas and vernacular to become among the most easily understood across the Arab world.[195] However, content was also imported from Britain, France, and the United States.[196]

64. Finally, the globalization phase begins in 1991 and continues until today.[197] Several notable developments at the beginning of the 1990s led to the onset of the globalization phase, beginning with the live coverage of the Iraqi invasion of Kuwait by CNN.[198] Following the liberation of Kuwait, several broadcast media initiatives emerged, including the London-based Middle East Broadcasting Network (MBC) intended for all Arab nations, and the establishment of Al Jazeera in Qatar in 1997.[199] Scholars who study this period often note that there are some channels with sectarian views, such as Al-Manar TV from Lebanon, as well as other political orientations, including that of the United States in its financing of Al Hurra news channel as well as BBC Arabic, which is financed by Britain.[200] The proliferation of satellite television also impacted the content available to viewers across the Arab world in the 1990s. In Kuwait, the government approved TV license to private industry by 1998. However, these efforts were subject to governmental approval by 2000.[201]

65. These three stages are important to consider due to their impact on the regulation of broadcast media as well as the effects of the broadcast media on the political environment and culture.[202] The increase in available television content created room for the voicing of more and diverse political thought, affected public relations, and led to the development of research analyzing the effectiveness of foreign governments'

191. *Ibid.*
192. *Ibid.*
193. *Ibid.*
194. *Ibid.*
195. *Ibid.*
196. *Ibid.*
197. *Ibid.*
198. *Ibid.*
199. *Ibid.*
200. *Ibid.*
201. *Kuwait.* Press Reference, http://www.pressreference.com/Gu-Ku/Kuwait.html (accessed May 15, 2017).
202. Muhammad Ayish. "Television Broadcasting in the Arab World: Political Democratization and Cultural Revivalism." Chap. 5 In Arab Media: Globalization and Emerging Media Industries, edited by Muhammad Ayish Noha Mellor, Nabil Dajani, Khalil Rinawi, 85–102. Cambridge, UK: Polity Press, 2011.

ability to shape Arab public opinion.[203] Further, game shows and reality television became popular throughout the Arab world, driving research agendas examining the portrayal of gender, religion, and other cultural dimensions on television.[204] In Kuwait, there is a multitude of available stations for viewers today. Approximately seven are government-controlled through the Ministry of Information, mostly in the Arabic language. Other private entertainment, political, and social channels also are available.

TV

TV	*Kind*	*Public or Private*
KTV1	General Arabic	Government
KTV2	General English	Government
KTV Sport	Sports	Government
KTV Sport Plus	Sports	Government
KTV Ethraa	Cultural	Government
KTV Arabe	Documentary	Government
KTV Plus	Entertainment	Government
Al Qurain	Popular Heritage	Government
KTV Al Majlis	National Assembly	Government
Kuwait Space Channel	International viewers	Government
Alafasy TV	Islamic	Private
Al Rai TV	General	Private
Funoon TV	Entertainment	Private
Scope TV	General	Private
Alwatan TV Alwatan Plus Alwatan Ghanawi Alwatan radio TV	The license was stripped from Alwatan & all stations were closed	Private
Al-Kout TV	General	Private
Al-Adala TV	General	Private
Alsabah TV	General	Private
Al-Bawadi TV	General	Private
Alshahed TV	General	Private
Rawasy TV	General	Private
m3ali.tv	Islamic	Private

203. *Ibid.*
204. *Ibid.*

D. *Print Media*

66. The freedom of the press in Kuwait goes back to before 1956 when publications were opened to anyone as long as they were not offensive to the government. But, in 1956, with the opening of the Government Printing Press, the new press laws implemented in Kuwait helped create an opinionated press leading to a marketplace for more newspapers.

67. Abdul Aziz Al-Rushaid is the founder of the first Kuwaiti magazine called *Mujallat Alkuwait,* which translates to Kuwait Magazine. It was printed in Egypt in 1928 but stopped after two years.[205] In 1946, a moment in the history of the freedom of the press occurred in Kuwait when students in Egypt published a magazine called *AlBe'thah.* This gave the boost for the establishment of the first monthly magazine published in Kuwait called *Kathmah* in 1948, specialized in literature. In the same year, the country's first Printing Office was established. Many publications appeared during the years of 1950 and 1959, but did not last due to financial and technological difficulties as well as the lack of intellectuals.[206,207] In 1954, the Publication Department first published the official Kuwaiti newspaper called *Kuwait Alyawm.*[208]

68. In 1961, *Al-Rai Al-Aam* was the first Kuwaiti weekly newspaper established and printed in Beirut. One year later, *Al-Taleea* the weekly opposition newspaper was established, and in 1967, *Al-Nahda,* a social magazine started in Kuwait. The second newspaper, *Alseyassah,* was launched in 1965. By the 1970s, more and more newspapers started, including *Alqabas* in 1972, *Alwatan* in 1974, and *Alanba* in 1976. The English newspaper *Kuwait Times* was established in 1961, and in 1977 *The Arab Times* was introduced. Since their establishment, all newspapers are privately owned and operated. Government newspapers were discontinued due to private competition.[209] Additionally, after the 2006 Press and Publication Law became active in Kuwait, the number of daily newspapers reached 15. Besides newspapers, there are many magazines with general and specific interests such as *Al-Arabi* established in 1958, *Al Forgan, Al-Yaqza, Mishkat, Al-Nahda, Al-Majales, Al-Balagh,* and a monthly magazine called *Homat Alwatan* published by the Ministry of Defense.

69. In 1976, the Kuwait News Agency (KUNA) was established to gather news and disseminate information about Kuwait to an international audience. KUNA, which is considered the voice of the Ministry of Information, provides information on various political and socioeconomic issues and conducts research.[210] Kuwait Journalist Association was established in 1964 aiming to strengthen ties of friendship between

---

205. Nabeel A. Jurdi & Ali A Dashti. *Communication Policies in the State of Kuwait.* 96 Annals of The Faculty of Arts XIV (1994).
206. M. Almashiki. *The Media in the Arab Gulf.* (Alfalah Publishing, 2008).
207. M. Alshanoofi. *Tareekh Ale'elam Fi Alkuwait Wal Khaleej.* (Department of Mass Communication, 1999).
208. AldiwanvAlamiri. *The Initials in Kuwait History.* http://www.da.gov.kw/eng/picsandevents/first_time_in_kuwaits_history.php
209. *Kuwait.* Press Reference, http://www.pressreference.com/Gu-Ku/Kuwait.html (accessed May 15, 2017).
210. *Ibid.*

journalists in Kuwait and Arab Countries, increase local honesty, protect the rights of members, and facilitate ways for doing their journalism duties (Association).

Kuwaiti Newspapers

Name of Newspaper	*Kind*	*Year*	*Editor in Chief & Owners*	*Owner*
Al-Seyassah[1]	Daily	1965	Ahmad Al-Jarallah	Ahmed Al-Jarallah
Al-Qabas[2]	Daily	1972	Walid Al-Nusif	Kuwaiti merchant families
Al-Anbaa[3]	Daily	1976	Yousef Khalid Al-Marzouq	Khalid Al-Marzouq
Al Rai – Alrai-Alaam[4]	Daily	1995-2006	Majed Yousuf Al-Ali	Jassim Al Boodai
Al-Wasat[5]	Daily	2007	Adnan Al-Wazzan	Alwzzan Family
Annahar[6]	Daily	2007	Emad Jawad Bukhamseen	Jawad Bukhamseen
Al-Shahed[7]	Daily	2007	Sabah Al-Sabah	Sabah Al-Sabah
Al-Jarida[8]	Daily	2007	Khalid Alhelal	Mohammad AlSager
Al-Sabah[9]	Daily	2007	Barakat Al-Hudaiban	Al-Sabah for Press, Publishing & Distribution
Al Kuwaiteya[10]	Daily	2011	Zuhair Al Abbad	Al-Awraq Al-Kuwaitia for Media Services
Kuwait Times (English)[11]	Daily	1961	Yousuf Saleh Alyan	Yousuf Saleh Alyan
Arab Times (English)[12]	Daily	1977	Ahmed Al-Jarallah	Ahmed Al-Jarallah
Al-Dostour[13]	Weekly	2007	Allam Al-Kandari	National Assembly
Al Khaleej[14]	Weekly	2009	Ahmad Behbehani	Ahmad Behbehani,
Al Taleea[15]	Weekly	1962–2016	Abdullah Al-Nibari	Not available
Al-Watan[16]	Daily	1974–2015	Khalifa Al Ali Al Sabah	Ali Al-Khalifa Al Ali Al Sabah

AlRay AlAam[17]	Daily	1962–1995	Abdulaziz Fahed Al Massaeed	Abdulaziz Fahed Al Massaeed
Alam Al Yawm[18]	Daily	2007–2014	Ahmad Al Daas	Ahmad Al Daas &Ahmad Al Jabr Al Shemmeri
Al Daar[19]	Daily	2008–2013	Abdulhussain Al-Sultan	Mahmood Haider
Al-Watan Daily (English)[20]	Daily	2008–2013	Khalifa Al Ali Al Sabah	Ali Al-Khalifa Al Ali Al Sabah
Al Huriyah	Daily	2009–2012	Reem Albaghdadi[21]	Mathni Al-Farij
Al Mustagbal[22]	Daily	2010–2012	Sultan Al-Adwani	Albath Alfadhae Al Arabi
Arrouiah	Daily	2008–2010	Saud Al Sebeiei	Shireeda Al Mousherji
Awan	Daily	2007–2010	Mohammad Al-Rumaihi	Howar Lile'elam
Assawt[23]	Daily	2008–2009	Fahad Alkashti	Yas Investment Company
Alkuwait Alyom[24]		1954	The State of Kuwait	Government's official newspaper

1. http://al-seyassah.com/
2. http://alqabas.com/
3. http://www.alanba.com.kw/newspaper/
4. http://www.alraimedia.com/
5. http://www.alwasat.com.kw/
6. http://www.annahar.com.kw/Annahar/Default.aspx
7. http://www.alshahedkw.com/
8. http://www.aljarida.com/
9. http://www.alsabahpress.com/
10. http://www.alkuwaityah.com/
11. http://news.kuwaittimes.net/website/
12. http://www.arabtimesonline.com/news/
13. http://www.dostor.org/

14. http://alkhaleej-kw.com/
15. Online account is suspended
16. http://alwatan.kuwait.tt/
17. http://alrayalaam.com/
18. Online account is suspended
19. Online account is suspended
20. Online account is suspended, but you can get the issue in this link: https://issuu.com/alwatandaily
21. She was the first editor in-chief after switched to women newspaper. (http://www.kuwaitnews.com/kuwait/locals/20347-2012-04-28-14-06-08)
22. http://www.almustagbal.com/content/page/1
23. http://www.alsawtnews.cc/
24. http://kuwaitalyawm.media.gov.kw/

E. Social and Online Media

70. Kuwait is among the world's more outspoken and connected nations.[211,212] The use of social media organically stems from a nation whose "democratic tradition may have played a role in Kuwait being among the first Arab countries to link to the then-backbone of the internet," wrote Kaposi[213] about a network connection established in 1992 at Kuwait University. By 1997, the private telecommunication sector provided Internet services, leading to the development of one of the highest Internet users per capita in the Muslim world by 1998.[214] Against this backdrop, the fact that Kuwaitis are avid social media users should not be surprising.

71. The penetration of Twitter into the Kuwaiti population is the highest in the world.[215] It is worth noting that Kuwaitis actively consume and produce more Twitter content than any other Middle Eastern nation.[216] Aladwani[217] cites Mourtada, Salem, Al-Dabbagh and Gaggani's[218] statistics that Kuwaitis make up 30% of all Middle Eastern Twitter messages despite making up "less than 1% of the population of Arab

211. Adel M Aladwani. *Facilitators, Characteristics, and Impacts of Twitter Use: Theoretical Analysis and Empirical Illustration.* 35 International Journal of Information Management. 15,25. (2015).
212. Mark Graham, Monica Stephens & Scott Hale. *Featured Graphic. Mapping the Geoweb: A Geography of Twitter.*45 Environment and Planning. 100–102. (2013).
213. Ildiko Kaposi. *The Culture and Politics of Internet Use among Young People in Kuwait.* 8 Cyberpsychology: Journal of Psychosocial Research on Cyberspace. 2 (2015).
214. *Ibid.*
215. Mark Graham, Monica Stephens & Scott Hale. *Featured Graphic. Mapping the Geoweb: A Geography of Twitter.*45 Environment and Planning. 100–102. (2013).
216. Adel M Aladwani. *Facilitators, Characteristics, and Impacts of Twitter Use: Theoretical Analysis and Empirical Illustration.* 35 International Journal of Information Management. 18. (2015).
217. *Ibid.*
218. R. Mourtada, and F Salem. *Social Media in the Arab World: Influencing Societal and Cultural Change.* Arab social media report 2, 1,28 (2012).

countries." Further, Aladwani cites statistics that demonstrate that the number of Kuwaiti tweets produced is higher than the sum of those produced by eighteen of twenty-two Arab countries.[219]

72. Arab cultural values and tendencies are reflected in their use of social and online media. For example, Sharif and Al-Kandari[220] revealed gender differences in uses of online bulletin boards by women in the six Arab nations that make up the GCC: Bahrain, Kuwait, Oman, Qatar, the United Arab Emirates, and Saudi Arabia. Given the limitations many parents place on their daughters, more than half of the women in their sample reported using online bulletin boards for at least three hours a day.[221] Further, Sharif and Al-Kandari[222] (2010) revealed a tendency not to endorse greater gender equality by the examined female users of online bulletin boards in the GCC. While the researchers called their findings "disappointing"[223] (Sharif & Al-Kandari, 2010, p. 49), they did not explore the possibility that this finding is a symptom of a larger tendency of women living in misogynistic environments to value gender roles that favor men[224] (Szymanski, Gupta, Carr, & Stewart, 2009; Tosone, 2009).

73. However, the scholars did find that the females used online bulletin boards to listen to different perspectives—a behavior that was interpreted to demonstrate the openness of Arab women. Stronger was the finding that women use these websites as a means to confirm existing attitudes, demonstrating the need for belonging and the conservative nature of society.[225] Despite recounting several women who have achieved high management positions at newspapers, news agencies, and universities, Dashti and Mesbah[226] (2016) explain that Kuwaiti society discourages women from "asserting their independence and individualism"[227] (p. 12). Regardless of the reasons underlying the phenomenon, there seems to be a tendency for women not to advocate for gender equality even when it is legal. Chapter 7 will delve into the phenomenon of self-censorship among journalists and academics—two groups to which communication and media laws can be applied, regardless of gender.

74. Kuwaiti society has a collectivist culture where both men and women are identified by others based on their social networks, and time is organized in such a way that individuals are expected to spend much time on these social relationships

---

219. *Ibid.*
220. Ahmad A. Sharif & Ali A Al-Kandari. *The Use of Online Bulletin Boards by Females in the Gulf Cooperation Council Countries.* 27 Telematics and Informatics. 42,50. (2010).
221. *Ibid.*
222. *Ibid.*
223. *Ibid.*
224. Dawn M. Szymanski, Arpana Gupta, Erika R Carr & Destin Stewart. *Internalized Misogyny as a Moderator of the Link between Sexist Events and Women's Psychological Distress.* 61 Sex Roles. 101–109. (2009).
225. Ahmad A. Sharif & Ali A Al-Kandari. *The Use of Online Bulletin Boards by Females in the Gulf Cooperation Council Countries.* 27 Telematics and Informatics. 42,50. (2010).
226. Ali A. Dashti & Hesham Mesbah. *The Perceptions of Female Media Professionals in Kuwait About Their Job: An Empowerment Perspective.* Feminist. 16 Media Studies 276,92 (2016).
227. *Ibid.*

and obligations—regardless of gender.[228] Despite this similarity, women must be careful when disclosing personal information for reasons "beyond safety concerns."[229] Kuwaiti women are considered indecent for disclosing personal information, for spending time with a man with the door closed or going on a date without a chaperone.[230] Thus, it should be unsurprising when almost double the number of Kuwaiti men post personal photographs compared to Kuwaiti women. The findings of Al-Kandari, Al-Sumait, and Al-Hunaiyyan[231] reveal that Instagram is not a rich enough medium for social connection to motivate the use of the medium; rather, entertainment is a much more motivating factor for both sexes. The scholars cite "regular censorship of moral content in cinemas and print media" in addition to the lack of available venues for single men and women to mix, such as nightclubs and concerts as a possible reason Instagram is used for entertainment purposes.[232]

75. Yet, the secondary motivations of Kuwaiti women and men's use of Instagram does differ.[233] For example, Kuwaiti women use Instagram to look for information while Kuwaiti men use it for social connection.[234] The conservative nature of Kuwaiti society may explain the freedom that is afforded only to men in connecting with others through social media websites while that freedom is denied to women. Once again, Arab social reality is reflected in the use of online and social media.

76. Even when the medium changes, gender differences in its uses remain. For example, Al-Kandari, Melkote, and Sharif[235] reveal that men are more likely to disclose less superficial information through Instagram and more likely to have public accounts than women. When women do have private accounts, the likelihood of their posting more honest images than those who did not increases.[236] The depth males disclose on public accounts reveals a barrier that faces only women and which is made up of possible fear, shame, or other negative experiences that are reserved for women in the Kuwaiti cultural context. Al-Kandari, Melkote, and Sharif[237] explain this "cultural prohibition" by highlighting the importance of complying with a patriarchal family structure and the cultural requirements that females are more deferential to elders and males and simultaneously "less democratically expressive of their true opinions and beliefs"[238] (p. 14). In other words, there is a censoring effect on women that is a part

228. Ali A. Al-Kandari, Fahad Y. Al-Sumait & Ahmed Al-Hunaiyyan. *Looking Perfect: Instagram Use in a Kuwaiti Cultural Context.* Journal of International and Intercultural Communication 1,18 (2017).
229. *Ibid., 5.*
230. *Ibid., 1, 18.*
231. *Ibid.*
232. *Ibid.,.*
233. *Ibid., 1, 18.*
234. *Ibid.*
235. Ali Al-Kandari, Srinivas R Melkote, and Ahmad Sharif. *Needs and Motives of Instagram Users That Predict Self-Disclosure Use: A Case Study of Young Adults in Kuwait.* 11 Journal of Creative Communications. 85,101(2016).
236. *Ibid.*
237. *Ibid.*
238. Ali Al-Kandari, Srinivas R Melkote, and Ahmad Sharif. *Needs and Motives of Instagram Users That Predict Self-Disclosure Use: A Case Study of Young Adults in Kuwait.* 11 Journal of Creative Communications. 14 (2016).

of the Kuwaiti culture that is true even when the medium is more visual in nature—like Instagram.

77. Fascinatingly indeed, this cultural tendency is within the context of a country with an increasing number of women's rights and economic opportunities—specifically in the media industry. For example, Dashti, and Mesbah[239] explain that there has been a notable increase in the number of women working in the media industry since the 1990 Iraqi invasion of Kuwait. Women hold positions in content development, production, and even management. Bibi Al-Marzouk became the first female editor-in-chief of a Kuwaiti newspaper in 1997, and Iqbal Al-Ahmad was named as editor-in-chief of the Kuwait News Agency in 2001.[240] In other words, the tendency for women to engage in self-censorship on a personal level in using online and social media is offset by the provision of professional opportunities for women.

78. The nuances of the inclusion of women's voices are rather complex and worthy of study. Kuwaiti women report that they are not fearful of isolation, which Dashti, Al-Abdullah, and Johar[241] suggest are the result of governmental support, international support, constitutional legality and an increased participation of women in education, travel, and political participation. Despite such positive attitudes, a study examining Kuwaiti women confirmed the operation of the spiral of silence theory both in-person and on Twitter.[242] In other words, Kuwaiti women are likely to calculate the majority opinion prior to expressing their own, measure the degree to which their opinions would be supported by the majority and then decide to silence minority perspectives.[243] However, their findings revealed that the decision not to communicate with unfamiliar people is due to the difficulty of calculating the opinion held by the unfamiliar person.[244] Clearly, the cultural values of Arabs are carried from the social reality to the mediated reality in great numbers.

79. In Kuwait, "the growth in the number of Internet users tells only one part of the story, though."[245] Kaposi[246] explains that the nature of the Internet changed between the early 2000s and the early 2010s. As the nature of the Internet changed, so did the way the Internet was used by Kuwaitis. Kaposi[247] cites a high rate of mobile phone penetration throughout the population as one of the factors contributing to social media use. Government, media, and business require people to use social media.[248] This use has been for a plethora of reasons—including developing friendship, finding

239. Ali A. Dashti & Hesham Mesbah. *The Perceptions of Female Media Professionals in Kuwait About Their Job: An Empowerment Perspective.* Feminist. 16 Media Studies 276,92 (2016).
240. *Ibid.*
241. Ali A Dashti, Hamed H Al-Abdullah, and Hasan A Johar. *Social Media and the Spiral of Silence: The Case of Kuwaiti Female Students' Political Discourse on Twitter.* Journal of International 16 Women's Studies 42(2015): 42.
242. *Ibid.*
243. *Ibid.*
244. *Ibid.*
245. Ildiko Kaposi. *The Culture and Politics of Internet Use among Young People in Kuwait.* 8 Cyberpsychology: Journal of Psychosocial Research on Cyberspace. 2. (2015).
246. Ildiko Kaposi. *The Culture and Politics of Internet Use among Young People in Kuwait.* 8 Cyberpsychology: Journal of Psychosocial Research on Cyberspace. (2015).
247. *Ibid.*
248. *Ibid.*

a potential spouse, accessing popular culture, and learning about health and current affairs.[249] So ingrained is the need for Internet access, that Kaposi[250] cites a newspaper article reporting an investigation of the installation of Internet routers in prison buildings.

80. How is Twitter used by different users in Kuwait? Aladwani[251] found that individuals produced approximately double the number of Twitter messages than the combined total of messages produced by government and corporations in Kuwait. Individuals had a higher number of followers, but businesses had a higher number of friends on Twitter. Individuals who produced tweets were more engaging than corporations.[252] Government Twitter accounts focused on employment, health, and education while businesses promoted their products and services.[253] Individual users wrote about topics such as education, travel, health, religion, and employment.[254] Moreover, individuals reported being motivated to post by "freedom of expression, privacy laws and social activism."[255] Although Twitter is used differently by government, businesses, and people, it is a space for robust public debate and the improvement of various parts of Kuwaiti life.

81. In Kuwait, activists have employed communication technologies to successfully affect political reform. Activists demanding electoral reform in 2006 used e-mail, blogs, and text messages to reach newspapers and legislators and to organize protests, some of which faced Special Forces at the gates of the Kuwaiti National Assembly.[256] The Orange Movement, which got its name by the color of clothes worn by activists, is an example of a nonviolent political movement where activists were successful in achieving their political agenda, in part due to their use of blogs, without being subjected to censorship.[257] The activists, who were mostly young and educated in the United States for approximately 4–6 years, employed grassroots organization methods to fight corruption by decreasing the number of electoral districts from twenty-five to five. The activists, who felt pessimistic because corruption was seen as part of the electoral system, wanted smaller districts because they would be more difficult for "the government to intervene and manipulate the political process."[258] Albloshi and Alfahad[259] noted that Kuwaiti newspapers did not support the movement, and *Al Watan* even mocked it and its leaders. Several blogs with credibility among Kuwaiti readers were "the core

249. *Ibid.*
250. *Ibid.*
251. Adel M Aladwani. Facilitators, Characteristics, and Impacts of Twitter Use: Theoretical Analysis and Empirical Illustration. 35 International Journal of Information Management. 15,25. (2015).
252. *Ibid.*
253. *Ibid.*
254. *Ibid.*
255. Adel M Aladwani. Facilitators, Characteristics, and Impacts of Twitter Use: Theoretical Analysis and Empirical Illustration. 35 International Journal of Information Management. 18. (2015).
256. Hamad Albloshi & Faisal Alfahad. *The Orange Movement of Kuwait: civic pressure transforms a political system.* In Civilian Jihad, 219,232. (Springer, 2009).
257. *Ibid.*
258. *Ibid., 221.*
259. *Ibid., 219, 232.*

of the movement."[260] Overall when online media first emerged in Kuwait, it was a place where harsher criticism of the government was tolerated than in newspapers.[261]

82. Prior to the Arab uprisings of the early 2010s, social media were used to advocate for political reform. It is extremely important to note that the "Kuwaiti authorities never attempted to ban blogging or take down sites."[262] Organizers of the movement cite the blogs' refraining from criticizing the regime and a possible underestimation of the influence of Kuwaiti bloggers as reasons for the lack of censorship.[263] Further, the movement included various segments across the political and ideological spectrum.[264] The riots led to the dissolution of parliament and elected representatives who opposed the Orange Movement did not win any parliamentary seats in the elections held on June 29, 2006.[265] By July 12, 2006, the new electoral system was passed by the National Assembly.[266]

83. In conclusion, the role of social media in Kuwait is quite complex. Social media have led to real social changes in terms of politics and gender. Social media in Kuwait are particularly effective due to the Kuwaiti culture's innovative nature when it comes to technological developments.

F. Online Newspapers and News Apps

84. In the year after the implementation of the 2016 Electronic media law, 365 publications applied for online news licenses. The latest official list from January 4, 2018 shows that 213 licenses have been issued by the Ministry of Information to date. The law gave the existing online news sites one year to apply for a license, which period ended on 24 July, 2017. While sites that failed to apply by the deadline are in violation of the law, the license application process remains open for these publications. The deadline does not concern new news sites that need to go through the license application process before starting their operations.[267]

II. Ownership Models

85. The ownership of media outlets in Kuwait must be understood within the context of its history. While Kuwait gained its independence from Great Britain in 1961, its newspapers date back to the late 1920s.[268] Daily newspapers began in the

260. *Ibid., 227.*
261. Ali A Dashti. *The Role of Online Journalism in Political Disputes in Kuwait.* Journal of Arab & Muslim Media Research. 91,112 (2009).
262. *Ibid.*
263. Hamad Albloshi & Faisal Alfahad. *The Orange Movement of Kuwait: civic pressure transforms a political system.* In Civilian Jihad, 219,232. (Springer, 2009).
264. *Ibid.*
265. *Ibid., 227.*
266. *Ibid., 219, 232.*
267. Mohammad Rashed. *"Alaelam" rasd almukhalafat baad entihae mudat tarkhees "aleliktroni" ghadan.* (Aljarida, 2017, accessed Jan. 27, 2018 http://www.aljarida.com/?previous=2017-07-24).
268. Fayad Kazan. *Kuwait.* In Mass Media in the Middle East. (Greenwood Press, 1994).

1960s, which is the time period to which the tradition of an independent Kuwaiti press can be traced.[269]

86. The laws that regulate the establishment of various media outlets—including newspapers and broadcasting stations—have changed over time. The first media law regulating newspapers can be traced back to 1956, before Kuwait's independence.[270] The laws have changed dramatically over time, and the number of newly licensed newspapers in Kuwait tripled three years after the 2006 publication law.[271] This law decreased "state-imposed barriers of entry" which restricted newspaper ownership in Kuwait.[272] Even a decade before this law was passed, scholars observed that "Kuwaiti media have progressed both quantitatively and qualitatively,"[273] which can be explained by its pluralistic demographic structure, high political participation rates and cultural characteristics that make it "unlike the media of the other Gulf countries."[274]

87. Thus, the fact that most Kuwaiti newspapers are owned by prominent families is noteworthy, as the media literature is consistent with Herb's[275] observation that Kuwaiti people are culturally more prone to negotiating power with political and economic elites.

88. Scholars do not have a consensus on how Kuwait's media ownership affects the editorial stances of newspapers. For example, Kazan[276] states that the editorial stances of newspapers depend on issues and change over time. Moreover, Kazan[277] explains that all of Kuwait's daily newspapers have both defended and criticized the government and parliament while refraining from engaging in taboo topics—namely the monarchy and religion.

89. The same newspapers that Kazan[278] refers to as liberal are referred to as conservative by Rugh.[279] In other words, there is notable disagreement on the political orientations and editorial stances of newspapers that are likely to be indicative of greater problems scholars have in comparing liberals and conservatives in Kuwait to those in other nations.

90. Selvik[280] makes sense of these differences by explaining several points. First, he explains that the decreasing of political barriers to newspaper ownership gave

269. Kjetil Selvik, Jon Nordenson &Tewodros Aragie Kebede. *Print Media Liberalization and Electoral Coverage Bias in Kuwait.* 69 The Middle East Journal. 255,276. (2015).
270. Fayad Kazan. *Kuwait.* In Mass Media in the Middle East. (Greenwood Press, 1994).
271. Kjetil Selvik. *Elite Rivalry in a Semi-Democracy: The Kuwaiti Press Scene.* 47 Middle Eastern Studies 477,496 (2011).
272. *Ibid., 478.*
273. Fayad Kazan. *Kuwait.* In Mass Media in the Middle East. 147 (Greenwood Press, 1994).
274. *Ibid.*
275. Michael Herb. The Origins of Kuwait's National Assembly. (2016, London School of Economics and Political Science, http://eprints.lse.ac.uk/65693/1/39_MichaelHerb.pdf).
276. Fayad Kazan. *Kuwait.* In Mass Media in the Middle East. (Greenwood Press, 1994).
277. *Ibid.*
278. *Ibid.*
279. William A. Rugh. *Arab mass media: Newspapers, radio, and television in Arab politics.* (Greenwood publishing group, 2004).
280. Kjetil Selvik. Elite Rivalry in a Semi-Democracy: The Kuwaiti Press Scene. 47 Middle Eastern Studies 477,496 (2011).

voice to "previously marginalized groups like the Salafis and the Shi'a."[281] Second, newspapers are used in Kuwait as a way to demonstrate "prestige and recognition" to new entrants to the economic elite strata of society. Third, newspapers are used as political tools to buy support for various political agendas—an important consideration in a nation where political parties and related regulations of political organizing are absent. Thus, Selvik observes that there are "signs that members of the ruling family use media outlets to attack each other by proxy"[282] and provide funding in order to ensure that their agendas are secured. Selvik explains that newspapers are seen as civil society tools, as he warns of the dangers that blurring state and society can pose to Kuwait's democracy.

91. Despite this confusion, Kazan[283] states that some newspapers have attracted individuals more interested in religion—such as *Al-Watan*. As sectarianism has risen in the decade after the September 11, 2001 terrorist attacks on U.S. soil and the subsequent removal of Saddam Hussein from Iraq's government, several newspapers have discontinued their operations for political reasons that are not completely unrelated to religion. *Al-Watan* is one of these newspapers and so is *Al-Dar*, which Selvik[284] describes as a newspaper established in April of 2008 by a prominent Shi'ite businessman interested in advocating "against the Sunni Islamist and tribal opposition."[285] *Al-Watan* continued to publish an electronic version of its paper from outside of Kuwait, which led to a new regulation of electronic laws in 2015. Chapters 3 through 5 will outline the sources of Kuwaiti media law at a greater depth.

92. Newspapers are the medium to which Kuwaitis were accustomed to obtain information on issues salient in the public sphere,[286] even though similar deregulations of television and radio occurred. It is fascinating to observe that although the Kuwaiti government was the first of 10 Arab states to invest in television, the government permitted a wealthy merchant to establish the first television station privately until it was able to develop a government-run system to take it over.[287] The trend for government-controlled television began in the 1960s and ended in the 2000s when private television and radio stations were allowed to be licensed.

281. *Ibid., 492.*
282. *Ibid., 493.*
283. Fayad Kazan. *Kuwait.* In Mass Media in the Middle East. (Greenwood Press, 1994).
284. Kjetil Selvik. Elite Rivalry in a Semi-Democracy: The Kuwaiti Press Scene. 47 Middle Eastern Studies 477,496 (2011).
285. *Ibid., 485.*
286. Kjetil Selvik, Jon Nordenson &Tewodros Aragie Kebede. *Print Media Liberalization and Electoral Coverage Bias in Kuwait.* 69 The Middle East Journal. 255,276. (2015).
287. William A. Rugh. *Arab mass media: Newspapers, radio, and television in Arab politics.* (Greenwood publishing group, 2004).

III. Infrastructure

A. Cable/Fiber-Optics Penetration

93. In order to understand the development of fiber optics in Kuwait, it is necessary to provide the relevant context that sheds light on the function and importance of fiber optics. Certain infrastructure requirements need to be met for Internet access to be available in different countries across the globe.[288] These infrastructure requirements can be considered in three levels: international, national and access networks.[289]

94. The first level of infrastructure required for nations across the globe to access the Internet is international and regional.[290] Data travels in several ways across the globe, and the Middle East and North African region generally is well-connected to the Internet. In this world region, data travels in several ways, including "submarine cables, terrestrial fiber, microwave, and satellite transmission accounting for a smaller amount."[291] Submarine cables, "buried in the sea beds that spans entire oceans,"[292] carry the majority of the information that travels across the world.

95. Kuwait is connected to several submarine cables including "FLAG, FOG, SMW3, SMW4, Falcon, and GBI,"[293] Kuwait is also connected to the Gulf Cooperation Council Interconnection Authority (GCCIA), which is based out of Saudi Arabia,[294] Although the GCCIA leases its fiber-optic cables to Kuwait,[295] Kuwait's Central Agency for Information Technology[296] has reported that this has not translated into improved Internet services for the end-users.[297]

96. The second level of the infrastructure that enables online connectivity, the national level, can explain this. There is a point at which the international communication infrastructure needs to be distributed within the country.[298] Historically, Kuwaitis

288. Natalija Gelvanovska, Michel Rogy & Carlo Maria Rossotto. *Infrastructure Deployment and Developing Competition.*" In Directions in Development-Information and Communication Technologies, 59–99, (2014).
289. *Ibid.*
290. *Ibid.*
291. *Ibid., 59.*
292. Ryan W. Neal. *Underwater Internet Cables: 'Submarine Cable Map' Shows How the World Gets Online*. International Business Times 2 (2014).
293. The Central Agency for Information Technology. *Consolidated Kuwait National ICT Indicators Report.* (2016, accessed Jun. 7, 2017, https://www.e.gov.kw/sites/kgoarabic/Forms/FinalConsolidatedEnglishReportSinglePages.pdf).
294. Natalija Gelvanovska, Michel Rogy & Carlo Maria Rossotto. *Infrastructure Deployment and Developing Competition.*`" In Directions in Development-Information and Communication Technologies, 59–99, (2014).
295. *Ibid.*
296. The Central Agency for Information Technology. *Consolidated Kuwait National ICT Indicators Report.* (2016, accessed Jun. 7, 2017, https://www.e.gov.kw/sites/kgoarabic/Forms/FinalConsolidatedEnglishReportSinglePages.pdf).
297. *Ibid.*
298. Natalija Gelvanovska, Michel Rogy & Carlo Maria Rossotto. *Infrastructure Deployment and Developing Competition.*`" In Directions in Development-Information and Communication Technologies, 59–99, (2014).

accessed the Internet through dial-up connections which utilized copper cables for the data transfers.[299] Smith[300] reported that some Kuwaitis partially blame the political environment for their failure to invest in infrastructure. In 2016, a report cited *The Kuwait Times* announcing the beginning of a privatization process for information-technology infrastructure that would be overseen by a regulatory body established in 2014, the Communication and IT Regulatory Authority (CITRA) .[301] According to Kuwait's Central Agency for Information Technology[302] (2016), approximately 15–25% of the Kuwaiti population had access to fiber-optic connections by 2013. An estimated 130,000 connections were fiber optic by 2015.[303] However, this number is expected to increase by 2019 to approximately 200,000 connections.[304]

97. Generally, there are two categories of access networks: fixed and mobile.[305] Fixed broadband technologies are ones where the user must be located in a specific physical location in order to access the Internet.[306] These include wired, wireless, and satellite connections.[307]

98. Fixed connections can take on three wired forms.[308] First, they can be made of copper wires that connect to a digital telephone network.[309] Second, cable television networks can also supply Internet services that are wired.[310] Third, fiber-optic networks are newer networks that are wired.[311]

99. Some fixed connections are not wired. For example, wireless connections require the use of technology referred to as Worldwide Interoperability for Microwave Access (WiMax).[312] Finally, when wired and wireless technologies are not available, satellite connections are a third option for wired Internet access.[313] Fixed connections can be contrasted with mobile broadband connections.[314]

299. The Central Agency for Information Technology. *Consolidated Kuwait National ICT Indicators Report.* (2016, accessed Jun. 7, 2017, https://www.e.gov.kw/sites/kgoarabic/Forms/FinalConsolidatedEnglishReportSinglePages.pdf).
300. Matt Smith. *Kuwait Internet Firm Blasts Price Cuts, Infrastructure*. Reuters, (accessed May 15, 2017 http://www.reuters.com/article/net-us-kuwait-internet-idUSBRE88Q11U20120927).
301. Telegeography. *Moc Kuwait's Fixed Infrastructure to Be Privatised* (accessed May 15, 2017, https://www.telegeography.com/products/commsupdate/articles/2016/03/22/moc-kuwaits-fixed-infrastructure-to-be-privatised/).
302. *The Central Agency for Information Technology. Consolidated Kuwait National ICT Indicators Report. (2016, accessed Jun. 7, 2017,* https://www.e.gov.kw/sites/kgoarabic/Forms/FinalConsolidatedEnglishReportSinglePages.pdf*).*
303. *Ibid.*
304. *Ibid.*
305. Natalija Gelvanovska, Michel Rogy & Carlo Maria Rossotto. *Infrastructure Deployment and Developing Competition.'*" In Directions in Development-Information and Communication Technologies, 59–99, (2014).
306. *Ibid.*
307. *Ibid.*
308. *Ibid.*
309. *Ibid.*
310. *Ibid.*
311. *Ibid.*
312. *Ibid.*
313. *Ibid.*
314. *Ibid.*

100. Mobile broadband technologies allow individuals to access broadband services without being confined to a specific physical location.[315] Mobile broadband technologies are sometimes categorized into generations of communication technologies. The fourth generation (4G) of mobile technology would provide a faster transfer of data than the third generation (3G) technologies.

101. It is important to note that Gulf nations are different from the rest of the MENA in how individuals access the Internet—through mobile broadband.[316] Kuwait is one of the only four countries to have access to 4G technologies before December 2012, and the penetration of mobile broadband in the Gulf is an estimated 64.8%.[317] In the next section, more details of the Kuwaiti mobile market will be described.

B. Mobile Market

102. According to a report by the Central Agency for Information Technology in Kuwait, the availability and use of mobiles is widespread in Kuwait. For example, a third of Kuwaiti homes have fixed-line telephones which is a rate far below the 99.7% of the Kuwaiti population that has a smart phone. There are 8.7 million mobile telephone subscriptions in Kuwait, which is almost double the population. In contrast, there are approximately 473,000 fixed telephone subscriptions. In fact, there are approximately 840,000 mobile data subscribers—which is almost double the number for fixed telephone subscriptions. Fixed telephone connections are available across 100% of Kuwait, where voice data is transmitted rapidly and accurately[318] through digital exchanges. Almost all households have access to a telephone.

103. In addition to other uses, Kuwaitis use their cell phones to access the Internet. Similarly, there are twice as many mobile subscriptions as fixed subscriptions to access data. In fact, approximately 60% of Kuwaiti homes have a computer or a tablet, but 50% have a tablet. This translates to low-level usage of computer, and the statistics for a computer used by all members of a household was quite low at 28%. Yet, 80% of Kuwaiti households have access to the Internet. The majority of Kuwaiti households access the Internet through their mobile phones. Many households purchase Internet access through their mobile operators, separately from the Internet access they access on their mobile phones. Among the services purchased by mobile operators are MIFI, dongle and USB modem services.

104. The Internet is used in different ways and for various purposes. Social networks are widely used regardless of the user's age. WhatsApp is a text-messaging application that is commonly used regardless of the nationality of the user. While Kuwaitis use Instagram, Twitter, and Snapchat more frequently, expatriates are more likely to use Facebook. The most commonly used online activities involve communication, with instant messaging, e-mail and social networking websites being the most reported activities online. Among activities to receive information, Kuwaitis are likely to receive

315. *Ibid.*
316. *Ibid.*
317. *Ibid.*
318. V4 Telecom. *Fixed Line Service.* (2015, accessed Mar. 12, 2017, https://www.v4telecom.co.uk/fixed-line-service).

news and information as well as explore links on social networks to access external websites.

105. According to CAIT, the Internet is used to formulate political opinions among individuals. Kuwaitis also react to current events through the Internet, with approximately 20% having used the Internet to contact a government official or politician. While televisions are found in 91% of Kuwaiti households, Kuwaitis agree that the Internet is becoming a much more essential source of entertainment and information than television, radio, or newspapers. Individuals feel the Internet is both accurate and reliable as a source of information and entertainment. However, a study by Elareshi, Ziani and Gunter[319] revealed that Kuwaiti university students are more likely to follow national news on social media. This suggests that Kuwaitis' reliance on newspapers may be shifting from the printed versions to online versions. This is important to note because newspapers are an important source of political information in Kuwait.

106. The entire nation of Kuwait is covered by a mobile network, and 97% of Kuwait is connected to a fourth Generation Long Term Evolution (4G LTE) network.[320] A 4G LTE network is considered one of the fastest for data download, as it downloads between 5–12 megabits per second.[321] There are four ISPs (FASTtelco, QualityNet, Gulfnet, and KEMS) responsible for offering fixed connectivity services to enterprises and consumers under the supervision of the Ministry of Communication.[322] These four Internet service providers use fixed connections that are both established and maintained by Kuwait's Ministry of Communication, the agency that regulates them. The Internet service providers then provide their services to individual consumers and businesses.

IV. Technological and Economic Developments on Media Markets

A. Changes to Regulatory Bodies

107. By 1857, the Ottoman and British empires realized the needs for telegraphic messages after a number of revolts and wars spread across Europe and Asia. *Alqabas* published a letter written by Sheikh Jaber Mubarak Alsabah on October 24, 1916 asking the British political agent to provide previously denied water and shelter from rain to Kuwaiti laborers who had been contracted by Great Britain to link two Iraqi ports, Al-Faw and Umm Qasr, to Kuwait by cable.[323] On December 4, 1916, the first

319. Mokhtar Elareshi, Abdul-Karim Ziani & Barrie Gunter. *How GCC University Students Get Local News and Information*. 2 Studies in Media and Communication. 1,12 (2014).
320. The Central Agency for Information Technology. *Consolidated Kuwait National ICT Indicators Report*. (2016, accessed Jun. 7, 2017, https://www.e.gov.kw/sites/kgoarabic/Forms/FinalConsolidatedEnglishReportSinglePages.pdf).
321. J.D. Biersdorfer. *Q&A: The Difference between 4G and 4G LTE*. The New York Times, 2012.
322. The Central Agency for Information Technology. *Consolidated Kuwait National ICTIndicators Report*. (2016, accessed Jun. 7, 2017, https://www.e.gov.kw/sites/kgoarabic/Forms/FinalConsolidatedEnglishReportSinglePages.pdf).
323. Alelectrony, Moharer Alqabas. "Hajat Alhikomatayn Alothmaniya Walberitaniya Wara Insha'a Albarq Fe Alkhaleej: 100 'Am Ala Iftitah Maktab Altelegraph Fe Alkuwait." Alqabas, Dec. 29, 2016.

telegram office was established to send electronic messages to India, Great Britain, and other Arab states.[324]

108. A century later by 2017, the Kuwaiti Ministry of Communications (MOC) was engaged in a major transition that would remove the regulation of telecommunication from its responsibilities[325] (Hamza, 2016). On January 8, 2017, the official gazette of the State of Kuwait, *Alkuwait Alyom*,[326] published an Amiri decree that demonstrates the transfer of responsibilities of the Minister of Communication to the Minister of Service Affairs.[327] This transition heralds a change in the regulatory authorities and methods for the regulation of telecommunication. Employees of the MOC would continue to be employed under the ministry's new name, the Ministry of Services. However, the regulatory authority for telecommunication-related services would be moving to CITRA.

109. Historically, the MOC was in charge of telegram and postal services in addition to telecommunications.[328] In May 2014, the government implemented the Law No. 37 called "Telecoms Law" moving the power of the MOC as primary regulator of the telecommunications to the newly-formed Commission dividing telecommunication activities by service (sending or receiving and transmitting of information) and networks (using any national of international networks such as the Internet) between public and private.[329] This law makes violators, whether public or private, liable to three years imprisonment or a fine ranging from KWD 50,000 to KWD 500,000 or both for the violation. The law will be explained in greater detail in Chapter 7.[330]

B. *Digital Television*

110. Technological advancements in communication technologies have affected the Middle East in important ways. For example, Coll[331] explained that fax machines were utilized to send dissident messages by Saudi Arabian Islamists in the 1990s. Then, Coll[332] explained that Gulf dissidents' messages were transferred via satellite to Middle Eastern broadcast media. By the early 2000s, text messages were used to undermine parental control on gendered communications across the Gulf.[333]

324. Waseem Hamza. *Abul: Awda'a Alalameen Fe Almowasalat Lan Tataghayer*. Alqabas, Dec. 17, 2016.
325. *Ibid.*
326. Alkuwait Alyom. *Marsoom Raqam 5 L'sanat 2017 Fee Sha'an Ikhtisas Wazir Aldawlah L'sho'on Alkhidmat.*" In 1322 (The State of Kuwait., 2017).
327. *Ibid.*
328. Ministry of Communication. *The History of Ministry* (accessed May 17, 2017, http://moc.gov.kw/English/history.html).
329. DLA Piper. *Key Telecommunications Laws, Regulations and Policies*. https://www.dlapiperintelligence.com/telecoms/index.html?t=laws&c=KW
330. *Ibid.*
331. Steve Coll. *In the Gulf, Dissidence Goes Digital*. Washington Post 29 (2005).
332. *Ibid.*
333. *Ibid.*

111. However, television is a particularly important medium to the Gulf States. The Arab League[334] established Arabsat in 1976. Four satellites were to be operated by an intergovernmental organization that regulates the transmission of content to Africa, the Middle East, and Europe. These technologies have given rise to satellite news to be broadcast across the Arab world, including Al-Jazeera in Qatar and Al-Arabiya from Saudi Arabia.[335]

112. Historically, television was broadcast in analog or digital. In Kuwait, the transition to digital has complications because the installed infrastructure must survive a hot and dry climate.[336]

In 2016, a U.S. manufacturer from the state of Illinois, GatesAir[337], completed the second of three phases to support an improved digital TV network covering about 80% of urban areas and many desert regions in Kuwait. This move from analog to digital will provide high quality programming and media services.

C. *Social Media and Digital Convergence*

113. In reality, the world of communication technology changes rapidly. In January 2016, Netflix[338] expanded its international operations. Kuwaitis were able to access movies and television shows through the Internet on their computers, tablets, and smartphones. As local and international media organizations compete for audiences in Kuwait, the digital media landscape grows more complex.

114. Further, many newspapers have developed apps to compete with social media and other technologies for the dissemination of news. In Kuwait, Internet use has increased since it was introduced in the 1990s. In 2000, there were 150,000 Internet users and as of June 2016, it reached 3,202,110 with 79.9% penetration rate, and 2,300,000 Facebook users.[339]

115. According to the 2016 Global Information Technology Report, Kuwait is ranked 61 in networked readiness.[340] The International Telecommunication Union

334. David Ostroff. *Engines of Content Diversity: A Brief Chronicle of Communication Satellite Policies*. In Diverse Mediawerelden: Hedendaagse Reflecties Gebaseerd Op Het Onderzoek Van Frieda Saeys, Edited by Sofie Van Bauwel and Elke Van Damme, 161–75 (Academia Press, 2010).

335. Shahira Fahmy, Wayne Wanta & Erik C Nisbet. *Mediated Public Diplomacy: Satellite Tv News in the Arab World and Perception Effects*. 74 International Communication Gazette 728,749 (2012).

336. Dimension PR. *Gatesair Completes Phase Two Rollout of Dvb-T2 Digital TV Network in Kuwait*. (accessed Mar. 12, 2017, http://www.tvtechnology.com/thewire/gatesair-completes-phase-two-rollout-of-dvbt2-digital-tv-network-in-kuwait/6784/view).

337. *Ibid.*

338. Netflix. *Netflix is now available around the world*. (accessed Mar. 7, 2017, https://media.netflix.com/en/press-releases/netflix-is-now-available-around-the-world).

339. Internet World Stats: Usage and Population Statistics. *Middle East*. (accessed May 17, 2017, http://www.internetworldstats.com/middle.htm).

340. World Economic Forum. *Innovating in the Digital Economy*. (accessed May 17, 2017, http://www3.weforum.org/docs/GITR2016/GITR_2016_full%20report_final.pdf).

(ITU)'s "Measuring the Information Society Report" placed Kuwait 53 in the Internet Communication Technology Development Index.[341]

V. Sources of Media Law

116. There are several sources of media law in Kuwait, and some of them carry more weight than others. In the next section, we will outline the constitutional provisions on free speech. More details will follow with the inclusion of legislation passed by the National Assembly and other types of regulations, including ministerial bylaws. The texts of these laws, which appear in the Arabic language, have been translated and contextualized to clarify various aspects of Kuwaiti regulation of the media.

341. International Telecommunication Union. *Kuwait.* ITU Development Index (2016, http://www.itu.int/net4/ITU-D/idi/2016/#idi2016countrycard-tab&KWT).

Part I. Freedom of Speech

Chapter 1. Constitution

117. Noteworthy are several articles of the Constitution that deal with the freedom the press. Articles 36 & 37 of the 1961 Constitution specifically seek to protect the freedom of expression and the freedom of the press in Kuwait, but on the other hand, prohibit some content from individual denigration or criticism. The law defined the content that may cause the suspension of newspapers or jailing journalists if they publish materials that make blasphemous suggestions concerning God (Allah), the Prophet, his Companions, and the Quran, or criticizing the Amir's self-identity, government's secrets, and disseminating any information that may be construed to inflict harm on the economy, violate the country's ethical code, or encourage criminal behavior. Besides these subjects, the local press is free to publish what it wants in accordance with the stipulations articulated in the 1961 Press and Publication Laws, which clearly stated, "Freedom of printing, writing and publishing is guaranteed within the limits of this law."[342] "The law remained active for more than forty-five years, and because it was passed in the same year the Constitution was put in practice, many clashes and controversial points arose between the two."[343] Although the 1961 press laws are no longer in effect, it is important to get an understanding of it because it is the foundation on which the 2006 press laws were formed.

118. "Article 35 of the 1961 Press and Publication Law gave the Kuwaiti Government the authority to suspend any print publication or cancel a newspaper's license if it is found serving a foreign entity that acts against the country's national interest, and/or if it is found that a newspaper switches from a nonpolitical to a political publication.[344] In accordance to the 1961 Law, the Kuwaiti Government limited licenses to only the established five local owners. Since then, it has refused to grant new licenses for new daily newspapers. As a result, the same five families have monopolized the press market. By 2006, however, the new Press and Publication Law of 2006 removed this restriction and the market opened up, fostering an environment that allowed for the entry of new newspapers."[345]

342. USA International Business Publications. *Kuwait Internet and e-commerce investment and business guide: Regulations and opportunities*. 35. (Intl Business Pubns, 2009).
343. Ali Dashti. *The Effect of Online Journalism on the Freedom of the Press: The Case of Kuwait*. 46 (University of Stirling 2008).
344. Abdullah, M. *Kuwait Press. Kuwait: Magazine of Gulf and Arabian*. 196–205. (1985).
345. Ali Dashti. *The Effect of Online Journalism on the Freedom of the Press: The Case of Kuwait*. 46, 47 (University of Stirling 2008).

119. Article 39 deals with the right to privacy "The freedom of postal, telegraphic and telephonic communications is safeguarded and their secrecy is guaranteed. Censorship of letters or disclosure of their secrecy shall not be permissible save in such cases as are set out in the Law and in conformity with the procedure stipulated therein." Messages meant all sorts of messaging including mailing, telegram, telephone in which in need to ensure the confidentiality.

120. The "Kuwaiti Government, together with the approval of the National Assembly in March of 2006, passed a new press law containing some 33 Articles with four key changes. Unlike the previous 1961 Law, the new law gives any party that is denied a license the right to appeal in court. In addition, a prior judge order is required to cancel a license, to suspend a newspaper, or to detain a journalist. As such, the freedom of the press as it appears in Kuwait is considered by many scholars throughout the world to be one of the freest in the Arab world, but this did not occur in a vacuum. It was due in large part by the progressive orientation of the Kuwaiti Government's laws and regulations. Today Kuwait has eight new daily newspapers, which is substantially more than the previous five Arabic and two English newspapers."[346]

346. *Ibid., 59.*

Chapter 2. Legislation from the National Assembly

121. However, the power of the freedom that was given to the National Assembly was a big concern for the government felt this freedom of speech and press could lead to fragmentation in the society and political unrest.[347] After the dissolution of the National Assembly in 1986, the Crown Prince Sheik Saad Al-Sabah justified this action by explaining that freedom of the press would be worthless without a sense of responsibility, which is important for the national interests and social unity of Kuwait.[348]

§1. 1962 Press Law No. 3

122. The Press and Publications Law of 1961 was produced in the process of preparation for independence. It set the basis for governing the media in Kuwait.[349] This law has been amended and modified several times to give the government the power over the press, to satisfy immediate needs, and to fit with the current changes especially with the new communications technologies which forced the government in 2006 to accept the reality and approve a new press law. In accordance with the Constitution, the new law gives the government the authority to suspend newspapers or jail journalists for criticizing the Amir, disparaging God and the prophets, tarnishing public morals, violating the national interest or security, or creating divisions among the people.[350] It did stop issuing license for new newspapers. However, the law included many several vaguely worded phrases.[351]

123. AlSaudi and Taher[352] summarized the main criticism to the 1961 law in six points. First, they believed it gave power to administrative authorities to issue or withdraw licenses outside of judicial control. Second, the flexibility and vagueness of the laws left broad space for interpretation. A third criticism was the excessive punishment of offensive publications either by imprisonment or harsh fines. Fourth, the pre-publication censorship was subject to criticisms. Fifth, the law prevented the circulation of foreign publications under the pretext of maintaining public order or morals or the sanctity of religions. Finally, it remained inadequate for both printing and publications, despite amendments made to it.

124. In 1971, the law was amended with more restrictions. For example, section III did guarantee the freedom of printing, publishing, and writing, but Articles 23, 24, 25, and 26 prohibit criticism or comment on God, religious personalities, publishing

347. Kamal Osman Salih. Kuwait: Political Consequences of Modernization, 1750–1986. 27 Middle Eastern Studies. 46,66. (1991).
348. *Ibid.*
349. Naomi Sakr. *Media Policy as a Litmus Test of Political Change in the GCC.* Constitutional Reform and Political Participation in the Gulf 132 (2006).
350. *Ibid.*
351. Human Rights Watch. *Restrictions on Freedom of Expression.* (accessed May 14, 2017, https://www.hrw.org/reports/2000/kuwait/kuwait-06.htm).
352. A. AlSaudi & A. Taher. *Aldemoqratiya Alkuwaitiya: Altareekh, Alwaqe'a, Almustaqbel.* 186,187. (Al-Arabai for Publishing, 2011).

official state secrets, writings that may jeopardize relations between Kuwait and other countries, publishing news or information that may affect the value of the national currency or economic situation, and publishing news or information that violates public morality.[353] The law created criteria to issue or renew permits for journalists, news agencies, or correspondents.

§2. Postal Law No. 1 of 1970

125. The website of the Ministry of Communication[354] contains an English translation of Law No. 1 of 1970, in which the organization of the postal system is laid out in 11 articles. Although the website labels these eleven articles as Chapter 1, there is no information beyond these eleven articles available. In this section, all ten articles will be described. The postal law is important because magazines, advertisements, and other forms of media were historically received by mail.

In the first article, the law establishes a public postal system in accordance to international conventions. In the second article, the law explains that the relevant ministry is responsible for several aspects of the postal system—including both printing and providing different types of stationary, stamps, and envelopes. The relevant ministry is also responsible for opening and closing various post office locations. Further, the responsibility of receiving mail and distributing improperly is laid onto the relevant ministry in the second article.

126. The third article explains that the state does not oversee the postal system in certain circumstances. For instance, correspondence cannot be sent to places outside the distribution area or sent by private postal services. Further, the postal system would not deliver mail of government affairs. In the fourth article, violations of postal services are outlined. For example, postmen may not evade clearance fees, keep correspondences received by the post office, or deliver mail to someone who is not the specified recipient or someone the recipient lives with.

127. According to the fifth article, a fine equivalent to ten times the costs of clearing mail that gets seized can be imposed. According to the sixth article, postal services must guarantee privacy except in the cases that are specified after the sixth article. The seventh article explains that postmen are allowed to view mail when they are found in a garbage can, when the relevant government authority is investigating a misdemeanor or felony, when the recipient is a merchant that has declared bankruptcy, or in other cases where it is legal to do so. The eighth article forces the postal authorities to gain judicial approval before opening documents or packages.

128. The ninth article explains that when members of the Kuwait judicial system have opened mail and reached the objectives for which the mail was opened, they must mark it as having been reviewed. The tenth article defines violations to privacy of the postal correspondence in three ways: First, when the content of the mail is purposefully viewed; second, when mail is disclosed to the postal authority; and third,

353. M. Odine. *Middle East media: Press freedom in Kuwait*. 1 Journal of Advanced Social Research. 177, 190 (2011).

354. Ministry of Communication. *Law Organizing Postal Works.*(accessed May 17, 2017, http://moc.gov.kw/English/Laworganizingpostalworks.html).

when administrative or official documents are provided as proof that mail was sent or received. The eleventh article provides an oath that all postal employees in Kuwait must take, in which they pledge against violating the provisions and to respect the privacy of mail. The eleventh article states that the relevant minister is to provide further procedures.

§3. Press and Publication Law No. 3 of 2006

129. The Journalists Association in Kuwait, established in June 1964, aims to (1) strengthen the relationship between JAK's members and other journalists in the Kuwait and Arab states; (2) raise journalist's professional standards in Kuwait and the Arab world; (3) defend the interests of its members and create best practices in professional journalism in accordance to public interest (Association). The seven members of the management council are elected every two years.

130. Several websites list Law No. 3 of 2006 in both English[355] and Arabic.[356] In this section, the law is summarized such that each article is represented briefly. Following the law, an explanatory note accompanying the law is also summarized.

131. In March 2006, the National Assembly approved the government's new press law which contains 33 Articles with four key changes from 1961s Press and Publishing Law. The most important changes of the new law consist of giving a party that is denied license the right to appeal in court and a new requirement of a prior judicial order to cancel a license, to suspend a newspaper, or to detain a journalist. The new law opens the door for licensing after it has been suspended for years. Today, there are 15 daily newspapers (13 in Arabic and 2 in English). The new titles attracted famous and fresh columnists to join them with promises of more freedom or better compensation. These new laws include provisions requiring a minimum of KWD 250,000 in capital to start a daily newspaper. Also, a university degree is a prerequisite for a newspaper license. Further, it increased the amount for fines on publishers and journalists to KWD 20,000. The law includes provisions holding foreign television correspondents and radio stations responsible for spreading banned materials and applies fines as stated in the law against them. Finally, only the criminal division and judges are authorized to temporarily suspend a newspaper for urgent matters.[357]

132. Law No. 3 for the year 2006 on Press and Publications was translated by the Doha Centre for Media Freedom.[358] The first article clearly states that the "Freedom of the press, print, and publishing shall be guaranteed in accordance with the provisions

355. Doha Centre for Media Freedom. *Law No (3) for the Year 2006 on Press and Publications-Kuwait.* (accessed May 14, 2017, http://www.dc4mf.org/sites/default/files/press_law_kuwait.pdf).

356. Alkuwait Alyom. *Qanun Raqam 3 Lesanat 2006 Fe Shaan Almatboat Walnashr.* (State of Kuwait, 2017).

357. *Alqabas Tansher Nas Qanun Almatbuat Walnashr Almotamad Min Alhikooma Altathalem Fe Hal Rafth Altarkhees Khilal 60 Yawman Amam Alqadaa Aledara.* (Alqabas, 2005).

358. Doha Centre for Media Freedom. *Law No (3) for the Year 2006 on Press and Publications-Kuwait.* (accessed May 14, 2017, http://www.dc4mf.org/sites/default/files/press_law_kuwait.pdf).

of this Law."[359] Then, the second article defines terms used in the law. Print was defined as any "writing, drawing, photo, or saying whether solely or accompanied by music or other forms of expression whether they are affixed to a supporting stand by traditional means or by any other means or kept in saving dockets or magnetic or electronic devices or in others devices that are prepared for circulation against return or without return."[360] A typography was defined as an "entity or natural person who, by himself or through others, copies the prints by machines or devices which he uses for this purpose."[361] A newspaper is defined as a "newspaper, magazine, or any other print which is issued under the same name periodically at regular or irregular intervals even if it is mere translation or transfer from other prints."[362] Further, circulation is defined as the "selling of the print or offering it for sale or distribution or affixing it on any supporting stand, such as on the fronts of shops or walls or others by making in any way available for a number of persons, whether this is done against return or without return."[363]

133. Further, the second article defines roles for personnel working in the media industry. First, a chief editor is defined as the responsible person for "the actual supervision on the newspaper and its contents based on the authorization from the issuing licensee. Second, a deputy chief editor" is defined as "the person who satisfies the qualifying conditions set for the post of the chief editor, and he is the responsible person who does the actual supervision of the newspaper and its contents in the absence of the chief editor."[364] Next, a publisher is the natural person or entity who is in charge of preparation of the print for publishing, production, or distribution and circulation. Moreover, a writer is defined as any person who writes in the newspaper regularly or irregularly. Finally, "an editor is defined as any person who works on editing the newspaper professionally whether he is one of the correspondents, or news analyzers, or the person who is conducting press investigation, or translators, or artists or photographers."[365] In 2016, a fourth law was added requirements for what parts of electronic media and web pages are counted as print media, which was published on the third page of issue 1,274 of Kuwait Alyom.

134. The first section of this law deals with printed materials. Article 3 states that any person may establish a print house for publishing or distribution or translation after obtaining a license by following these conditions. First, he/she must be a Kuwaiti national with full-fledged citizenship. Second, he/she must have good conduct and reputation and must not have been convicted of a crime involving dishonor or dishonesty. Third, he/she must have at least obtained the general secondary diploma or its equivalent. Fourth, he/she must be the owner or utilizer of a suitable location for the activity.

135. Article 4 addresses license termination procedures while Article 5 talks about license transfer. Article 6 explains the procedures for the typographer to follow

359. *Ibid.*
360. *Ibid.*
361. *Ibid.*
362. *Ibid.*
363. *Ibid.*
364. *Ibid.*
365. *Ibid.*

before printing any print, and Article 7 deals with the sale and circulation of imported print materials.[366]

136. The second section of this law deals with newspapers. It begins with Article 8, which states that the newspaper shall not be subject to any prior censorship. Article 9 sets the capital amount to start a daily newspaper after obtaining the license that shall not be less than KWD 250,000 (USD 817,991). Article 10 sets the conditions to issue a newspaper. He/she must be a Kuwaiti national and 25 years of age with full eligibility, conduct, and reputation without being convicted of crime or dishonesty. A higher qualification degree of high school or equivalent is required. Article 11 explains the date it takes (ninety days) to issue the license by the ministry and the procedure to take if it was rejected.

137. Article 12 gives the licensee three months after the approval to start the procedure by satisfying four criteria.[367] First, the licensee must provide proof of a monetary deposit at the Ministry, a financial guarantee of KWD 100,000 (USD 327,432) for a daily newspaper and KWD 25,000 (USD 81,858) for others. Second, the licensee must provide the name of the editor-in-chief and the deputies with written acceptance of their positions. Third, the licensee must state the expected release date of the first issue of the newspaper, which shall not exceed one year from the date of submitting the statement. Finally, the licensee must provide the name of the printing house that will handle the printing of the newspaper along with a copy of the printing contract. Article 12 concludes by explaining that if any of the mentioned conditions is not fulfilled, the license will be considered cancelled.

Article 13 deals with the leasing or assigning a newspaper's license which will be void if it was done without the approval of the competent Ministry.[368]

138. Article 14 explains the situations in which the license will be cancelled by law. First, newspapers that do not produce issues without an acceptable excuse from the competent Ministry for a period exceeding three months (daily newspaper) and six months (other types). A second reason for the cancellation of the license includes a situation whereby the licensee was a national entity and its legal capacity was revoked for any reasons. A third reason for the cancellation of a license is a death without a legal heir. Further, "if the heirs within six months from the date of the death and after the approval of the competent Minister, did not transfer the license to their names or to the name of any other person while taking into account what was stipulated under Article 10 of this Law."[369] Fourth, failure to adhere to any of the conditions that are listed under Article 10 of this law by the licensee leads to a cancellation of the license. Article 14 explains that the concerned party shall be notified of the cancellation of the license in any of the mentioned cases. In any other cases, the license of the newspaper

366. Matt J. Duffy. *Media Laws and Regulations of the GCC Countries: Summary, Analysis and Recommendations.* Doha Centre for Media Freedom (accessed May 15, 2017, http://www.dc4mf.org/sites/default/files/gcc_media_law_en_0.pdf).

367. *Ibid.*

368. *Ibid.*

369. Doha Centre for Media Freedom. *Law No (3) for the Year 2006 on Press and Publications-Kuwait.* (accessed May 14, 2017, http://www.dc4mf.org/sites/default/files/press_law_kuwait.pdf).

may not be cancelled except by a final judgment which is issued by the competent court or based on the request of the licensee.

139. Article 15 states that without prejudice to the text of Article 10, the Chief of the Criminal Division or "the Judge of the Urgent Matters, if necessary and based on a request by the public prosecution, may issue a decision on suspending the issuing of the newspaper temporarily for a period not exceeding two renewable weeks during the investigations or the court interrogations."[370]

140. Article 16 set the conditions for newspaper's editor-in-chief. First, the editor-in-chief "must be a Kuwaiti national who attained the age of thirty years with full eligibility."[371] Second, "the editor-in-chief must have good conduct and reputation, and he must not have been convicted in a crime involving dishonor or dishonesty, unless his reputation was restored to him."[372] Third, "the editor-in-chief must have obtained an academic degree or its equivalent, or he must have practiced the profession regularly for a period not less than five years, provided that his educational qualification shall not be less than the general secondary certificate or its equivalent. Finally, the editor-in-chief must be employed full-time."[373]

141. Article 17 provides the characteristics of the editor-in-chief which he or she "must search for accuracy and truth in everything" before publishing "news, information, or data."[374] "The chief editor must publish, free of charge, any reply or correction or refutation that he" or she "receives from the competent ministry or from the other government entities or from any natural or entity person, whose name was mentioned or indicated in a writing or drawing or symbol which was published in the newspaper, and this shall be done on the date that is determined by the concerned party and in the same place of publishing and in the same letters and fonts which the article, the subject of the reply or correction or refutation, was first published."[375]

142. Article 18 addresses the responsibility of those who represent foreign newspapers, their correspondents and representatives of news agencies, and the foreign radio and television stations which shall obtain licenses from the competent Ministry in order to practice their work inside Kuwait.[376] The competent Ministry may issue a warning to the representative or correspondent or delegate, or it may cancel the license of a foreign newspaper, if it was evident that the news and information which was reported contained violation of the provisions of this law.

143. The third section deals with matters prohibited from being published in print or newspapers and the penalties of violating this law. Article 19 prohibits any sort of meddling, defamation, slander, or mocking that prejudice the divine, the Holy Quran, the prophets, his noble companions, prophet's wives "or persons who are part of the Prophet's family" using "any forms of expression that are stipulated under

370. *Ibid.*
371. *Ibid.*
372. *Ibid.*
373. *Ibid.*
374. *Ibid.*
375. *Ibid.*
376. Matt J. Duffy. *Media Laws and Regulations of the GCC Countries: Summary, Analysis and Recommendations.* Doha Centre for Media Freedom (accessed May 15, 2017, http://www.dc4mf.org/sites/default/files/gcc_media_law_en_0.pdf).

Article (29) of the Law No (31) for the year 1970."[377] Further, Article 20 prohibits criticizing or challenging the Amir, and "no statement shall be attributed to him" without a "special written permission from the Amiri Diwan."[378,379]

144. Article 21 shows 10 conditions by which the law prohibits publications.[380] First, "disdain or contempt the Constitution of the State."[381] Second, disdain or insult judges or prosecutors or what is considered infringing on the integrity and impartiality of the judiciary "or publish something which the courts or the investigating authorities decide" as a secret.[382] Third, "insulting the public morals or instigating to violate the public order or to violate the laws or to commit crimes, even if the crime did not occur."[383] Fourth, "news about secret communication and publishing of agreements and treaties which the government of Kuwait" achieves "before publishing them in the official gazette, except by a special permission from the concerned ministry."[384] Fifth, "influencing the value of the national currency or what would lead to shake the economic status of the country or publishing news about the bankruptcy of businessmen, commercial companies, banks or money exchangers, except by a special permission from the competent court."[385] Sixth, "revealing what goes on in any meeting or what is written in the papers or documents or decrees, or any papers or prints which the Constitution or any law decided that they are to be kept in secret, even if the published topic was true, publishing is limited to the official statements that are issued in that regard."[386] Seventh, "infringement on the dignity of the persons or their lives or religious beliefs," and instigating hatred or disdain of any class of the society or to publish information about their financial statuses or to reveal a secret which "would harm their reputation or wealth or their trade names."[387] Eighth, compromising "the private life of the employee or a person who is charged in a public service or attributing statements or acts not true to him which would cause harm or insult to his person."[388] Ninth, damaging the relationships between Kuwait and other Arab countries or allies if done through media campaigns. Finally, if "the specialized newspaper went beyond the purpose of the license which is granted to it."[389]

145. Article 22 gives the competent minister the right to prohibit publishing of any commercial advertisements or others in accordance with the conditions and rules contained in a decision issued by the Minister. In Article 23, the public prosecution

---

377. *Law No. 8 of 2016 Regarding the Regulation of Electronic Media.* (The Kuwait Times, Feb. 14, 2016).
378. *Ibid.*
379. *Ibid.*
380. Matt J. Duffy. Media Laws and Regulations of the GCC Countries: Summary, Analysis and Recommendations. Doha Centre for Media Freedom (accessed May 15, 2017, http://www.dc4mf.org/sites/default/files/gcc_media_law_en_0.pdf).
381. *Ibid.*
382. *Ibid.*
383. *Ibid.*
384. *Ibid.*
385. *Ibid.*
386. *Ibid.*
387. *Ibid.*
388. *Ibid.*
389. *Ibid.*

shall have the competency, without others, to handle the investigation, to take action, and to make the pleading regarding all crimes that are stipulated under this Law, provided there shall be a specialized prosecution for these crimes. Further, Article 24 specifies the Criminal Chamber of the Full Court is the competent court to decide on all criminal lawsuits that are stipulated under this Law, and their judgments shall be appealed before the Court of Appeals. The rulings issued by the Court of Appeals may be objected to by cassation before the Court of Cassation. Article 25 states that the criminal case for the crimes stipulated in this law cannot be filed anymore if it is not reported to the Public Prosecution's Office within three months from the date of publication. In addition, the compensation's lawsuit cannot be filed if it was not pleaded within a year from the date of publishing.

146. Article 26 states that any violation of the provisions of the First Section's Articles is punishable by a minimum fine of KWD 500 (USD 1,636) and maximum fine of KWD 1,000 (USD 3,273). If the print contradicts with the national interest or if it served a foreign authority or state or if it infringes on the social or political system of Kuwait, the penalty shall be a fine not less than KWD 3,000 (USD 9,819) and not more than KWD 10,000 (USD 32,730).

147. Article 27 relates to the editor-in chief, reporter, and author's punishments under four conditions. First, the editor-in-chief's publication in the newspaper, prohibited under Article (19), will be penalized with imprisonment for a period not exceeding one year and a fine no less than KWD 5,000 (USD 16,365) and not exceeding KWD 20,000 (USD 65,460) or by one of these two penalties. Second, the editor-in-chief's publication in the newspaper, prohibited under Article (20), will be penalized with a fine no less than KWD 5,000 (USD 16,365) and not exceeding KWD 20,000 (USD 65,460). Third, the editor-in-chief's publication in the newspaper, prohibited under Article (21), will be penalized with a fine no less than KWD 3,000 (USD 9,819) and not exceeding KWD 10,000 (USD 3,273). Fourth, any other violation of the provisions of the Second Section of this Law will be fined no less than KWD 1,000 (USD 3,273) and no more than KWD 3,000 (USD 9,820). The Criminal Court (*almahkamah aljazaiyah*) may, in any of the previous cases, order to cancel the license or to close down the newspaper for a period not exceeding one year and confiscate the published issue as well as the supporting stand on which it was affixed to destroy it and to close down the printing shop which was used to make the print.

148. Article 28 states that if an instigation was published to overthrow the ruling regime in the country and this instigation included induction to change this system by force or through illegal means or by urging to use force to change the social and economic system that exists in the country or to embrace creeds which aim at destroying the basic statutes of Kuwait through illegal means, the editor-in-chief and the article writer shall be penalized by the penalty which is stipulated under Article (29) and paragraph (1) of the Law No (31) for the year 1970 on Amendment of Some of the Provisions of the Penal Law No (16) for the year 1960.

149. The fourth section includes concluding provisions. Articles (29, 30, 31, 32, and 33) give the competent Minister to issue the law and the procedures should be taken to implement the law. The translation of the explanatory note of the law appears in English on many websites and was only briefly modified, including the Doha Centre for Media Freedom:[390]

> Accompanying the law is an explanatory note, and an English translation of it and its five articles is included here. Four of its five articles refer to a section of the law previously described. The explanatory note begins by stating that freedom of expression is considered one of the basic rights of man, and it is one of the rights for which the Constitution guaranteed its protection and preservation, as provided by Article (36) of the Constitution (Freedom of opinion and academic research is guaranteed, and each person shall have the right to express his opinion and to publish it by saying or in writing or other means, and this shall be in accordance with the conditions and situations outlined by the law). Guaranteeing the freedom of expression is the basis of the democratic system, and its organization is a necessity in the legal state; however, such organization must not be a reason for restricting it so as to prevent its practice or to suspend its aimed contents. Distinguishing between guaranteeing the freedom of expression and the other freedoms which the Constitution and the law guaranteed their protection is considered one of the most delicate issues and the most intriguing and interesting matters. The Constitution's guarantee of the freedom of expression would retreat if such freedom missed its social value, or if its exercise was attached with something that would threaten the freedoms of the citizens. The different means of the press media, such as prints and publishing means are some forms of exercising the freedom of expression. The technological advancement of the means of media like the radio, television, and electronic information networks helped facilitate the spread of information effectively, and publishing is no longer limited to the news and political events; instead, it extended to cover all aspects of the public and private life. On January 26th, 1961, the law of prints and publishing No (3) for the year 1961 was enacted, and over the years of working with it, many amendments were introduced to it in order to satisfy immediate needs. However, they were not sufficient enough to modify the law as to make the law adequate and regulating for the affairs of prints and publishing in their advanced intellectual and artistic concepts. Based on the forgoing and on the developmental role that is expected from the means of print and publishing in their many fields and in order to bridge the gaps in the legislative development that regulate these means, the attached law was prepared. The law includes five sections: a preface section and four other sections. They cover the affairs of prints and newspapers along with the matters that are prohibited from publishing, the determined penalties and the concluding provisions.

The explanatory note includes four articles. First, it states that the first article in the preface section addressed the guarantee of the freedom of the press, printing, and publishing in accordance with the provisions of this Law. The second article dealt with defining the terms that are used in the law, namely defining the meanings of print,

390. Matt J. Duffy. Media Laws and Regulations of the GCC Countries: Summary, Analysis and Recommendations. Doha Centre for Media Freedom (accessed May 15, 2017, http://www.dc4mf.org/sites/default/files/gcc_media_law_en_0.pdf).

typographer, newspaper, chief editor, deputy chief editor, publisher, circulation, writer, editor, competent minister, and the competent ministry.

The second article of the explanatory note states that the first article of this section includes the provisions related to prints, where the third and fourth articles of the section regulated the conditions required for application for license to establish a print house or to utilize it or to open a shop for selling or renting prints or publishing and distribution or translation or an office for advertisements and publicity or an art production establishment in relation with this law. It also covered the conditions that must be satisfied by the license applicant whether he is a natural person or an entity, and it specified the procedures of terminating or suspending the activity of the print house or the licensed shop or changing its name or location. The law also designated the executive regulations for outlining the regulating rules regarding the same. The fifth article of the law outlined the provisions on regulating the procedures for assigning the license to others and the case of the death of the licensee. The sixth article stipulated that the typographer shall submit a written notification to the Ministry before assuming printing of any print and to indicate his name and address. It stipulated that it is permissible to print and circulate and publish any nonperiodic print provided that the names of the typographer, the publisher, and the author are stated. It also specified that two copies of the print shall be submitted at both the competent Ministry and at the Kuwait National Library before entering circulation or publishing, in accordance with the conditions and procedures outlined by the executive regulations. The seventh article permitted the entry and circulation of prints imported from abroad after obtaining permission for them from the competent ministry, and after making sure that they do not contain what is prohibited from publishing in accordance with the articles stipulated under the third section of this law. It also considered the local distributor responsible in case of violating any of the provisions of this law and that he shall be penalized according to its provisions and without prejudice to any severer penalty stipulated by any other law. Thus, the second article of the explanatory note contextualizes Articles 3–7 of the law.

Further, the third article of the explanatory note states that the second section included many provisions related to the newspaper, where Article 8 of the law stressed that newspapers shall not be subject to any prior monitoring. Article 9 outlined that no person may issue a newspaper except by a license issued by the competent authority and that the licensing shall not be issued except to the owner of an establishment or a company which has a capital of not less than KWD 200 and KWD 50,000. Articles 9 and 10 regulated the conditions for obtaining a license for issuing a newspaper. These included the license applicant and the department to which he submits the application and the contents of application for license. As for Article 11, it authorized the competent Minister to issue a decision on rejection or approval of the application within ninety days from the date of its submission. It also regulated the procedures of appealing, before the administrative department, the decision passed on rejection of the application, in accordance with the procedures stipulated by the Decree by Law No 20 for the year 1981. It also determined a period of sixty days from the date of notification of the decision or from the date of elapse of the ninety-day period indicated for appealing the decision. Article 12 of the law determined the amount of financial guarantee which the licensee must deposit with the treasury of the ministry or the bank guarantee bond and the period during which he shall submit. It also stipulated that the name of the chief editor and his deputies shall be specified along with the date of issuing the first issue and provided that this date shall not be more than one year from the date of submitting this statement along with the name of the print house, which will take charge of printing the newspaper and at the end its considers the license annulled in accordance with the law in case of not fulfilling the commitments specified by the previous clauses, and it authorized the minister to extend the date to a period not exceeding one month. Article 13 stated that any lease of the license for issuance of a newspaper shall be considered null and void, and this shall also be applicable to selling or assigning the license if it was done without the approval of the competent Ministry. Article 14 of the law stipulated a provision of canceling the license under situations listed under the article. It also tasked the competent ministry to notify the concerned party regarding the cancellation of the license in the cases indicated under this article; it also added that in cases other than these limited cases, no license of a newspaper shall be cancelled except by a final judgment from the competent court or by the request of the license owner. Article 15 of the law stipulated that no cancellation of a license for a newspaper may be made except in accordance with a final judgment that is issued by the competent court. The Article authorized the Chief of the Criminal Department or the Judge of the Urgent Matters when necessary and based on the request from the public prosecution to temporarily suspend issuing of the newspaper for a period not exceeding two renewable weeks, during the investigation by the public prosecution or during the court interrogation. Articles 16 and 17 of the law listed provisions related to the conditions that must be fulfilled by the chief editor and his duties.

Article 18 stipulated that the representatives of the foreign newspaper, their correspondents, delegates of the news agencies, and radio and television stations shall obtain the license from the competent Ministry in order to practice their work inside Kuwait.

The fourth article of the explanatory note states that the third section of the Law regulates the matters that are prohibited from publishing in the print or the newspaper along with the penalties. Article 19 of the Law prohibited meddling in matters related to God, the Holy Quran, the prophets, the noble companions, or wives of the Prophet, peace be upon him (PBUH), or persons of the family of the Prophet, peace on them, by meddling, disdaining, mocking, or criticizing in any means of expression that are stipulated under Article No 29 of the Law No 31 for the year 1970 on Amendments of Some of the 20 Provisions of the Penal Law No 16 for the year 1960. The term Companions means any person who saw the Prophet Muhammad (peace be upon him), who was a Muslim and a believer in the Prophet, died as one, and shall have regard to especially Prophet's wives and the members of his family (peace be upon on them). The term Members of the Family (peace be upon them) shall mean the Prophet's family and relatives who believed in him and who lived in his time and saw him in reality (peace be upon him).

Article 20 stipulated that no meddling may be made to the person of the Amir by criticism, and that no statement shall be attributed to him, except by a special written permission issued from the Amiri Diwan. Article (21) listed the matters prohibited from publishing.

Article 22 of the Law provides that the competent Minister shall issue a founded decision on prohibiting the publishing of any commercial or other advertisements in accordance with the conditions and rules that shall be issued in a decision by the Minister. Article (23) specified the competent authority which shall investigate, take action, and prosecute all crimes that are stipulated under this Law, namely the public prosecution solely and non-others, provided that a prosecution entity shall decide on these crimes. Article No (24) stipulated the competence of the Criminal Department in the Full Court of First Instance to decide on all the penal lawsuits that are stipulated under this law, that its rulings shall be appealed before the Court of Appeals, and that the appeal by cassation shall be before the Court of Cassation.

Article 25 of the law covered the periods related to prescription or cancellation of the penal lawsuits related to crimes stipulated in this Law along with the compensation lawsuits. Article 26 listed the penalties related to violating the provisions of this law without prejudice to any severer penalty stipulated under any other law. Article 27 outlined the penalties that shall be imposed on the chief editor and the article writer or author in case of violating the prohibition which is stipulated under Articles 19, 20 and 21 of the law and without prejudice to any severer penalty stipulated in any other law. It authorized the penal court in any of these situations to order cancelling the license or to suspend the newspaper for a period not exceeding one year. If the publishing included an instigation to overthrow the ruling regime of Kuwait, Article 28 of the Law stipulated punishment of the chief editor and the article writer by the penalty that is determined under the first sub article of Article No 29 of the Law No 31 for the year 1970 on Amending Some of the Provisions of the Penal Law.

The fifth article of the explanatory note states that the fourth section of the law included concluding provisions, where Article 29 authorized the competent minister to issue a decision regarding the audio, visual, and audio-visual prints and to appoint employees who shall be in charge of proving the occurrence of violations of the provisions of this Law, preparing their reports and minutes and forwarding them to the public prosecution.

Article 30 stipulated publishing of the judicial decisions and rulings related to implementing the provisions of this Law in the official gazette. Article 31 authorized the competent Minister to issue the executive regulations and the decisions required for implementing the provisions of this Law within six months from the date on which the law comes into effect. Article 32 stipulated the abrogation of the Law No (3) for the year 1961 on promulgation of Prints and Publications Law. Article 33 provided implementation of law from the date of its publishing in the official gazette.

§4. Audio-Visual Law No. 61 of 2007

150. In 2007, the National Assembly ratified the Audio-Visual Media Law No. 61/2007. The Law, which has three sections with twenty-one articles, aims to control, set conditions, prohibit precise materials, and apply punishments to limit the negative practices of satellite channels.[391]

151. Article 1 defines the words and phrases used in this law. Here, a figurative translation is provided because it can be telling of the types of regulated aspects of audio-visual media. First, visual and audio media are defined as any TV or radio broadcast that reaches the public or certain groups through signals, images, sounds, or drawings that are not private correspondence by means of stations, channels, waves, and other modern broadcasting means of TV or radio. Next, broadcasting is defined as the act of sending works, visual programs, or audio programs through electromagnetic waves via satellite or other means, regardless of their description or nature, enabling the public to receive them through technical means in various terms. In contrast, rebroadcasting is defined as receiving and rebroadcasting private channels from inside Kuwait to be received inside Kuwait using modern technology according to the prepaid system.

152. Further, a channel is defined as having a transmitter for satellite broadcasting or audio broadcasting. In contrast, programs are defined as visual or audio materials of any kind or any part thereof transmitted by the licensee to the public. In addition, frequency is defined as a package of allocated electromagnetic waves whether it is visible or audible transmitted in space used to broadcast or rebroadcast. A broadcasting license is defined as permission for the licensee to establish and operate a channel in accordance with the executive regulations. Finally, a licensee is defined as an individual, company, or organization that has obtained the broadcasting license in accordance with the provisions of this law.

153. After the first article, the law is divided into 3 sections. The first section is from Articles 2–10, the second section is from Articles 11–14, and the third section contains Articles 15–21. The first section, which contains Articles 2–10, explains the process to obtain the license, the conditions, the regulations, and the cancellations of the license.

154. The second section explains the prohibited materials to broadcast, the responsible individuals, and the punishments. For instance, Article 11 stated fourteen matters that are prohibited by this law to be broadcast, which include insulting Almighty God (self-divine), the angels, the Holy Quran, Islam, the prophets, the companions of the Prophet Mohammad, his wives and his family, the incitement to overthrow the government, criticism of the Amir, defaming or belittling members of the judicial system and the public prosecutions, creating hatred, influencing the value of the national currency, harming the dignity of persons, the disclosure of secret information, and damaging the relations between Kuwait and other countries.

155. Further, Article 13 identified the punishment that will apply to the general manager, the producer, the broadcaster, or the responsible personnel if they violated the law which includes (1) no more than one year in prison or financial penalty no less than KWD 5,000 (USD 16,000) and no more than KWD 20,000 (USD 65,000) or both punishments. (2) Penalty no less than KWD 3,000 (USD 9,800) and no more than KWD 10,000 (USD 32.800) where the court has the right to request the cancellation

391. Amnesty International. *The 'Iron Fist' Policy: Criminalization of Peaceful Dissent in Kuwait.* (2015, accessed, May 17, 2017, https://www.amnesty.org/en/documents/mde17/3080/2015/en/).

of the license or postponed the license for a period no more than a year. Article 14 gives the minister, in accordance with the conditions and the regulations of the law, the right to prohibit or ban the transmission of any commercial.

156. The third and final section deals with the final provisions of the law. In Articles 15 through 21, the regulation claims that public prosecution is solely responsible for investigating the claims. Further, the law states that the Criminal Division of the Plenary Court is the competent court to arbitrate all criminal cases.

§5. Protection of National Unity Law No. 19 of 2012

157. In 2012, the Amir issued an emergency decree called the National Unity Law which contains five Articles criminalizing any content (in publishing, broadcasting, and social media) considered offensive to religious "sects" or groups. It penalizes those convicted with high fines ranging from KWD 10,000 (USD 36,000) to KWD 100,000 (USD 327,947), and as many as seven years in prison.[392]

Article 1 prohibits initiating or advocating or encouraging any means of expression as stated in Article (29) of Law No. 31 for the year 1970 to hate or disrespect any group of society or to provoke sectarian or tribal strife or spread ideas calling for superiority over any race, group, color, origin, religion sect, sex or pedigree. Incitement to an act of violence for that purpose includes radio and TV broadcasting, publishing, printing, retransmitting, producing, or circulating any visual or audible content, print, or broadcast false rumors leading to the above mentions actions. These provisions apply to every person who personally commits an act or accomplices in the crime if committed wholly or partly in the territory of the State of Kuwait. One of the means of expression is information networks, blogs, and other modern communication.

158. Article 2 and Article 3 deal with the kinds of punishment for those who violate Article 1 of this law which includes maximum seven years in prison and a minimum of KWD 10,000 (USD 36,000) to maximum of KWD 100,000 (USD 327,947) fines or one of these punishments.

159. Article 4 gives the court the right to discharge the offender of the law if he or she informed the authorities of the existence of the criminal agreement on committing the crime before it begins to be carried out, and the court may exempt the penalty if the notification is made after the completion of the crime and before starting the investigation. The court also can make the exemption if the offender helped the authority to arrest the rest of the perpetrators.

160. The explanatory note of the law states that due to the various backgrounds of the people living in Kuwait and the Constitution which gives equal rights to all citizens with no discrimination, and in accordance with UN and international human rights laws, is what forced Kuwait to adopt this law to protect the national and social unity in Kuwait.

392. U.S. State Department. *Kuwait.* (accessed May 17, 2015, http://www.state.gov/j/drl/rls/irf/religiousfreedom/index.htm?year=2012&dlid=208398).

§6. Telecommunications Law No. 37 of 2014

161. In May 2014, the new Communications Law No. 37 of 2014 was approved to regulate, supervise, and censor the ICT sector, which falls under the telecommunication regulatory authority. The Telecommunications Law creates a Commission for Mass Communications and Information Technology (CMCIT) which serves as an independent organization under the supervision of the Minister of Communications who has the power to grant or refuse licenses to companies that provide Internet cable, satellite, and land and wireless phone connections. Furthermore, the law gives the commission the right to impose harsh penalties on users who create or send inappropriate messages and the power to suspend communication services on the grounds of national security.[393]

162. The key features of the new law include a requirement for licensing, through the commission, before any telecommunication network or service.[394] Further, the commission's board has the power to set the terms and conditions to issue licenses. Also, the law states that the commission is responsible for setting prices of fees required to obtain a license to establish and operate a public telecommunications services.[395] Next, the law states that the commission sets the quality standards and takes measures to ensure compliance with these standards.[396] The law also requires a required annual report be submitted to the commission regarding the technical, administrative, and financial aspects of the licensees business.[397] Finally, in order to prevent the transmission of "breaching material," the commission may require, on the expense of the licensee, to provide and install devices, equipment, and programs.[398]

163. The law has 12 sections and 91 Articles. In the first section, Article 1 defines the phrases and the meaning of the terms used in the Law. In the second section, Article 2 deals with issues related to the establishment of the Telecommunications Regulatory Commission. Article 3 states the tasks that the commission will manage. Articles 4–10 deal with the Board of Directors of the commission, while Articles 12 and 13 deal with the Commission's financial resources. Articles 14 and 15 are related to the replacement of the Ministry of Telecommunication with the commission.

164. The third section includes Articles 16–25. Article 16 prohibits owning, operating, managing, or servicing any communication networks without license. Articles 17–21 deal with issues related to establishing, managing, and operating communication networks. Articles 22, 23, 24, and 25 set the conditions to issue and obtain the license.

165. The fourth section includes Articles 26–31. Articles 26–32 in which Article 30 and 31 clearly stated the prohibition and obtaining radio stations on Kuwait's territory, ships, or plain without a license except for the Armed and Security forces, ships, foreign aircrafts, land transport, and transit services.

---

393. International Labor Organization. *Kuwait (311).* (accessed May 17, 2017, http://www.ilo.org/dyn/natlex/natlex4.detail?p_lang=en&p_isn=99822&p_country=KWT&p_count=311).
394. DLA Piper. Key Telecommunications Laws, Regulations and Policies. (2016, https://www.dlapiperintelligence.com/telecoms/index.html?t=laws&c=KW).
395. *Ibid.*
396. *Ibid.*
397. *Ibid.*
398. *Ibid.*

166. The fifth section includes Articles 33–42, which deal with licenses renewal, modification, and cancelation. The sixth section includes Articles 43–46, which are concerned with the approvals and clearance of communication devices.

167. The seventh section includes Articles 47–58. Articles 47–55 are about monitoring the licensees, and they protect the beneficiaries and set the conditions for the service provider how to deal with the complaints and disputes cases. Article 51 states that telephone calls and private communications are confidential matters and that it is illegal to infringe the privacy, otherwise, the violator will be liable under the legal responsibility.

168. In the eighth section, Articles 56–58 deal with competition provisions. In the ninth section, Articles 59–63 discuss the judicial procedures of the authority to monitor the implementations of this law. In the tenth and eleventh sections, Articles 64–83, which deal with penalties and fines, specified the punishments on the violators of this law; the violations include breaching public morality, provoking panic, outrage of modesty, or libel. Finally, Articles 84–91 set the final provision of the law.

§7. Law No. 4 of 2016

169. Law No. 4 of 2016 provides an amendment to Law No. 3 of 2006 such that the definition of the law is applicable to websites and electronic media. In its explanatory note, the amendment is contextualized by explaining the technological and sociological impact of the diffusion of websites and social media among users. In this context, print refers to all these new sources of media that were not proliferated when the 2006 law was passed. Further, it explains the rise of a phenomenon in today's professional media environment in which media, news, or individual accounts associate actions or words with people that did not say or behave as the reports suggest. These accused people are unable to take judicial action toward these news or other media websites due to the lack of available legislation to regulate these websites as happens with print media. Thus, the publications law is adjusted in order to ensure regulations and punishments that Law No. 3 of 2006 proposes to electronics users that commit violations that the law considers criminal. This law was published in Alkuwait Alyom on February 7, 2016 in accordance to Kuwaiti law, which is also noted both in the second article of the law and the explanatory note.

§8. Penal Code

170. The Penal Code in Kuwait is another source of law that outlines criminal punishment for various laws. In fact, former parliamentarian, Dr. Hassan Johar,[399] who participated in the drafting of the 2006 publication law mentioned that the committee for media law reform was challenged with the task of liberalizing media regulations without contradicting various bodies of the law. Some of these offenses are relevant to professionals working in the media and communication industry. So central is this

399. Johar, Hasan A. (2017).

awareness that readers should examine the Penal Code when they mention the publication law.

171. Kuwait's defamation laws can be found in Articles 209 through 216 of its Penal Code.[400] In Article 209, defamation is defined as harming the reputation of an individual in a public space where it is audible or visible. In a comparison of international norms to the provisions of the laws in several Arab countries, Duffy and Alkazemi[401] found that Arab nations tend not to allow truth as a defense for defamation cases. In other words, the wording of the law makes defamation punishable even if a reputation is deservedly harmed—limiting the journalists' ability to combat corruption.

172. Journalism is not the only type of specialization within the mass media to be affected by the Penal Code. For example, Articles 205–208 punish promotional communication activities that relate to gambling, alcohol, drugs, and narcotics.[402] While these regulations will be explained in more detail in Chapter 5, it is worth noting that communication professionals and students must be familiarized with the Penal Code Number 16 of 1960 as well as its amendments.[403]

173. Other parts of the Penal Code outlaw insulting communication. For example, Articles 134 and 135 of the Penal Code relate to insult laws. Article 134 punishes insulting employees with a maximum jail sentence of 3 months as well as a fine. This punishment gets multiplied if this insult is targeting a court of law or any of individuals within it during a session. Article 135 specifically protects public servants from being insulted. The law provides for additional penalties in case there is resistance. Human rights lawyers Amal Clooney and Philippa Webb[404] made eight recommendations to the United Nations on protecting insulting speech that has been used around the world to limit free speech.

174. Other articles within the Penal Code, Law No. 16 of 1960, as well as its amendments are also related to communication. For example, Articles 143 and 144 punish those who witness a crime and fail to report them.[405] Along the same lines, Article 145 punishes false reports to a public official, whether it is written or stated orally.[406] Further, UNESCO[407] reports that some of the Penal Code articles protect intellectual property.

400. Matt J. Duffy & Mariam Alkazemi. *Arab Defamation Laws: A Comparative Analysis of Libel and Slander in the Middle East.* 22 Communication Law and Policy 189,211 (2017).
401. *Ibid.*
402. Alkuwait Alyom.*Qanun Raqam 16 Lianat 1960 Bi Isdar Qanun Aljazaa.* (1960).
403. *Ibid.*
404. Amal Clooney & Philippa Webb. *The Right to Insult in International Law.* 48 Colum. Hum. Rts. L. Rev (2016): 1.
405. Alkuwait Alyom.Qanun Raqam 16 Lianat 1960 Bi Isdar Qanun Aljazaa. (1960).
406. *Ibid.*
407. United Nations Educational Scientific and Cultural Organization. *Kuwait.* (2009, accessed Jun. 7, 2017, http://www.unesco.org/culture/pdf/kuwait_cp_en).

§9. Copyright Laws

175. According to a report by the United Nations Educational, Scientific and Cultural Organization (UNESCO),[408] Kuwait is a signatory to several international treaties that recognize intellectual property rights and combat piracy. According to the UNESCO[409] report, some of these include Law No. 10 of 2003 of the GCC Unified Customs Law, Regulation 200 of 2003 in the Customs Law Implementing Regulation, and the 50th of Customs Instructions of 2003. Kuwait is also a signatory to several international treaties pertaining to copyright.[410] Further, several other Kuwaiti laws dealing with criminal law and criminal procedure, including laws 16 and 17 of 1960 and their amendments, are relevant according to the UNESCO[411] findings. Also, decree 67 of 1980 and its amendment, Law No. 15 of 1996, are part of the civil law that deal with issues relevant to copyright and intellectual property law.

176. Finally, Ministerial Decree 30 of 2003, issued by the Ministry of Information, sets some bylaws relating to copyrights. This decree regulates books, printed materials, academic theses and dissertations, genealogical trees, and stamps. It also states that works must be registered with the National Library of Kuwait and refers to a procedure in which the library can accept or deny a work via the registration process. Thus, it is important to recognize that law Law No. 22 of 2016 (On Copyrights and Related Rights) is not the only regulation that can be used in cases where copyright is relevant.

177. Before assessing the changes introduced in Law No. 22 of 2016, the revoked old law of 64 of 1999 on Intellectual Property Rights should be discussed to highlight the development of copyright legislation in Kuwait. Law No. 64 of 1999 nullified any previous legislation which contradicted it—an important development in civil law, where the focus on laws are extremely important. Further, the law was a domestic legislation that dealt exclusively with copyright protections. This legislation defined the works to which copyright applied, as well as its limitations.

178. According to the 1999 law, the definition of a work to which the copyrights apply could range from a computer program, to a literary work or a public speech. The definition included work that was verbal, visual, audio, technical, and/or scientific. For example, architectural, topographical, and geographical maps, sketches and plans were protected whether they were two- or three-dimensional in addition to computer programs, including databases and programs among other similar works. Similarly, cinematographic and audio-visual works were also covered whether they were produced by hand or through a more elaborate process that required industrial techniques. Literal and oral works were covered, whether lectures, speeches, dramatic performances—including pantomime—or musical composition that did not include words.

179. Further, the 1999 law included original works, translated works, and titles that were original. The law protected adaptations, summaries, explanations or any other work in which an original work appeared in a new form, as long as the original author's rights were observed. In other words, the materials used to create the work did not disqualify the work from protections. Further, a creative work did not need to

408. *Ibid.*
409. *Ibid.*
410. *Ibid.*
411. *Ibid.*

be registered for the copyright to apply to it. Although photographs were protected under the 1999 copyright law, this protection did not affect other photographers' ability to capture similar photos from the same location and under the same conditions. In other words, there were some limits to the copyright law. Among these limitations, national folklore was considered as owned by the State of Kuwait.

180. The duration of copyright was established at the lifetime of the author plus fifty years, and this time period was calculated to start a year after the death of the author. In cases of joint ownership, when more than one author is involved, the copyright was extended until fifty years has passed from the death of the author who died last. In the case the work being anonymous or when an author used a pen-name, the copyright extended for fifty years until after the death of the author, under the condition that there was no doubt who the author was. Authors were expected to enjoy economic gains for their creative works.

181. The authority to enforce the law was granted to several legal agencies within Kuwait, ranging from customs officers at the borders to police officers and officials employed by the Ministry of Information.[412] Several civil societies were identified by UNESCO[413] as being interested in issues relating to intellectual property rights in Kuwait. These groups aim to protect brands, increase public awareness among other goals.

182. The year 2014 saw important developments in copyright law in Kuwait. First, the country ratified the Berne Convention for the Protection of Literary and Artistic Works. Second, Resolution No. 1070 by the Council of Ministers transferred copyright administration to the National Library of Kuwait. Authors or publishers can register and deposit artistic works at the National Library to ensure conservation of the author's intellectual property.[414]

183. Lastly, Kuwait was moved from the Watch List to the Priority Watch List of the US Trade Representative[415] (USTR)'s Special 301 Report for its failure to introduce to the National Assembly "long-overdue copyright legislation" consistent with Kuwait's international commitments as well as the government's failure to resume effective enforcement against copyright and trademark infringement[416] (USTR 2015, p.53).

184. Partly in response to international pressure, in May 2016, Kuwait's National Assembly unanimously approved the draft of what became Law No. 22 of 2016 (On Copyrights and Related Rights).The new law covers the copyright and related rights of natural and legal entities, Kuwaitis and foreigners who have permanent residency in Kuwait as well as foreign nationals who belong to one of the Member States of the

412. *Ibid.*
413. *Ibid.*
414. Ahmed ElKlatawy & Karim Marouny. New Copyright Law in Kuwait. (2016, accessed Dec. 2, 2017, http://www.tamimi.com/en/magazine/law-update/section-14/october-6/new-copyright-law-in-kuwait.html).
415. Office of the United States Trade Representative. *Special 301 Report.* (2015, accessed Dec. 2, 2017, https://ustr.gov/sites/default/files/2015-Special-301-Report-FINAL.pdf).
416. *Ibid., 53.*

Berne Convention, the World Trade Organization, or the World Intellectual Property Oragnization.[417]

185. The new law grants moral and economic rights to the work of an author. Economic rights allow the author to benefit financially if their work is used by others, while moral rights grant the author continuation of control over their work. According to the provisions of the law, authors preserve the right to permit or prohibit the use and exploitation of their work.

186. Several provisions of the old law were left unchanged, including the duration of copyright set at the lifetime of the author plus fifty years. However, compared to the old law, the new copyright law introduced stronger penalties, including imprisonment and fines, for unauthorized uses of copyrighted work. Prison sentences can now be issued for between six months to two years, compared to a maximum of one calendar year in the 1999 law. The old law maximized fines at KWD 500 (approximately USD 1,650), whereas the 2016 law sets fines between KWD 500 and KWD 50,000 (USD 1,650 and USD 165,000). Finally, the new law also allows three-month temporary closures of offending establishments and the revocation of their trade licenses in case of repeat offenses.[418]

187. The law was lauded for protecting copyrighted works from unauthorized publication, reproduction, public broadcast or rebroadcast, public communication, translation, adaptation, rental, or the making available of the work to the public including via computer, the Internet, information networks, communications networks, or other means.[419]

188. Article 1 of Law No. 22 of 2016 defines "written work" as original literary, artistic, or scientific works, whatever the type of work or the means of its expression, importance, or the purpose of its creation or composition.[420] Article 4 establishes situations where copyright legislation cannot be applied, including for principles, intangible ideas, texts of laws, court rulings, judicial decisions, and news.[421] Article 5 makes provisions for national folklore as owned by the public and supported by the National Council for Culture, Arts and Literature. Article 6 states that the moral rights of authors and their successors cannot be waived off or confiscated. Article 8 authorizes the National Council for Culture, Arts and Literature to exercise the moral rights to the work of authors who die without an heir, or for anonymous works.

189. Article 38 confirms the National Library is in charge of establishing a register for depositing works, sound recordings, radio shows, and performances. The National Library also has the prerogative of monitoring and inspecting the enforcement

417. Ahmed ElKlatawy & Karim Marouny. New Copyright Law in Kuwait. (2016, accessed Dec. 2, 2017, http://www.tamimi.com/en/magazine/law-update/section-14/october-6/new-copyright-law-in-kuwait.html).

418. Vanessa Delnaud & Marian Fayek. *Enforcement of IP Rights in the GCC: 2016 Highlights.* (2017, accessed Dec. 2, 2017 http://www.mondaq.com/x/576036/Patent/Enforcement+of+IP+rights+in+the+GCC+2016+highlights).

419. Ahmed ElKlatawy & Karim Marouny. *New Copyright Law in Kuwait.* (2016, accessed Dec. 2, 2017, http://www.tamimi.com/en/magazine/law-update/section-14/october-6/new-copyright-law-in-kuwait.html).

420. *Ibid.*

421. STA Law Firm. *Kuwait: New Copyright Laws in Kuwait.* (2017, accessed Dec. 2, 2017, http://www.mondaq.com/x/637952/Copyright/New+Copyright+Laws+In+Kuwait).

of the law by examining printing presses, libraries, and publishing houses. Should the Library refuse to register or deposit works, Article 39 states the right of an author to lodge a complaint against the decision.

190. Article 29 of the law has been highlighted as an interesting change offering exceptions to copyright.[422] The article relies on an open formulation to define exceptions to copyright infringement as uses that do not conflict with the normal exploitation of the work and do not prejudice the legitimate interests of the author. Among the 20 examples for permitted use provided by the article are private or personal use with no direct or indirect financial outcome, scientific research, quotations for purposes of criticism, enlightenment, study or information, software backup, and conversion to copies accessible for the blind. Apart from uses listed in Article 29, additional exceptions are provided for press reports, for noncommercial, educational uses as well as for libraries and archives.[423]

191. Punitive measures for copyright violations are found in differing legal sources in Kuwait. For example, materials that violate copyright law—including the original—can be confiscated and even destroyed in addition to tools that have been used to produce the violations.

192. Article 37 of Law No. 22 of 2016 grants customs authorities the right to deny customs clearance to goods if they violate copyright or its related rights. Additionally, Article 40 establishes the public prosecution as the sole authority to investigate and prosecute crimes related to Law No. 22, while cases fall under the jurisdiction of the Criminal Division in the High Court.

§10. 2015 Cybercrime Law No. 63 of 2015

193. In January 2016, Kuwait started implementing the new Cybercrimes Law, Law No. 63 of 2015, which includes 21 articles approved by the National Assembly in June 2015. Many world organizations such as Amnesty International, Reporters without Borders, Freedom House, and Human Rights Watch expressed their concern regarding this new cybercrime law which restricts the right of freedom of expression and online activism in Kuwait. The new law includes restrictive measures for online freedom,[424] and sets penalties for criminal offenses such as the hacking of electronic systems, unauthorized data retrieval, pornography, fraud, and human trafficking.[425]

194. Article 6 of the law includes similar elements to the Press law also stated in this new law but made explicit for digital media. Thus, in accordance to Articles

422. Al-Balushi, Riyadh (2017), "Overview of the Kuwaiti Copyright Law of 2016," 28 January. http://www.riyadh.om/2017/overview-of-the-kuwaiti-copyright-law-of-2016/, last accessed Dec. 2, 2017.
423. *Ibid.*
424. FH. Kuwait. https://freedomhouse.org/report/freedom-press/2016/kuwait (accessed Jan. 17, 2018).
425. Kuwait's New Cybercrimes Law Restricts Free Expression and Targets Online Activists. IFEX: The Global Network, Kuwait's new cybercrimes law restricts free expression and targets online activists. (2016, accessed May 14, 2017, https://www.ifex.org/kuwait/2016/01/22/cybercrimes_law/).

19, 20, and 21 of the 2006 Press Law, either insulting religious figures, criticizing the Amir or the judicial system, potentially damaging Kuwait's relations with other countries, or publicizing classified information can all lead to imprisonment or fines. Reporters without Borders believes this law is designed to target local activists who practice their freedom online, leading the country to be an oppressive state.[426]

195. Furthermore, Article 7 related to Article 28 of the Press Law which outlaws the use of the Internet to "overthrow the ruling regime in the country when this instigation included an enticement to change the system by force or through illegal means, or by urging to use force to change the social and economic system that exists in the country, or to adopt creeds that aim at destroying the basic statutes of Kuwait through illegal means."[427,428] Amnesty International believes this law is designed to stifle free speech in Kuwait in which the new law with the current legislations helps increase the arrest and persecution of people who make comments online such as on Twitter.[429]

196. The law recognizes what may be considered criminal acts, such as data alteration (i.e., forgery), unauthorized access to an electronic network, dissemination of unlawfully accessed information, and online use for human trafficking. Amnesty International stated that this new law conflicts with the international law because it did not clearly and precisely define the crimes.[430] On the other hand, this law is also in contradiction with human rights law because it fails to meet the three-part test to restrict the freedom of expression. The three parts include that human rights must be provided by law, must pursue a legitimate aim as enumerated under Article 19 (3) and be necessary and proportionately applied within the context of a democratic society.[431]

197. On the other hand, Reporters without Borders stated that Article 4 of the new law is very broad and not specific. For example, item 4 of Article 4 stated that "Whoever establishes a website or publishes or produces or prepares or creates or sends or stores information or data with a view to use, distribute or display to others via the Internet or an information technology device that would prejudice public morality or manages a place for this purpose" did not address what constitutes "prejudice to public morality."[432]

---

426. *Ibid.*
427. FH. Kuwait. https://freedomhouse.org/report/freedom-press/2016/kuwait (accessed Jan. 17, 2018).
428. Kuwait's New Cybercrimes Law Restricts Free Expression and Targets Online Activists. IFEX: The Global Network, Kuwait's new cybercrimes law restricts free expression and targets online activists. (2016, accessed May 14, 2017, https://www.ifex.org/kuwait/2016/01/22/cybercrimes_law/).
429. Amnesty International. *Kuwait: Electronic Crimes law threatens to further stifle freedom of expression.* (2016, accessed May 14. https://www.amnesty.org/en/latest/news/2016/01/kuwait-electronic-crimes-law-threatens-to-further-stifle-freedom-of-expression/).
430. *Ibid.*
431. Reporters without Borders. *New Cyber Crimes Law Restricts Free Expression and Targets Online Activists.* (2016, accessed May 14, 2017, https://rsf.org/en/news/new-cyber-crimes-law-restricts-free-expression-and-targets-online-activists).
432. *Kuwait's New Cybercrimes Law Restricts Free Expression and Targets Online Activists.* IFEX: The Global Network, Kuwait's new cybercrimes law restricts free expression and targets online activists. (2016).

198. Before the new media, the government used Article 25 of the National Security Law to prosecute people in violation of this law, which prohibits public insults of the Amir or "mocks God, the prophets and messengers, or the honor of his messengers and their wives." Since 2011, about 63 people were prosecuted for their critical views in views on Twitter, Facebook, blogs, other social media platforms, and at protests.[433]

§11. Kuwait Electronic Media Law No. 8 of 2016

199. In July 2016, the Ministry of Information implemented the new inclusive electronic media law (No. 8/2016) to manage and regulate electronic media.[434] The National Assembly overwhelmingly approved the law with thirty-seven members in favor and four against.[435] The new law which includes 27 Articles is intended to regulate all-web-based publications including newspaper and online news websites, news services, social media, website polls, online television, and bulletins. Accordingly, in order to operate, all the mentioned services should obtain a license from the government.

200. In its explanatory note of the law, which has been translated into the English language,[436] the government justified its move to adopt this law as being due to the Internet technology which created a fast spread of information, and reaching mass audience in short time with low expenses creating a new media phenomenon forced the government to produce this law in order to manage and regulate the online space. Thus, the new electronic media became an important part of life that needs to have a new legislation in line.

201. The government stated two main reasons for adopting this law. The first reason is to strengthen the freedom of speech and the rights to obtain information and make it accessible to everybody. The second reason is to create up-to-date legislation to better serve and use new media, and to ensure the rights of everyone to the freedom of opinion, freedom of expression, and the right of access to information while maintaining the principles and foundations of different beliefs

202. Article 1 of the Electronic Media Law defined the terms that associated with online news activities such as electronic media, electronic publication, electronic domain, electronic content, and other terms relevant to the law. The definition of electronic media includes electronic content that is produced, developed, upgraded, dealt with, broadcast, published, or reached through the Internet or any other communications network. Similarly, "electronic publication" is defined to include the copying, broadcasting, sending, or receiving of electronic media content through the Internet or any other communications network. An electronic domain is defined as the domain registered on the Internet or any other communications network, by which electronic sites are entered. Similarly, a website or electronic media facility is defined as the page, link, or electronic application that is issued within a certain time, has a

433. *Ibid.*
434. Alkuwait Alyom. *Law 8.* (State of Kuwait, 2016).
435. *Nod to Electronic Media Law-Shias Boycott.* (Arab Times, 2016, accessed May 17, 2017, http://www.arabtimesonline.com/news/nod-to-electronic-media-law-shias-boycott/).
436. *Law No. 8 of 2016 Regarding the Regulation of Electronic Media.* (The Kuwait Times, Feb. 14, 2016).

certain electronic address and domain, and is issued or hosted or extends through the Internet or any other communications network. Electronic content consists of text, audio or fixed, moving or multimedia content, which includes any mentioned structure, which is developed, produced, upgraded, or dealt with by electronic means or any type of content that is turned into electronic form, which is published and reached through the Internet or any other communications network. An electronic paper is a website or other electronic means through which electronic content that includes news, topics, columns, and multimedia of journalistic or information nature is published, whether regularly or not.

203. Similarly, information or electronic commercial advertisement services refers to content that includes promotion of works, services, products, or individuals through the Internet or any other communications network. An owner of the site or the electronic information media tool is the natural or legal person to whom the site or the electronic information media facility is proven to belong to. A responsible manager is the natural person appointed by the site owner or the electronic information portal, responsible for the administrative and judicial side of the the site's or the electronic information facility's content. Blocking is disallowing audiences from reaching the site or the electronic information facility.

204. The law continues by providing the right to manage electronic media without prior censorship in Articles 2 and 3. As stated in Article 2 "…there is no prior censorship on what is circulated of content via electronic sites and facilities." Article 5 lists the electronic sites the law applies to, namely, electronic publication houses, electronic news agencies, electronic journalism, news services, information service facilities, and commercial advertisements. The article also applies to electronic versions of paper newspapers and audio-visual satellite channels. However, it states that the rules of this law do not apply on the domain or facility or a personal electronic account, whose user is not characterized to be of specialized professionalism.

205. Further, Article 6 clearly states that those who operate any of the above list should obtain a license (ten years and renewable) from the Minister of Information. Article 8 sets the conditions to apply for the license as stated in the law including the Kuwaiti nationality and a minimum age of 21 years. The applicant must be of good repute, and not previously sentenced for a felony or a crime that violates honor or trust, unless his status was restored. Further, the applicant must name the site or electronic information facility, and it must not be in violation of public order or general or public decency or identical to the name of another site. The applicant must have a specific location for the activity mentioned in the license.

206. Next, Article 9 provides in detail the legal requirements for the manager of the site or news service. The manager who will be responsible for the published content should be a Kuwaiti of not less than 21 years of age. The manager must have at least a general secondary certificate or its equivalent, and the manager must be of good repute, and must not have been convicted for a felony or an honor violating crime, unless his status was restored. Finally, the manager must not manage another licensed site or electronic information facility.

207. The license as stated in Article 16 can be revoked under several conditions. First, if the licensee is a legal person, and his legal personality is lifted for any legally set reason. Second, if the licensee loses any of the requirements mentioned in Article

8 of this law. Third, if the responsible manager's post becomes vacant, or if the appointed manager loses one of the conditions that he must meet, and the licensee does not appoint a replacement that meets the set conditions within the designated period of Article 10 of this law. Fourth, if he licensee rents out the license. Fifth, if the licensee sells the license or waives it without the approval of the ministry. Sixth, if the licensee does not practice the licensed activity during the period mentioned in Article 13 of this law. Seventh, if the license period ends, without a renewal request within six months of its expiry. Seventh, if the licensee dies, and does not have a legal heir, or if the heirs do not transfer the license within the period mentioned in Article 14. Finally, the license cannot be revoked without a court order that must be implemented or a written request from the licensee along with the conditions mentioned above.

208. In case the company violates any of the mentioned conditions or the company practiced without a license, it will be fined a minimum of KWD 500 and a maximum of KWD 5,000 as stated in Article 19, public prosecution is responsible of all crimes mentioned in the law as stated in Article 21.

209. This law brought two different viewpoints against and in support of the law among the public, government officials, MPs, and academics[437438439] not to mention the confusion created on whether a personal account is included or not which made the spokesperson for the Ministry of Information state clearly that the law will not be applied to personal accounts and its only purpose is to manage, not control, the freedom of speech online ("Alelam Alkuwaitiya: Qanun Alelam Alelekroni La Yashmal Alhisabat Alshakhsiya,"). Those who opposed the law claim that the electronic law will take away youth's freedom. On the other hand, the speaker of the Kuwaiti National Assembly Mr Marzouq Al-Ghanim believes that the law will stop chaos in the country but freedom is a fundamental constitutional principle that cannot be touched. Furthermore, the Information Minister Sheik Salman Al-Homoud Al-Sabah asserted that the new law will not touch people's freedom and it is made to manage the media. However, Dr. Mohammad Al-Faili, professor of constitutional law at Kuwait University, explained that any successful legislation must be an outcome of a realistic experience and this new technology which stripped the power from the state will affect the legislative path because the emergence of new means of expression made two routes, either to put special rules for these means or stay with the general rules already in practice.[440,441]

210. The law also heavily relies on Law No. 3 of 2006, the press law, which prohibits the publication of certain matters in Articles 19, 20, and 21. Article 19 prohibits meddling in matters relating to God, The Holy Quran, prophets, the companions of

437. M. Abdullah. *Mashroo Alelam Alelektroni.* (2015, Aljarida, accessed May 14, 2017, http://www.aljarida.com/articles/1468435509747917700/).

438. *Alelam Alelectroni Muhalafat Wa Eyoob.. Walhikooma Tueed Alnathar Feh.* (2015, Aljarida, accessed May 14, 2017, http://www.aljarida.com/articles/1462436984316940600/).

439. *Almukhtasoon Walqanuniyun Min Halaqat Niqash Elelam Alelektroni: Yuharem Alhuriyat Walshabab Bishaklah Alhali.* (2015, Alerada, accessed May 14, 2017, http://alerada.net/2015/04/27/26717).

440. *Alelam Alelectroni Muhalafat Wa Eyoob.. Walhikooma Tueed Alnathar Feh.* (2015, Aljarida, accessed May 14, 2017, http://www.aljarida.com/articles/1462436984316940600/).

441. *Almukhtasoon Walqanuniyun Min Halaqat Niqash Elelam Alelektroni: Yuharem Alhuriyat Walshabab Bishaklah Alhali.* (2015, Alerada, accessed May 14, 2017, http://alerada.net/2015/04/27/26717).

Prophet Mohammad (Peace Be Upon Him), his wives, and his family. This type of meddling includes defamation, slander, or expressions of mockery regardless of how it is expressed, which is stated in Article 29 of Law No. 31 of 1970 which is an Amendment of Some of the Provisions of the Penalty Law No (16) for the year 1960. Further, Article 20 outlaws any challenge that can be made to the head of the State of Kuwait, and no statement shall be attributed to him except by a special written permission from the Amiri Diwan.

211. Finally, Article 21 prohibits ten other types of expression. First, expressions of disdain or contempt at the Constitution of the State is prohibited. Second, it prohibits expressions of disdain or insults aimed at judges or members of the public prosecution or to state something that is considered as a disparagement of the integrity and impartiality of the judicial system or to publish something which the courts or the investigating parties decide to maintain in secret. Third, it is not permissible to insult public morals or instigate to violate the public order or to violate the laws or to commit crimes, even if the crime did not occur. Fourth, it is not permissible to publish news regarding official secret communications and publishing of agreements and treaties which the government of Kuwait concludes, before publishing them in the official gazette, except by a special permission from the concerned ministry. Fifth, it is not permissible to influence the value of the national currency or what would lead to worries about the economic status of the country or publishing news about the bankruptcy of businessmen or the commercial companies or banks or the money exchangers, except with a special permission from the competent court. Sixth, it is not permissible to reveal what goes on in any meeting or what is written in the papers or documents or decrees, or any papers or prints which the Constitution or any law decided that they are to be kept in secret or not to publish them, even if the published topic was true, and the publishing was limited to the official statements that are issued in that regard. Seventh, it is not permissible to infringe upon the dignity of the persons or their lives or religious believes, and instigating hatred or disdain of any of the society's strata or to publish information about their financial statuses or to reveal a secret which would harm their reputation or wealth or their trade names. Eight, Article 21 prohibits the encroachment into the private life of an employee or a person who is charged in a public service, or attributing statements or acts not true to him which would cause harm or insult to his person. Ninth, it is prohibited to cause harm to the relationships between Kuwait and other Arab or friendly countries if that is done through the press campaigns. Finally, the Article states a prohibition to publications by newspaper that go beyond the purpose of the license which is granted to it.

212. A note is included in the law to pay attention to an amendment to the aforementioned press law. An amendment to Law No. 3 of 2006 on press and publications was published in "Kuwait Al-Youm" national gazette's February 7, 2016 issue, which adds material published online under publications covered by the law.

§12. Tribal Elections Law

213. In 1998, the Kuwaiti National Assembly issued a Law No. 9 to be added as a new item No. 5 to Article 45 of Law No. 35 of 1962 on the elections. The new law punishes all who prepared or participated in organizing a preliminary election or invited for it, which is carried out on unofficial procedures stipulated by the election law before the set date for the elections to choose one or more of belonging tribe or sect to run officially alone in the main elections, which is called tribal primary elections or Intikhabat Fareya.

214. According to a study conducted by the Kuwait National Assembly, there are mixed views regarding this law.[442] The supporters of the law believe that the candidate who won the election is representing the entire country and not a group of people, a tribe, or a specific religion, and that these kinds of tribal primary elections will increase sectarianism and tribalism in the country at the expense of national belonging giving chance to those who have influence over the tribe or religion to prevent those who are most generous, most capable and able to serve the public interest. On the other hand, those who are against the law believe the freedom of opinion and expression is a right guaranteed by Article 36 of the Kuwaiti Constitution and this kind of election is part of this right. The tribal primary elections are also practiced according to Law No. 65 of 1979 regarding public meetings and gatherings that permit these kinds of meetings as long as they are in accordance with the procedures organized in accordance with this law. It is a legitimate tribal primary election within a big family and participation in these tribal primary elections is optional not mandatory. However, regardless of this law, people will circumvent around any law preventing these kinds of tribal primary elections.

215. From a legal point of view, this law was only limited to tribe and the sect's tribal primary elections, but did not include other groups such as merchants, parties, political blocs, and other associations. It is important to note that all those who have been charged with this crime have been acquitted of this charge.

216. Ministerial decree 143 of 2016 provides more conditions and regulations for media coverage, advertising, and promotion pertaining to elections of both the National Assembly and the Municipal Council. Prior to any National Assembly or Municipality's elections, the Minister of Information issues a decree regarding the conditions and regulations of media coverage, advertising, and promotion of the elections. Similar decrees have been issued for previous elections with 21 Articles.

217. Article 1 explains the period of the implementation for the decree which starts from the day it was published in the government's official newspaper or a call was made for the elections of the National Assembly or Municipality until the announcement of the final results. Article 2 prohibits publishing, broadcasting, or rebroadcasting calls for tribal primary elections, participation, advertisement, and the broadcast of any news or information about it during the elections. Similarly, Article 2 prohibits the publication, broadcast, or rebroadcast during the elections of information disturbing the freedom or the regulations of the elections by any means.

218. Article 3 calls for the media when covering the elections to distinguish between what is news and what is communicated for the purposes of promotion, which should be clearly specified as an advertisement. Article 4 prohibits media coverage from insulting any candidate either directly or indirectly using words, pictures, symbols, text, drawing, or other means. Article 5 stresses on the method of publicity or coverage

442. Kuwait National Assembly. *Dirasat Wabihooth: Tajreem Alentikhabat Alfariyah.* (2015, accessed May 17, 2017, http://www.kna.kw/clt-html5/run.asp?id=1183).

to not include financial inducements, offers, or promising to offer the voter something to vote in a particular way or to abstain from voting.

219. Article 6 calls for fair coverage of all candidates, and when conducting, publishing, or broadcasting results or opinions of the polls several conditions should be considered. First, the coverage should provide the organization which conducted the poll, the way it was conducted, the date it was conducted on, and the number of people that participated. Second, the media coverage should not publicize the statistics or results of the polls on the day of the elections. Finally, the media should not announce the results, the rates, or the percentages of the elections before the officials' announcement.

220. Article 7 prohibits the broadcast or rebroadcast of interviews, programs, or reports with or about any candidate for the National Assembly or Municipality before the start of the elections. Article 8 bans the broadcast or rebroadcast of reports, or audio-visual works that include a publicity or media coverage about any candidate or the elections in general unless it coincides with the Audio-Visual Media Law No. 61/2007. Article 9 explains the role of appointed staff or experts during the elections which include monitoring the media coverage of the elections to make sure not violating the law and to receive and investigate the complaints. Article 10 indicates the laws that will apply in case of violating this law. Finally, Article 11 cancels the previous Law No. 78 of 2012. Article 12 requests for the responsible body to implement the law.

§13. Censorship of Films

221. An article by *The Washington Post* stated a striking similarity between Kuwait and a small town in Alabama: both censored the 2017 Disney production of *Beauty and the Beast* for a positive portrayal of homosexuality.[443] A board member for the Kuwait Cinema Company was quoted by the BBC as having explained that the film was pulled from theaters after the Ministry of Information's censorship department deemed it offensive.[444] A Kuwaiti blog later published an update that the movie theaters themselves had pulled the movie, announcing that the pulling of the movie from the Ministry of Information was inaccurate.[445]

222. Regardless of how this censorship went about, this event shows the importance of understanding how films are censored in Kuwait. Here, several decrees from the Ministry of Information were found that may shed light on the process of film censorship. While some of these regulations oversee the censorship, licensing, and distribution of films, others oversee who is permitted to watch them and where they are allowed to be shown.

223. First, ministerial decrees 31 of 2016 and 21 of 2013 both deal with the films, the licenses to display and distribute films, and the censorship of films. The 2013

443. Sudarsan Raghavan. *Disney's Hit "Beauty and the Beast" Is Banned in Kuwait for Its 'Gay Moment'*. (The Washington Post, 2017).

444. Mark. *Disney Pulled Beauty and the Beast from Kuwait Cinema *UPDATED** (2017, accessed Mar. 20, 2017, http://248am.com/mark/movies/disney-pulled-beauty-and-the-beast-from-kuwait-cinema/).

445. *Ibid.*

regulation has 19 articles. In the first article, it defines a film, a place for showing a movie and the regulatory bodies. Most strikingly, the definition of a film does not differ whether the content is actually recorded on film, electronically, digitally, and displayed in a movie theater or on a television. Article 2 states that films will be regulated for the purpose of protecting spiritual values, Kuwaiti customs and traditions, and to protect against disruptions to public order or national unity. Article 3 states that it is necessary for any theater, artistic space that either shows films or announces them to get a license. Article 4 makes the Ministry of Information's film censorship committee responsible for ensuring that the three laws that are followed: Laws 3 of 2006, 61 of 2007, and 19 of 2012. Further, the committee is responsible for an evaluation of each film and to determine an appropriate age for admission of audience members to the film, applications for films that will be screened, and a consideration of all complaints about the decisions they issue. Article 5 states that licenses for the management and operation of rooms in which films are displayed or distributed must be assigned to individuals who satisfy four criteria. The first of these criteria is Kuwaiti citizenship, and the second is a combination of a good reputation and the absence of a criminal record or evidence of a criminal behavior's rehabilitation. The third criterion is a high school diploma or the equivalent, which may be waived in the case the individual has sufficient experience. The final criterion is that the person should own or operate a theater in a suitable location. Finally, Article 5 ends with a clause to regulate in the case that the applicant is a legal person, as opposed to a natural person. In such a case, all the partners or founders of that legal person must be Kuwaiti citizens.

224. Then, several administrative tasks are outlined in the remainder of the Articles 6–11. Article 6 then states that the Minister of Information must decide on the licensing application within ninety days, as long as the submitted application is complete and follows all the instructions are provided. If the ninety-day period ends without a decision, the decision is by default a rejection. Article 7 requires separate licenses for each movie theater, validates a license for five years with the potential of a renewal that must be requested by the licensee and approved by the Ministry of Information—as long as the renewal is submitted three months prior to its expiration date. Article 8 makes the licensee responsible for notification of the relevant authority within the ministry if they should choose to disable or terminate the theater's operation, distribution activities, or any of the data in the original license application. Article 9 states that a ministerial approval is required for the sales or a license. If a licensee dies, the transfer of the license must be requested and the conditions of Article 5 must be followed. If such a transfer is not completed within six months of the death, Article 9 deems the license terminated. Articles 10 and 11 place rules on who is allowed to be appointed as a director of a movie theater. It is noteworthy that the Kuwaiti nationality is nevertheless a requirement and that an age requirement must be shown, visibly and prominently, in the same language as advertisements that appear for a film.

225. Article 12 states that movie theaters cannot display scenes from movies that have been censored by the committee. Article 13 states that any advertisements can be displayed only after a license is obtained. Article 14 states that the importation of equipment related to movie theaters cannot be conducted without a ministerial approval. Article 15 gives power to censorship officers from the Ministry of Information to prove violations, alter their procedures or minutes and submit them to the relevant investigators. The same article gives power to the Minister of Information to suspend any film, media, or advertisement if it contradicts this law or deviates from Kuwaiti customs and traditions, promotes public disorder, offends public morals, or disrupts national unity. Article 16 states that the Ministry of Information can also cancel or suspend the license or shut down the operation of movie theaters or film distribution companies in case there are violations. Article 17 outlines the service fees for various services provided in this law. Article 18 repeals Ministerial Resolutions 29 of 2011 and 73 of 2012. Article 19 makes the law effective on the date of the publication of the law, which is March 10, 2013.

226. This regulation is important because it is used as a legal reference in the subsequent 2016 regulation. Ministerial decrees 31 of 2016 also contains 19 articles. The articles are almost identical with some exceptions. For example, Article 7 of the 2016 regulation takes away the time period for which the license is valid and makes it the eighth article. Further, the tenth article of the 2016 regulation makes a license void if it is rented or leased. Finally, Article 18 makes the previous regulation void. Thus, this decree can be seen as an updated version of the previously described regulation.

227. Second, ministerial decree 30 of 2016 regulates the entry of children to cinemas, theaters, and similar spaces. The decree states that the directors of places where films are shown must satisfy four criteria when content would be seen or heard that is prohibited for children below a certain age. First, two signs—one in English and one in Arabic—must be placed in a prominent place outside the place where the film is shown. The sign must contain sufficient information on the type of restrictions shown and clearly state the age that is prohibited to watch or hear the content. A phrase must be used in this sign that states the following words, "not allowed for those under the age of ... to watch the show." This data must be presented in all forms of advertisements of the work. The directors are responsible for the verification of the age of child, which must be done by a civil identification, passport, or other government-issued identification that contains a photograph of the child and indicates his/her age. Finally, the directors are responsible for not allowing prohibited audience members from entering, watching, or listening to the content.

228. Third, ministerial decree 26 of 2016 deals with the determination of public spaces that can be used as cinemas or theaters. Several types of public spaces are outlined, including artistic and cultural institutions. Further, several commercial spaces are listed, including malls, clubs, hotels, restaurants, cafes, and beaches. Moreover, boats, yachts, and marinas are listed as spaces that can be considered a cinema or theater. In addition, wedding halls, Ramadan tents, other temporary tents, and other independent events can be considered a movie theater. Finally, the decree states that any place where a concert, show, song, film, or theater is presented to the public can be defined as a movie theater or cinema house. This definition is important because the definition determines the regulations that apply to it.

§14. Censorship of Books

229. Kuwait's Ministry of Information has two ministerial decrees that are relevant to publishing books and novels, published in 2015 and 2017. Both these decrees refer back to the publication law, Law No. 3 of 2006, and create a committee for the censorship of books. Both these decrees also make room for the Ministry of Islamic Affairs to opine on the legality of the written material.

230. Looking closer at Ministerial Decree 47 of 2015, it is worth noting that the decree consists of 11 articles and a preface. The preface begins by honoring the Kuwaiti Constitution's commitment to the Freedom of Expression, which should not be disrupted by public authorities. Yet, it adds a clause that there are necessary regulations that are upheld for the sake of protecting public safety, national security, as well as protection of order, health, and the rights and reputations of individuals. These protections are conducted by the issuance of license other administrative procedures as well as restrictions prescribed by the law.

231. The first article then states that all books and printed publications, including international magazines, are regulated by Law No. 3 of 2006. Further, any updated or otherwise modified editions are subjected to the same provisions. Article 2 suggests that several parties in the publishing industry, including the author, are responsible for filing out a form in the Publication Department to consult an electronic archive that determines whether a book or publication has been previously approved in order to prevent conflicting opinions. The third article suggests that there are three stages for controlling books and publications. First, officers would provide observations in writing. Second, the book is reviewed a second time with the initial officer, the head of the department and a specialized censor in management. The purpose of this review is to determine whether the book should be banned or if there should be a censorship of part of the publication. The third and final stage is to show the required censorship to the censorship committee of Kuwait.

232. Article 4 states that all religious books, including the Holy Quran, must be taken to the Ministry of Islamic Affairs in order to determine its legality or lack thereof. In addition, educational books must be sent to the Ministry of Education. Article 5 provides the only scenarios in which a book is allowed to be presented to the committee a second time. These three scenarios include a new edition that's different from the first, inclusion of new parts in the book, and the occurrence of political or social changes that required a second examination of the content of the printed materials. Article 6 states that the decision to permit or censor a book must be provided within three months of submitting it to the Press and Publication Administration. In case the decision is to ban or censor a book, Article 7 states that authors, publishers, and copyright holders would be given an official letter that explains the reason for the prohibition by the Head of the Press and Publications Department. Article 8 states that the authors, copyright holders, and publishers may issue within two months an appeal with specific reasons to challenge the decision made by the Book Censorship Committee and the Grievance Committee. Article 9 states that the Grievance Committee can either uphold the censorship or cancel it, with an order from the Management of the Press and Publication Department. Article 10 states that decisions by the Grievances Committee must be sent to the Assistant Undersecretary for Press, Publication and Publication

Affairs in order to complete the necessary procedures. Finally, the eleventh article cancels all previous laws that may contradict this one, as of the date of its publication which is May 16, 2015.

233. Two years later, Ministerial Decree 22 of 2017 can be viewed as an update of the previous regulation. The first article makes this resolution relevant for the control of novels, books, and other printed publications, and the second repeals the previous regulation. Article 3 makes the decision effective on March 13, 2017. Then, a list of rules is published in 14 articles. These rules are very similar to the previous 2015 regulations. However, Article 2 states that the Book Censorship Committee and the Grievance Committees are required to have members from the Ministry of Information as well as researchers, academics, and specialists in the humanities, culture, and fine arts. Further, the three stages contained in Article 3 of Decree 47 of 2015 are separated into three different articles in 2017 (Articles 6–8). Article 9 adds a thirty-day time limit for revisions to be made when certain parts of the publication are required to be changed or deleted. Further, the 2017 regulation uses the term "public interest" instead of providing the specific areas of concern that justify the censorship.

Part II. Regulation of Print Media

Chapter 1. The Journalists' Profession

234. In an international survey of Arab journalists, Pintak and Ginges[446] explain that Arab journalists feel a sense of responsibility for the people they serve. This responsibility includes the need to be fair and balanced and a commitment to be more independent.[447] In order to gain a deeper understanding of how the journalistic profession is conceived, it is important to review ethics of the profession.

235. In Kuwait, the factors that compromise the ethical standards to which communication professionals are held accountable are widely debated. For example, Onyebadi and Alajami[448] refute the claim that journalists have personal hardships due to insufficient salaries despite the fact that the journalists they interviewed had second jobs. The authors[449] attribute to cultural reasons and a lack of ethical standards a demand for gift solicitations among journalists and a willingness to accept gifts. More than half (55%) of the journalists they interviewed knew someone who would accept a bribe and 44.5% would accept a bribe if they knew someone who did so.[450] Gender and education did not affect a journalist's willingness to accept bribes.

236. Nevertheless, Selvik et al.[451] empirically demonstrated a bias in the coverage of the Kuwaiti parliament which they largely attribute to salaries that are insufficient. Regardless, Hafez[452] demonstrated that many Muslim-majority nations have some kind of ethical code to guarantee professional integrity that is analogue to those of more developed nations.

---

446. Lawrence Pintak & Jeremy Ginges. *Arab Journalists*. In The Global Journalist in the 21st Century, edited by David H Weaver and Lars Willnat, 429,442. (Routledge, 2012).
447. *Ibid.*
448. Uche Onyebadi & Fawaz Alajmi. *Gift solicitation and acceptance in journalism practice: An assessment of Kuwaiti journalists' perspective*. 17 Journalism 348,365 (2016).
449. *Ibid.*
450. *Ibid.*
451. Kjetil Selvik, Jon Nordenson &Tewodros Aragie Kebede. *Print Media Liberalization and Electoral Coverage Bias in Kuwait*. 69 The Middle East Journal. 255,276. (2015).
452. Kai Hafez. *Journalism Ethics Revisited: A Comparison of Ethics Codes in Europe, North Africa, the Middle East, and Muslim Asia*. 19 Political communication. 225,250 (2002).

Chapter 2. Journalists' Rights

237. Kuwaiti academics, journalists, PR practitioners, and media personnel have been calling for the enactment of code of conducts. In 1978, former Minister of Information, Sheikh Jaber Al-Ali, was the first to adopt the code of conduct making Kuwait a pioneer state in journalism.[453] Dr. Anas Al-Rasheed, media faculty at Kuwait University and former Minister of Information, put together in 2003 code of conduct to be used among the journalists in Kuwait.[454]

238. Al-Rasheed states that in accordance to the Islamic principles, the United Nations human rights, and the Kuwaiti Constitution, this code of conduct was designed to improve the efficiency and professionalism of Kuwaiti journalists.[455] The code includes 11 rights and 13 duties for journalists to consider when practicing journalism. Al-Rasheed explains that journalism is different from one society to another depending on the nature of the political system and the level of freedom, but this doesn't mean there are no universal traditions and customs that journalists should follow to protect the journalistic profession.

239. According to former minister of information Dr. Anas Mohammad Alrushaid, journalists are entitled to certain rights and have some responsibilities.[456] The journalists' rights include the right to obtain the information as well as the right to attend events and public meetings and report with honesty and fairness. Further, journalists have the right to conceal the source and not to be forced to disclose his/her sources. Also, journalists have the right to reject any command or publication that goes against his or her conscience and ethics. Journalists also have the right to participate and express his or her opinion with regard to the editorial policy of the newspaper. Journalists also have the right to learn and train with the latest in journalism and participate in programs that will improve his or her profession. Further, journalists have the right to provide conditions that guarantee a decent and just life in obtaining a fair wage. Further, journalists have the right not to be transferred to another work contrary to the nature his or her work without approval. Also, journalists have the right to be free to move and get some benefits, aid, or subsidies for international coverages as well as the right to enjoy recreational activities for the journalist and his or her family.

453. *Alrushaid Yadu Litafeel Alraqabah Althatiyah Wawadaa Mithaq Sharaf Sahafi.* (accessed May 17, 2017, http://beta.www.skedaddle.co.uk/Articles.aspx?ArticleID=277536&CatID=102).

454. Anas Mohammad Alrushaid. *Mashroo Mithaq Sharaf Sahaji: Wajhat Nathar Kuwaitiyah.* (Akwasat News, Jul. 19, 2003).

455. Kuwait News Agency. *Alrushaid Yuqadim Mashru Mithaq Sharaf Lilamilin fe Asahafah Alkuwaitiyah.* (2003, accessed May 17, 2017, http://www.kuna.net.kw/ArticlePrintPage.aspx?id=1352495&language=ar).

456. Anas Mohammad Alrushaid. *Mashroo Mithaq Sharaf Sahaji: Wajhat Nathar Kuwaitiyah.* (Akwasat News, Jul. 19, 2003).

§1. Role of Journalists as Watch-Dogs of Society

240. With freedoms come responsibilities, and there are some duties that a journalist should follow as stated in the code of conduct.[457] First, a journalist must demonstrate a commitment to this code of conduct, respect the Kuwaiti Constitution and laws, and not publish sectarianism or tribalism or hatred reports, and should defend the freedom of press and expression. Further, a journalist must be committed to the accuracy of their reporting, and journalists should not use their profession for self-interest and should refuse bribes. Journalists should practice his or her profession in accordance with the freedom given by the Constitution. Journalists should also refrain from using unethical methods to obtain the information. Journalists should also respect others' privacy and not to publish any information about them without their consent. Journalists should understand the importance of distinguishing between news and opinion and should distinguish between advertising and journalism. In order to ensure a fair trial, journalists should prevent the publication of names or photographs of suspects in the various cases unless they are transferred to the public prosecution. Journalists should prevent the publication of offensive images in news or press issues. Journalists should prevent the publication of images of dead bodies, victims of accidents, sexual assaults, or manipulations of digital images with the intent to excite. Journalists should respect the special-needs people. Journalists should demonstrate a commitment to publish balanced views of different opinions and the commitment to correct their mistake and apologize if needed. Journalists should also demonstrate a commitment not to glorify crime nor encourage violence or drugs.

§2. Journalists' Independence

241. Regardless of these important rights and duties, the press in Kuwait refrains from enforcing journalistic codes of conduct by encouraging journalistic independence. In fact, some journalists and academics believe the code of conduct restricts media freedom. Many journalists believe ethics are only in theory and not practical when practicing journalism in Kuwait, and the code of conduct is a tool to indirectly monitor the press to prevent journalists from practicing their role in the society.[458] Seeing the need for ethics in the communication profession, Faisal Albaidan[459] organized a code of conduct with 103 Articles in 2010.

---

457. *Ibid.*
458. *Cougar: Mithaq Alsharaf Alelami Takbeel Lilhuriyat Watanaqudan Lildemoqratiyah.* (Alrai, Jul. 9, 2008).
459. Faisal Albaidan. *Derasa Fe Akhlaqiyat Mihnat Alsahafa.* (Alaan, 2010).

Chapter 3. Journalists' Liability

§1. General Information on the Liability System

242. The Kuwaiti law addressed the personal liability rights indirectly using words such as personal reputation, privacy, freedom of expression, honor, and the right to control his image. Infringement of these rights under the Kuwaiti law can lead to either civil or criminal liability.[460] The law tries to balance between media freedom and personal rights. It sets restrictions on mass media to protect personal rights. Such restrictions include the prohibition of prejudice toward people's dignity, lives, religious beliefs, and incitement to hatred aiming to force the media not to use insult libel words or exposing the privacy of people.[461] However, in order to file legal negligence liability against the media, the person has to provide these three conditions:[462]

(1) The duty of care imposed on the mass media
(2) That the mass media were in breach of that duty
(3) That the claimant suffered damage caused by the breach of duty

§2. Who Will Be Held Liable?

243. Article 27 of Law No (3) for the Year 2006 on Press and Publications clearly stated who will be liable for violating the publishing law. It specified that both the editor-in-chief and the journalist or author will be held liable if they published, in a newspaper, something that was prohibited under Articles 19, 20, and 21 of the law. The penalty varies between imprisonment and fines or both penalties.[463] However, Articles 27 and 28 of the 2006 press law didn't consider the editor-in-chief as a main accountable of a deliberate crime in which the legislator equated the criminal intent with the unintentional mistake of the responsibility of the editor-in-chief and the reporter of the article switching out from the general rules of criminal responsibility.[464]

460. Thafar Alhajri. *Tortious Liability of Mass Media for the Invasion of Personal Rights: A Comparative Study between English Law and Kuwaiti Law*. International Review of Law (2014).
461. *Ibid., 14.*
462. *Ibid., 4.*
463. Doha Centre for Media Freedom. Law No (3) for the Year 2006 on Press and Publications-Kuwait. (accessed May 14, 2017, http://www.dc4mf.org/sites/default/files/press_law_kuwait.pdf).
464. A. AlSaudi & A. Taher. *Aldemoqratiya Alkuwaitiya: Altareekh, Alwaqe'a, Almustaqbel.* (Al-Arabai for Publishing, 2011).

§3. Defamation and Libel

244. Mansell et al.[465] explain defamation as "an alleged and intentional false communication" about an individual, and they address the tension "between the protection of an individual's reputation and the promotion of free speech, particularly political speech." However, the components of defamation may be interpreted differently from one country to another. For example, the United States focuses more on freedom of speech and press while Canada and the United Kingdom emphasize reputation at the expense of free speech.[466] In other countries like Kuwait, there is another type of defamation called lèse–majesté (LM) in which people receive sentences and fines for an offense violating the dignity of the ruler.[467] Judges and public prosecutors in Kuwait are also protected by media law from any defamatory speech.[468]

245. The defamation laws in the Gulf States (GCC) are mainly governed under the penal code, not the media law, and they focus on protecting individual reputation.[469] In their examination of the defamation laws of six Arab countries (Egypt, Jordan, Kuwait, Lebanon, Libya, and the UAE), Duffy and Alkazemi[470] found that none have a defamation law that aligns with international norms.

246. Articles 209–216 of the Kuwaiti penal code deal with the punishment of any defamatory actions. Article 209 specifically defined defamation as "any person, who attributes to another, in a public place or within the hearing range or sight of a person other than the victim, an occurrence that hurts his reputation."[471] Punishments vary and can include a monetary fine as well as a prison sentence.

§4. Privacy

247. Article 39 of the Kuwaiti Constitution protects the privacy of certain communication activities, such as telephone lines.[472] Alhajri[473] goes on to explain that this constitutional provision of freedom of communication applies regardless of whether the communication activity was conduction by postal mail, telegraphy, or through a telephone under most conditions. The understanding of privacy in Kuwait is nuanced,

465. Robin Mansell et al., eds. *The International Encyclopedia of Digital Communication and Society, 3 Volume Set*. 966. (John Wiley & Sons, 2015).

466. *Ibid.*

467. *Ibid.*

468. Matt J. Duffy & Mariam Alkazemi. *Arab Defamation Laws: A Comparative Analysis of Libel and Slander in the Middle East.* 22 Communication Law and Policy 189,211 (2017.).

469. Matt J. Duffy. *GCC Media Regulations Lead to Timid* Press (2013).

470. Matt J. Duffy & Mariam Alkazemi. *Arab Defamation Laws: A Comparative Analysis of Libel and Slander in the Middle East.* 22 Communication Law and Policy 189,211 (2017.).

471. *Ibid.*

472. Kuwait National Assembly. *Aldistour Alkuwaiti* http://www.kna.kw/clt-html5/run.asp?id=2024 (accessed Jan. 17, 2018).

473. Thafar Alhajri. Tortious Liability of Mass Media for the Invasion of Personal Rights: A Comparative Study between English Law and Kuwaiti Law. International Review of Law 4 (2014).

as homes are not permitted to be entered without permission from a homeowner unless another violation of the law has occurred.

248. Alhajri[474] explains that the Kuwaiti Electronic Transactions Law of 2014 protects the privacy of information related to one's employment, social status, health condition, financial liabilities, or other officially recorded information—unless other laws were violated that necessitate an exemption. Alhajri[475] explains that this privacy is intended to protect personal rights in situations where groups of people may be vulnerable due to religious beliefs, tribal affiliation, or cause reputation to their businesses.

249. In the information age, privacy is of global concern. Multinational technological companies collect information about users, which can add vulnerability to users navigating the worldwide web for health-related information.[476] It is unclear how Kuwaiti law would deal with such vulnerabilities, and it is also unclear which courts would have jurisdiction over such a legal question given the global nature of the worldwide web.

474. *Ibid.*

475. *Ibid.*

476. Scott Monteith, Tasha Glenn & Michael Bauer. *Searching the internet for health information about bipolar disorder: some cautionary issues.*" International journal of bipolar disorders (2013).

Chapter 4. Access to Public Information

250. Article 19 of the United Nations' Universal Declaration of Human Rights clearly deals with access to information. The article states, "Everyone has the right to freedom of opinion and expression; this right includes freedom to hold opinions without interference and to seek, receive and impart information and ideas through any media and regardless of frontiers."[477] Thus, access to information is an essential element for free speech. International Research & Exchanges Board[478] provided nine indicators for free speech, and two of them are related to access of information. In order to practice free speech, the information should be is easily available, the right of access to information should be equally enforced for media, journalists and citizens alike, and using news sources should not be restricted by law.[479] Freedom of information is one of the pillars of democracy that helps citizens monitor the government for corruption or mismanagement, creating transparent and accountable government.

251. Public officials cannot reveal confidential information without following a specific procedure to obtain permission to do so. Further, it is against the law to reveal information that is presented at governmental meetings, documents, or regulations before their release to the public—even if the information that was released unlawfully is true and consistent with official information.[480]

There is no legislation decree guaranteeing the right to access official information in Kuwait[481] (Freedom House, 2016). In 2009, the Kuwait Transparency Society drafted an access to information law but it did not end up seeing the light. In 2013, members of the National Assembly discussed legislation for right-to-information, which deals with various requirements including public information recordkeeping and process for information requests, but did not get through.[482] Despite this, the Ministry of Information may censor printed materials that are considered morally offensive, however, it does not regularly restrict access to news.[483]

477. International Research & Exchanges Board. *Media Sustainability Index*. (2017, accessed Apr. 11, 2017, https://www.irex.org/sites/default/files/pdf/media-sustainability-index-europe-eurasia-2017-full.pdf).
478. *Ibid.*
479. FH. Kuwait. https://freedomhouse.org/report/freedom-press/2016/kuwait (accessed Jan. 17, 2018).
480. Thafar Alhajri. *Tortious Liability of Mass Media for the Invasion of Personal Rights: A Comparative Study between English Law and Kuwaiti Law*. International Review of Law 4 (2014).
481. FH. Kuwait. https://freedomhouse.org/report/freedom-press/2016/kuwait (accessed Jan. 17, 2018).
482. Paul Ansah. *Blueprint for freedom*. 20 Index on censorship 3,8 (1991).
483. FH. Kuwait. https://freedomhouse.org/report/freedom-press/2016/kuwait (accessed Jan. 17, 2018).

Part III. Regulation of Audio-Visual Media

Chapter 1. Public Broadcasting

252. Public broadcasting is considered an important aspect of national development.[484] Labeling a nation as "developing" sometimes is seen as offensive; however, it's meant to describe a process in which nations are engaged to improve the quality of life for its people and promote freedom.[485] Although there is much progress to be made in media development in the Arab world, it "would be a mistake" to dismiss the progress of Arab broadcast media.[486]

253. The public broadcasting model is attainable in the Arab world, and particularly in the Gulf.[487] Ayish[488] relies on standards set by the United Nations Educational, Scientific and Cultural Organization (UNESCO) and analyzes these standards to define public broadcasting services. In his definition, public broadcasting is a tool for development that empowers citizens by providing information that is high in quality and diverse in content. To deliver such high-quality and diverse information, it is necessary for public broadcasting to be independent of government control and accessible to the public without cultural and economic obstacles.[489]

254. Although Gulf Arab states have progressive state broadcast systems, the potential for democratization set out through progressive state broadcast systems has not been actualized.[490] This is also true for Kuwait, despite scoring higher than other GCC states in terms of the status of its democracy. The four factors necessary to develop a public broadcasting system are present in Kuwait. First, editorial independence has been established by legislation set by audio-visual laws in Kuwait that allows a journalist to work in broadcast media without being a government employee.[491] Second, institutional autonomy, which refers to the operation and management of media

484. Gareth Locksley. *The media and development: what's the story*? (2009, World Bank, accessed Jan. 24, 2018, https://openknowledge.worldbank.org/bitstream/handle/10986/5924/472900PUB0Medi101OFFICIAL0USE0ONLY1.pdf?sequence=1&isAllowed=y).
485. Muhammad Ayish & Naomi Sakr. *Dynamics of Development in Arab Broadcasting*. 3 Middle East Journal of Culture and Communication. 3, 7. (2010).
486. *Ibid.*, *5*.
487. Muhammad Ayish. *Arab State Broadcasting Systems in Transition the Promise of the Public Service Broadcasting Model*. 3 Middle East Journal of Culture and Communication. 9, 25 (2010).
488. *Ibid.*
489. *Ibid.*
490. *Ibid.*
491. *Ibid.*

organizations so that they can take care of their own administrative and financial affairs, was developed in Kuwait after the Iraqi invasion in the 1990s.[492] Today, state-owned media in Kuwait have their own budgets that can be used to make creative decisions in which politicians do not interfere.[493] Third, nonstate broadcast competition exists in Kuwait in the form of private broadcast options as well as international programming coming from the Arab world and beyond.[494] Finally, examinations of program enhancement demonstrate that some programming in the Arab world pertains to religion while others relate to children, health, and tourism.[495]

492. *Ibid.*
493. *Ibid.*
494. *Ibid.*
495. *Ibid.*

Chapter 2. Private Broadcast

255. Soon after the 2006 press and publication law loosened regulations of print media in Kuwait, the audio-visual legislation (Law No. 61 of 2007) enabled private broadcast stations to be licensed. The terms of licensing and the termination of such licenses are listed in the second section of the law, which was briefly described previously (*see* Chapter 3, Section II, Subsection d).

256. To obtain a license, the company must be uniquely Kuwaiti that establishes and operates satellite radio and television or works with advertising and media in general. If the broadcast includes a visual element, the company should have an investment capital of at least KWD 500,000 (USD 1,500,000). A minimum of KWD 200,000 (USD 600,000) is set for broadcast that is limited to audio. Further, the licensee must be Kuwaiti, no less than 30 years old, of a good reputation, and free of criminal charges. These rules must be applied to the board of trustees of partner companies. Finally, the law states that it is necessary to follow all the technical, financial, and administrative requirements and to provide supporting documents required by the application process.

257. The licensee must find a general manager who is Kuwaiti, not below 30 years of age, and of a good reputation. Further, the general manager must either hold a university degree or have five years of relevant media experience. Finally, the general manager must be a full-time employee only.

The law also lists requirements of all licensed stations, including the saving of all broadcasted material for a three-month period. This material must be available to employees of the Ministry of Information when requested.

258. The license is subject to revocation under several conditions, including failure to broadcast for two years without requesting an extension and if the licensee does not broadcast within 60 consecutive days or 120 nonconsecutive days. If the conditions for which the license was granted are no longer satisfied, a license can be revoked. If the general manager no longer satisfies the licensing requirements and a minister does not approve it, a license can be revoked. If the license expires and is not renewed within three months of its expiration, a license can be revoked.

This law set standards that individuals and companies can follow to create private broadcasting organizations. The law can also be used to punish private broadcasters that violate the law. A case study of a license violation is provided in Chapter 7 (*see* section V).

Chapter 3. Program Standards

259. As previously stated, the term "developing nations" can be considered offensive because it implies a need for advancement. However, the standards of contents of public and private broadcast are not measured by independent watchdogs of the media in Kuwait. Thus, one area of development in media can pertain to the development of program standards. Three particular concepts are examined in developing standards for various television and radio programs across the world: impartiality, cultural diversity, and the protection of children. Although there is a need for advancement, some areas have been developed more than others—such as the protection of minors. Further, Kuwait's demographics make it unique in terms of the cultural diversity of the content. More details about each of these sections are provided in this section.

§1. Impartiality

260. Impartiality is not a regulatory issue for the media in Kuwait.

§2. Cultural Diversity

261. Many of Kuwait's media laws include provisions to protect the local culture. This needs to be contextualized by remembering that approximately a third of Kuwait's population is native to Kuwait and the rest consists of expatriates.[496] Further, Wheeler[497] explained that Kuwaitis demonstrate an openness to the global cultures due to the availability of foreign media. Access to the foreign media is enabled by the tendency of Kuwaitis to access latest technologies.[498,499] Thus, it should not be surprising that media regulations attempt to protect the local culture given that many developing countries are concerned about the loss of national identity due to an influx of global cultural goods like media products.[500]

496. The State of Kuwait's Central Statistical Bureau. *Alihsa'at alsikaniya: taqderat alsikan fe montasaf al'am*." (2013. accessed Mar. 12, 2017, https://www.csb.gov.kw/Socan_Statistic.aspx?ID=67).

497. Deborah Wheeler. *New Media, Globalization and Kuwaiti National Identity*. The Middle East Journal 432,444 (2000).

498. Eisa Al Nashmi, Johanna Cleary, Juan-Carlos Molleda & Melinda McAdams. Internet Political Discussions in the Arab World: A Look at Online Forums from Kuwait, Saudi Arabia, Egypt and Jordan. 72 International Communication Gazette. 719, 738. (2010).

499. Deborah L.Wheeler. *The Internet in the Middle East: Global Expectations and Local Imaginations in Kuwait*. (SUNY Press, 2006).

500. Thomas L. McPhail. Global Communication: Theories, Stakeholders, and Trends. (John Wiley & Sons, 2010).

§3. Protection of Minors

262. None of the Kuwaiti regulations examined make explicit references to children or minors in the laws translated for this manuscript. However, Sakr[501] retraces the arrival of television content specifically geared toward children in the Arab world back to the late 1990s. The majority was imported from Western media corporations and was dubbed into the Arabic language. By the mid-2000s, more local content began to emerge.

263. Children make a unique audience because they are vulnerable and need an environment that encourages their growth. Sakr[502] has documented rhetoric in the Arab world that calls for the protection of children from values beyond what is culturally acceptable. However, this protection must be accompanied with content that informs and educates children in an entertaining manner—a feat that often requires tax incentives to implement.[503] These conditions are supported by Article 17 of the United Nation's Convention on the Rights of the Child.[504]

264. The production of children's content is regulated through either formal regulatory legislation or informal self-regulating policies that organizations may adopt. The lack of regulations that support the development of media that is appropriate for children is "a political decision, not an innocent abstention from intervention."[505] In other words, this is a legislative "failure" which results in "other rules with benefits for other interest groups."[506]

265. Some developments have been made across the Arab world. For example, some organizations have focused on labeling media content with violent content that make it unsuitable for children.[507] There is a plethora of regulatory victories for children across the Arab world: children were banned from appearing in advertisements that are not targeting children in Tunisia, warnings must be used before content that may lead children to using harmful substances is aired in the United Arab Emirates, and ten hours of children's programs must be aired in Morocco.[508] Producers of content directed at Arab children complain of a lack of protection of their intellectual property and a lack of investment by Arab governments in the form of tax incentives or subsidies.[509]

266. In the case of Kuwait, it is important to remember that children are not considered citizens in Kuwait until the age of 18.[510] Yet, civic education programs are

501. Naomi Sakr. *Provision, Protection or Participation? Approaches to Regulating Children's Television in Arab Countries.* 163 Media International Australia. 31,41 (2017).
502. *Ibid.*
503. *Ibid.*
504. *Ibid.*
505. Naomi Sakr. *Provision, Protection or Participation? Approaches to Regulating Children's Television in Arab Countries.* 163 Media International Australia. 34 (2017).
506. *Ibid.*
507. *Ibid.*
508. *Ibid., 31, 41.*
509. *Ibid.*
510. Rania Al-Nakib *Human Rights, Education for Democratic Citizenship and International Organisations: Findings from a Kuwaiti UNESCO ASPnet School.* 42 Cambridge Journal of Education. 97,112. (2012).

being developed to help promote the rights of Kuwaiti children.[511] Further, Law No. 21 of 2015 was passed by the National Assembly to protect the rights of Kuwaiti children. These rights include provisions for access to paid maternal leave upon birth, education, healthcare, with particular clauses for vaccinations.[512]

511. *Ibid.*
512. Alkuwait Alyom. *Qanun Raqam 21 Lisanat 2015 Fe Shaan Riayat Altifil.* (State of Kuwait, 2015).

Chapter 4. Political Broadcasting

§1. Rules on Political Independence of Broadcasters

267. Kuwaiti laws and regulations do not place special emphasis on the political independence of broadcasters. State-run channels tend to reflect the political positions of the government, while critical and opposition perspectives can be aired on private channels and, increasingly, online.

As discussed in the overview of the country's media landscape, with the notable exception of Al-Rai TV, the privately owned television sector is dominated by satellite channels which can develop their own political flavor independent from the government, but not necessarily independent from the owners or groups backing them.

§2. Fair Representation in Election Periods

268. Since political parties are banned in Kuwait, there are only individual candidates contesting elections. Although the candidates may be affiliated with certain "blocs" (including Salafis, the Muslim Brotherhood, liberals), membership in a bloc is not a prerequisite for running for parliament, and many citizens decide to contest the elections as independent candidates.

Mainstream broadcast media coverage of the individual campaigns is inevitably fractured by the high number of candidates (ranging between 400+ and 200+ depending on the phase of the campaign) and follows regular procedures for news and current affairs reporting.

269. Ensuring fair representation of candidates was presumably the objective behind the Ministry of Interior introducing regulations on coverage of campaigns in the 2008 elections. The rules included requiring privately owned broadcasting stations to offer equal treatment to candidates and to provide unbiased coverage of candidates' campaign events.[513]

270. In 2012, the Ministry of Information decided to allocate free air time for prerecorded three-minute candidate campaign videos on KTV in an effort to promote "just and fair elections."[514] The practice continued in the 2016 snap elections where additional rules for media coverage of the elections were introduced in ministerial resolution 143/2016, discussed in detail under Section l. Tribal Elections Law.

513. *Democracy Reporting International & Kuwait Transparency Society.* Assessment of the Electoral Framework. http://democracy-reporting.org/newdri/wp-content/uploads/2016/02/dri_kuwait_report_08.pdf.

514. Kuwait News Agency. *Candidates" Elections Campaigns on KTV as of Jan 20 - Info. Min.* http://www.kuna.net.kw/ArticlePrintPage.aspx?id=2214890&language=en.

§3. Political Advertising

271. Candidate adverts in election periods were traditionally targeting newspapers as Kuwait Television was not allowed to carry political advertising.[515] The rise of private broadcasting, including satellite channels, and more recently the immense popularity of social media provided new outlets for audio-visual political advertising. Legislation, however, appears to be slow in catching up with the developments in campaigning. The campaign experts interviewed by Alqaseer[516] noted a lack of laws developed specifically for political advertising. Instead, the same laws regulated both commercial and political ads, and there were no stipulations requiring campaigns to declare the size of their advertising budgets or the source of the funding. The lack of transparency was also evident in practices such as selling TV-interview opportunities and advertising spots for candidates to purchase as a package, or offers of publishing false opinion polls to boost a candidate's chances.[517]

272. Ministerial resolution 143/2016, cited above, aimed to remedy some of the campaign abuses by insisting that audio-visual and electronic media must clearly distinguish between news coverage and political advertising by candidates, as well as listing technical specifications that must be included when publishing poll results. In terms of the contents of political advertising, the resolution bans mudslinging, or the public communication of offensive ideas about other candidates, but otherwise contains no additional restrictions beyond the terms of the laws regulating audio-visual media.

515. Jasem Alqaseer. *Political Advertising in Kuwait a Functional Discourse Analysis*. (University of South Carolina, 2013).

516. *Ibid.*

517. Jasem Alqaseer. *Political Advertising in Kuwait a Functional Discourse Analysis*. 41,42 (University of South Carolina, 2013).

Chapter 5. Regulations of Advertising

273. According to the Kuwaiti lawyer Talal Taqi,[518] there are different areas where regulations are in place that affect the advertising industry. These restrictions include affect religion, the Kuwaiti Constitution, judicial authorities, international relations, Kuwait's head of state, the value of the national currency, and medications that affect weight management among others. Further, Taqi[519] explains advertising cigarettes, gambling, legal services, nutritional supplements, sexual services, and sexual products are subjected to regulations that protect the national culture, ethics, and mores. Moreover, there are regulations on ads that protect trademark, protect the use of images of private citizens for commercial purposes, manage the use of public signs, and provide consumer protections when there is a sale or fraudulent advertisement.

274. For this section, Taqi provided several regulations that he cited in his article. It is noteworthy to examine the diverse sources of these regulations that affect the media industry. Some regulations on advertising come from the Ministry of Commerce and Industry, while others are laws passed in the National Assembly or in the Penal Code.

275. Let us consider some of the legislations passed by the National Assembly that include regulations of advertising. Law No. 15 of 1995, which regulates tobacco products, contains a clause prohibiting the advertising of tobacco, its derivatives, and cigarettes in the State of Kuwait.[520] Further, Law No. 62 of 2007 outlaws commercial cheating which is determined as deception with regard to the quantity of goods sold as well as several elements of the quality, including the nature and place of origin.[521] Article 2 of Law No. 62 of 2007 criminalizes the publication, including leaflets, of products that contain elements from human beings, animals, pharmaceutical products, agricultural products or other natural products when they are unfit for human consumption, false, or expired, among other conditions.[522] An explanatory memo that accompanied the law in Alkuwait Alyom explained that it was an update of Law No. 20 of 1976 that serves to protect the Kuwaiti economy and the interests of both Kuwaiti merchants and consumers.[523] Thus, there are some legislations that regulate advertising that have been made effective for the purposes of protecting Kuwaiti public health as well as the Kuwaiti economy.

276. The Ministry of Commerce and Industry is interested in the regulation of the Kuwaiti economy, and it oversees the regulations that may affect the media when it comes to consumer protections. For example, Ministerial Decree 361 of 2015 by

518. Talal Taqi. "*Advertising and Promotion in the State of Kuwait.* (2017, accessed May 14, 2017, http://www.hg.org/article.asp?id=32357.
519. *Ibid.*
520. Alkuwait Alyom. *Qanun Raqam 15 Lisanat 1995 Fe Shaan Mokafahat Altadkheen.* (State of Kuwait, 1995).
521. Alkuwait Alyom. *Qanun Raqam 62 Lisanat 2007 Fe Shaan Qama'Alqash Fe Almoamalat Altejariyah, 62 C.F.R.* (State of Kuwait, 2007).
522. *Ibid.*
523. *Ibid.*

the Ministry of Commerce and Industry regulates sales.[524] In Article 31, it references consumer protections laws that require special licenses in order to promote products and services when the prices are reduced.[525] The license includes a list of products or services that are to be included in the sales, a list of excluded offers that are valid, as well as verifications of the sales before and after the sales are publicized.[526] Further, Article 17 allows consumer protection advocates and individuals to complain when a violation of the law has taken place.[527] The law also sets punishments, in Kuwaiti Dinars, for various violations of the law.[528] Thus, it is important to consider the Ministry of Commerce and Industry when analyzing regulations of advertisements.

277. Finally, the Penal Code, mentioned in Chapter 3, also provides penalties for the promotion of gambling in Article 205.[529] The article creates different punishments for those who commit a public offense related to gambling than those who manage or organize gambling events or shops.[530] The act of gambling is defined as a game in which the probability of winning or losing depends on uncontrollable factors, defined by luck.[531]

278. Similarly, the Penal Code provides punishments for the promotion of alcohol in Articles 206, 207 and 208.[532] Article 206 states that any person who imports, manufactures or promotes wine or other drinks that have an intoxicating effect. The punishment in Article 206 states that the punishment shall not exceed KWD 100 (USD 300), a six-month period in jail, or a combination of either penalty. Article 2016 has three sub-articles that punish those who buy, sell or promote alcohol up to three years and for KWD 300 (USD 900), extend the punishment to fifteen years in some cases, and outlines penalties for people intoxicated in public, visible from public, in a private place or found in an intoxicated state. Article 207 penalizes those who facilitate the illegal use of narcotics by a jail sentence that is up to seven years or KWD 7,000 (USD 21,000). Finally, Article 208 states that there is a two year imprisonment sentence and KWD 2,000 (USD 6,000) fine for people who participate in the sales or use of recreational drugs without a prescription provided by a licensed healthcare professional.[533]

§1. Signage Law

279. Resolution of the Municipal Council number M.B/Q 11/387/15/2006 regulates advertising in the form of signs. These signs are addressed in several articles of the law by categorizing them by size and by type, including the location of the

524. Alkuwait Alyom. *Qarar Wizaree Raqam 361 Le'am 2015 edited by Wizarat Altijarah Walsina'ah.* (State of Kuwait, 2005).
525. *Ibid.*
526. *Ibid.*
527. *Ibid.*
528. *Ibid.*
529. Alkuwait Alyom.*Qanun Raqam 16 Lianat 1960 Bi Isdar Qanun Aljazaa.* (State of Kuwait, 1960).
530. *Ibid.*
531. *Ibid.*
532. *Ibid.*
533. *Ibid.*

billboards, purpose of the billboard. The 26 articles in this regulation includes punishments for failure to adhere to the regulation and also the fees expected for various types of billboards.

280. The first seven articles provide definitions of signs, provides procedures for regulations for when they are required, licensed and violated while granting the Municipal Council the power to regulate these processes. The first article defines advertising as a method to inform various segments of Kuwaiti society regardless of the method used—whether it is audio, visual, or verbal. Further, the article expressively states that the advertisement can be made of paper, glass, wood, or any other material to achieve this goal. The second article requires all individuals to display a billboard on the premises of his/her business, regardless of the nature of the business—whether it is professional, industrial, or related to the crafts. The third article lays out the requirements to receive a license from the municipality, including the required fees and a deposit to which governmental organizations are made exempt. The licenses can only be used by the party to which it was authorized, and must include certain information including a location, time period for which it is valid and commercial name among other requirements. The fourth article gives the Municipality the power to revoke the license without liability or compensation. The fifth article states that shop signs are valid as long as trade licenses while billboard licenses are authorized for one years, except when the license indicates otherwise. Article 6 places responsibility on the licensee to maintain the billboard and gives the Municipality the power to remove it and deduct related costs from the deposits paid in the process of obtaining a license. The seventh article gives the Municipality the power to place conditions on various billboards that must be followed.

281. Articles 8–10 suggests regulations that are consistent with the environment in which the billboards are placed. For example, the eighth article ensures that all signs and billboards do not violate public mores, public order or religious jurisprudence (Islamic Sharia). Further, the ninth article prohibits erecting billboards on archeological sites, places of worship, road signs, traffic signs, trees, government organizations, or on the walls of buildings with posters. Audio advertisements are also prohibited in the ninth article, except for when it is authorized. Finally, the tenth article prohibits the advertisement of tobacco products as well as health-related products, services or devices for humans or animals without an approval of the Ministry of Health.

282. Articles 11–13 lay out guidelines for the appearance of billboards as well as the requirements for licensing applications. For example, the billboard needs to be in Arabic but can be accompanied by a trademark or translation into a foreign language. The design of the billboard needs to look attractive and consistent with the design of the buildings on which they are posted. The billboards are not to resemble traffic signs in color or shape, and must not obstruct vision, or ventilation of the buildings. Further, these billboards should not make buildings more susceptible to fires or electrical problems or cause damage to pedestrians or neighbors. Billboards are not to be made of perishable materials and should not threaten or disturb people inhabiting the building. Further, the billboard needs to be safely fastened. Finally, applicants for a license must submit technical information to the Municipality about the materials of the billboard and how it was assembled. Each billboard must include the number of the license and the dates for which it is valid. Article 12 states that the license must be presented to officials of the Municipality when they request it. Article 13 grants the Municipality the power to remove billboards without advanced notice and outlines a process for appealing this decision that ends in court.

283. The resolution consists of 26 articles, and it categorizes billboards in many ways, including size, type and purpose of the billboards. For example, Article 14 begins by providing regulations for different types of billboards. These types include billboards on roofs, on the sides of buildings, at shopping malls, in parking lots, on taxi-cabs, on buses, on fences of private but nonresidential buildings and in the airport. Further, Article 14 provides different standards for advertising firms and some other organizations that meet certain regulatory standards are also allowed to represent some of their clients in billboards depending on size, according to Article 14. The sizes, which are listed in the metric system, range from 120 centimeters by 80 centimeters to 20.1 meters by 1.80 meters. There are five different sizes, and another category includes billboards on bus stops. Article 15 provides regulations on billboards that are projected, lit in a box, placed on refrigerators, or flown aerially.

284. Other articles deal with the purpose behind the erection of the billboard. For example, Article 16 states that only government authorities are allowed to provide directions to various institutions and official buildings. Similarly, Article 17 regulates political advertisements for elections, social advertisements for weddings in which the public is invited, and civil society events.

285. Articles 18–21 outline the fees for types of billboards as well as requirements for the licensing process. The list includes annual fees per square meter of the billboard, subject to some conditions, as well as deposits equivalent to half the cost of the billboard. Some of the conditions under which fees may increase include the use of a third-party trademark and projection.

286. Finally, punishments are included at the end of the resolution. These punishments can include the issuance of a violation notice as well as a fine that ranges between KWD 300–KWD 1,000, which is roughly equivalent to USD 1,000–USD 3,300. Article 22 allows for public officials to confiscate advertising materials, while Article 23 allows for public officials to enter premises on which billboards are erected.

§2. Ministry of Information's Decree 32 of 2012: Regulations of Radio Advertisements

287. The decree begins by defining various terms. For example, a commercial (*ali'lan altejari*) is an ad that promotes products or services for the purpose of making a profit. A commercial is contrasted to an education advertisement (*ali'lan altawa'awey*), which is made for the purpose of persuading or informing— such as public service advertisements—for the purpose of organizing society. Other distinctions are made to differentiate between sponsorship of an ad and the announcement of prizes given by an organization, which is called "advertisement in return for prizes."

288. These definitions are important in several ways. First, the legal definitions do not necessarily follow terminology of social scientific disciplines that explore advertisements. Second, the legal definitions are used in later articles to justify the differing prices for various radio ads in Kuwait. For instance, the price of a "complex ad" is increased by 30% in Article 5. Here, it is worth noting that a complex ad is defined as one that contains multiple advertising aspects and contrasted to an ordinary ad which contains single advertising aspect in Article 1.

289. Article 2 explains that the pricing system is calculated in seconds, with an initial ten-second frame. The prices are set for any additional frames such that an extra second would require the entire next frame to be an expense of the advertiser. Ads that exceed a minute are to be calculated by adding additional frames to the cost of a minute.

290. For 103.7 FM, a ten-second ad costs KWD 40, and every additional five seconds results in an additional KWD 5. For 99.7 FM, a ten-second ad costs KWD 30, and every additional five seconds results in an additional KWD 5. For Program Two and other radio channels, the initial ten-second frame costs KWD 20, and every additional five second results in additional KWD 5. The prices are only listed for government-run stations, and it can be assumed that the ministry can only regulate cost of advertising on channels the government owns.

291. An interesting observation to extract from this regulation is the difference in price for an advertisement of the same length depending on the channel in which it is aired. For example, the 103.7 FM radio station is KWD 10 (approximately USD 32) more expensive than the 99.7 FM radio station. It is unclear why the prices vary, as the 103.7 FM station broadcasts primarily in the Arabic language while 99.7 FM station broadcasts more international content in a country where expatriates outnumber nationals.

292. Nevertheless, the variations in pricing of radio ads in Kuwait's government-run stations are interesting because they demonstrate a prioritization of some kind. For example, educational advertisements that meet certain conditions that deal with factors such as the advertiser's intent to make financial gain, enjoy discounts that are unavailable to other types of organizations. Further, Kuwaiti charities, public service nonprofits, sports organizations, tourism organizations, art production companies, theater houses and ministries receive a 50% discount according to Article 7.

293. Some of these priorities are related to the financial interests of the Ministry of Information. To illustrate, consider that Article 8 provides advertising agencies with a 25% discount in comparison to a 5% discount for direct advertisers. Benefits privileged to ad agencies are not unlimited, however. Article 14 provides a maximum of KWD 1,500. to ad agencies that spend KWD 40,000. in one fiscal year.

294. This regulation is extremely important for professionals in the media industry not only because it relates to pricing. The regulation also provides a minimum timeframe in which professionals are expected to plan, modify or cancel scheduled advertisements. For instance, Appendix 1 requires submission of the advertisement, at minimum two working days before the desired broadcast date. It continues to require that forms requesting the booking are to be both printed and clear among other conditions. Similarly, two working days are required prior to the cancellation or amendment of a reserved ad space. Finally, the regulation includes clauses that accommodate cultural considerations. For example, the ads should not conflict with public mores, religious values or other legal codes.

§3. Ministry of Information's Decree 82 of 2012: Regulations of Television Advertisements

295. This Decree is similar to the Law of 61 of 2007, which regulates audio-visual media described, in Chapter 3. The regulation begins by defining terms that are used throughout the document. Many of the definitions are similar to the previously described regulation of radio advertisements, including the differentiation between commercial in contrast to educational advertisements and ordinary advertisement as opposed to a sponsored advertisement.

296. However, there are some additions included that put into consideration the visual nature of television. For instance, graphics are advertisements defined as materials shown on the screen or part of a screen in an artistic manner. Additionally, the term "program cast" refers to the list of individuals who appear in an ad, and which is provided in a written format at the end of an ad. Moreover, a defining clause explains that there are some items that are only available for sale through a television broadcast.

297. Then, several articles of the regulation provide discount for outlined Kuwaiti organizations, much like those for the previously described radio regulation. The timeframe for the television ads are also to be measured in seconds. The regulation outlines various methods for setting the prices, also based on the type of advertisement, the channel on which it is meant to appear, and the type of organization which is advertising. Certain prohibitions are also outlined. For example, Article 19 states that advertisements cannot be exchanged for advertising services.

298. Unlike the radio advertising regulation, advertisements on television prices range between KWD 40 (USD 120) and KWD 410 (USD 1,230) for an ad on Kuwait Television Channel One (KTV1). An ordinary ad goes for KWD 40 in the first ten seconds and then increases by a different amount for every additional five seconds. The additional amount progressively declines by KWD 5 after an initial increase in KWD 25, followed by a KWD 20 decrease, and so on. Advertisements are most expensive between 7:56 p.m. and midnight, which is described as peak times for KTV1. The second and third channels of Kuwaiti television, along with any other publicly owned television channel, range between KWD 25 (USD 75) to KWD 210 (USD 630) depending on the time of day and length of the ad. Once again, the regulation affects government-owned television stations.

§4. Advertising Healthcare Products

299. A law and two ministerial decrees are worth considering because of their references to media and promotional communication activities. First, Law No. 38 of 2002 and Ministerial Decree 437 of 2002 (putting into effect that same law) from the Ministry of Health, define the mass media ambiguously such that it includes messages that can be seen, heard, or otherwise disseminated. The decree suggests that a license must be obtained from the Ministry of Health when a health-related product is advertised as well as consent prior to the publication or broadcast of an advertisement. The legislation defines health-related products such that it includes a variety of substances with plant, animal, or chemical composition and such that it includes veterinary medicine in addition to human medicine.

300. A more recent ministerial decree that can be examined is the Ministry of Health's Decree 134 of 2014, which sets guidelines for marketing alternatives to mother's milk. The 2014 decree also includes bus advertisements, lectures at conferences, and other types of communication in the definition of advertising.[534] Further, the decree sets requirements for communication provided for educational purposes, including ensuring accuracy of information, providing bilingual information in English and Arabic, and avoiding the impression that alternatives to breast feeding are better than a mother's milk.[535] Despite the fact that these regulations affect the work of communication professionals, they are not set by the Ministry of Information. Thus, communication professionals should be aware of the Ministry of Health's regulations when dealing with topics that affect human or animal health.

§5. Competition Laws

301. In 2007, the first legislation, namely Law No. 10 of 2007, was passed to protect competition in Kuwait. The law defines market control as a person, or set of people, gaining a market share that exceeds 35% in a particular industry.[536] However, the specific industry did not explicitly mention the media and communication industry. It is worthy to note that Article 6 states that this law does not apply to projects owned or operated by the state. In Article 7, the law states that it is applicable to situations in which intellectual property law is abused to negatively affect free trade and economic competitiveness. Article 10 creates a body to regulate Kuwaiti economic competitiveness. When a 2014–2015 report was examined, specific references relevant to the media and communication sector could not be found.[537]

534. Alkuwait Alyom. *Qarar Wizaree Raqam 134 Lisanat 2014*. (State of Kuwait, 2014).
535. *Ibid.*
536. Alkuwait Alyom. *Qanun Raqam 10 Lisanat 2007 Fe Shaan Himayat Almonafasa, 10 C.F.R.* (State of Kuwait 2007).
537. Markaz Altamyeez Belidara. *Taqrir Alkuwait Liltanafisiya 2014–2015*. Markaz Altamyeez Belidara, Kuwait University College of Business Administration, accessed May 14, 2017, http://www.kuwaitncc.org/reports/KNCC201415.pdf).

Part IV. Cross Ownership Regulation

302. As discussed earlier, in Chapter 2, Part II, newspapers in Kuwait have been privately owned by Kuwaiti families since the beginning, while broadcasting was government-run until the licensing of private channels began in the 2000s. Of the five old newspaper titles, the proprietors of two acquired a domestic TV license when the state monopoly on broadcasting was lifted. The parent companies of Al-Rai and Al-Watan were operating both a paper and a commercial TV channel until the closing down of Al-Watan in 2015 for alleged license violations (for details of the case *see* Part VII).

303. While mature media markets tend to gravitate toward concentration of ownership, including cross-media ownership, the same phenomenon cannot be observed in Kuwait. The families that own media outlets maintain a balance in the ownership structure across the media scene that has not allowed for aggressive expansion on the part of any single company. Even though there is an economical incentive, mergers and acquisitions have not been a characteristic feature of media in Kuwait, and in terms of ownership, the media remains diverse and pluralistic. Consequently, media laws and regulations have also been unconcerned with the issues that would arise from consolidation.

Part V. Supervision: Media Regulator

304. It is important to pay attention to the authority issuing the regulation, as the diverse sources of regulations on communication demonstrate the complexity of the legal system. Unlike the common law system where the judge is allowed to interpret a law so that it is applicable when a precedent does not exist,[538] the civil law system does not allow for a case to stand where a regulation does not exist. Thus, the importance of individual regulations, which is further complicated by a variety of institutions that issue them, is heightened in this legal environment.

305. Unlike larger and more developed nations where a specific governing institution will regulate the media, various governing bodies in Kuwait regulate communication in different ways. As previously demonstrated, Kuwait has a Ministry of Information. However, the Ministry of Health may regulate the advertising of healthcare products and the Ministry of Commerce may regulate promotional material pertaining to sales. While by no means comprehensive, this section aims to shed light on different kinds of regulatory authorities as applied to religious communication—an important consideration in Muslim societies.

§1. Regulations of Religious Speech

306. In his book, *Heavy Metal Islam*, Mark LeVine[539] states that Kuwait's Ministry of Islamic Affairs is criticized for being secular by one of his Egyptian informants. The example that LeVine[540] is given to demonstrate the secular nature of the governmental institution is an advertisement on television encouraging youth to pray. The ad shows young children pausing a video game to pray when they hear the call to prayer. Although LeVine[541] points out that the ministry has actually sponsored the ad, he points out how his Egyptian informant believes this kind of advertisement sends the wrong message. Levine[542] does not elaborate on exactly what is wrong with this message, but his example demonstrates the different government ministries that may have passed decrees or other regulations that may affect the communication industry.

307. On June 1, 2016, defamation of religion charges were dropped against a Kuwait University professor, Dr. Shaikha Al Jassim. After this decision was made,

538. Daniel J Castellano. *Common Law and Civil Jurisprudence*. http://www.arcaneknowledge.org/histpoli/commoncivil.htm
539. Mark LeVine. *Heavy Metal Islam: Rock, Resistance, and the Struggle for the Soul of Islam*. (Crown, 2008).
540. *Ibid.*
541. *Ibid.*
542. *Ibid.*

she wrote in an article calling the dropping of charges "a victory for Kuwaiti judiciary and the Kuwaiti people" because the judicial ruling differentiated between freedom of expression and contempt of religion.[543] While details of this case will be discussed at greater depth in the blasphemy section of the final chapter, this case demonstrates that religious communication is regulated in the State of Kuwait.

308. One such regulation deals with print media that pertains to the Quran, the Holy Scriptures of Islam, and other material that is religious in nature. Law No. 10 of 2011 creates a public authority that is responsible for printing and distributing the Holy Quran, narrations of the prophet and related knowledge.[544] The first article suggests that this independent authority would be supervised by the Minister of Islamic Affairs and the second article declares that it would be funded by the Kuwaiti public budget. The third article suggests that it can also be financed by donations, gifts, wills, or other types of contributions that the administration agrees to accept. The fourth article suggests that the authority would aim to care for Quranic sciences of various kinds, including reports, Islamic studies and any other needs that are required for Muslims inside the State of Kuwait as well as Islamic publications required internationally. The fifth article lists 14 responsibilities of this authority, including printing the Holy Quran, translating it to different languages, recording recitations of it, and developing studies and publications for people around the world. The sixth article states that the authority would include Kuwaiti nationals, after the approval of the Minister of Islamic Affairs, for a period of two years and that the Cabinet of Ministers would decide on their compensation. The tenth article prohibits printing of the Holy Quran except with permission of the authority, whether it is inside or outside of Kuwait. The same article punishes all those who violate this with a penalty that is between KWD 3,000–KWD 5,000 (approximately USD 9,000–USD 15,000) as well as shutting down of the printing house for at least three months. Further, the article goes on to say that this punishment does not affect any other, harsher punishments that may be required by any other law. An explanatory memo that accompanies this law suggests this law is necessary for proselytization, and that such activities require institutionalization and funding—two provisions that are clearly stated within the law. This regulation clearly demonstrates that there are some communication activities that are regulated by Kuwait's Ministry of Islamic Affairs.

543. Shaikah Aljassim. *Shokr Watalab.* (Alqabas, 2016, accessed Jun. 7, 2017 https://alqabas.com/author/sheikhaal-jassem/).

544. Alkuwait Alyom. *Law 10.* edited by Ministry of Islamic Affairs. (2011).

Part VI. Kuwait Media Law in International Perspective

309. Communication law is part of a legal system that can be understood as a set of written rules that govern living together in a society. Although the principles underlying the law in democratic societies are reflections of universal ideals, each legal system is developed in specific national contexts, and it is in these contexts that they are enforced. In order to understand the laws that govern a land, it is necessary to consider them as part of particular social and cultural settings that both shape and are in turn shaped by law. Furthermore, the adoption of laws occurs in specific historical moments and is the outcome of a complex interplay of social, cultural, and political forces that define those historical moments. From the perspective of politico-cultural approaches to comparative analysis adopted in this chapter, communication law is "a cultural phenomenon" that "reflects national, regional and international mentalities or logics."[545]

310. A handful of areas of communication law—censorship, defamation, and blasphemy—were selected for this chapter to demonstrate the radically different solutions lawmakers and courts have adopted in dealing with similar issues across different politico-cultural contexts. The countries featured for comparison with Kuwaiti communication law are the United States and the United Kingdom, with occasional references where relevant to the French legal system and the European Convention on Human Rights. The USA and the UK were chosen primarily for the reason that at different points in its history, Kuwait has belonged to the "spheres of interest" of these countries. As discussed in Chapter 1, Britain exerted significant influence on the development of the legal and political system of Kuwait during the protectorate period, while "creeping Americanization"[546] has been a marked feature of social, cultural and political life in Kuwait since its 1991 liberation from Iraqi occupation. The inclusion of France in this comparative chapter is necessary because of the impact the French legal model had on Kuwait: on gaining independence in 1961, Kuwait chose to introduce a French-based civil law system (*see* Chapter 1 above). Additionally, the European Convention on Human Rights (ECHR) is relevant for discussing freedom of expression because both Britain and France ratified the Convention, and it was incorporated into domestic British law under the Human Rights Act of 1998. Although the ECHR is not

545. Lyombe S Eko. New Media, Old Regimes: *Case Studies in Comparative Communication Law and Policy*. (Lexington Books, 2012).
546. Meshal Al-Sabah. *Gender and Politics in Kuwait: Women and Political Participation in the Gulf.* 174. (IB Tauris, 2013).

formally a Constitution, its provisions are the functional equivalent of constitutional norms and signal the "internationalization" of constitutional law.[547]

547. Michel Rosenfeld & András Sajó. The Oxford Handbook of *Comparative Constitutional Law*. (Oxford University Press, 2012).

Chapter 1. Freedom of Speech: Constitutional Provisions

311. Eko's[548] politico-cultural approach can be demonstrated through a comparative analysis of constitutional provisions for freedom of speech, expression, and the press. Constitutions are the foundational documents of states, articulating a vision the founders have of the socio-political order they are be questing to future generations of the country.

312. Freedom of speech is enshrined in modern constitutions, but there are differences in the precise articulation of such free speech guarantees. In the United States, the First Amendment[549] states:

> Congress shall make no law respecting an establishment of religion, or prohibiting the free exercise thereof; or abridging the freedom of speech, or of the press; or the right of the people peaceably to assemble, and to petition the government for a redress of grievances.

313. The concise wording of the First Amendment has inspired multiple schools of interpretation, both in legal scholarship and US judicial practice. These approaches are concerned with how to interpret the First Amendment when the rights of free speech come into conflict with other rights recognized as fundamental in democratic societies.[550] The balancing approach dictates that when rights are conflicting, the courts must weigh them and decide which one needs to trump the other. There are those who advocate an absolutist theory of the First Amendment and believe that speech is meant to have absolute protection from government interference. From this perspective, the phrase "Congress shall make no law" needs to be taken literally, meaning that no other right can outweigh freedom of speech. In practice, absolutism has never commanded a majority position in the courts, but it remains influential and is evoked in First Amendment arguments.[551] Others advocate a preferred position theory that claims the rights of free speech and press are to be favored over other rights when they come into conflict, and the government must demonstrate sufficient reason for removing constitutional protection from speech in a particular situation.

314. The consistent preference given to free speech rights makes the First Amendment "exceptional," and it contributes to American exceptionalism as a distinguishing characteristic. Eko relies on a definition of exceptionalism as "a theory that a nation, region, or political system is exceptional and does not conform to the norm."[552] American exceptionalism proclaims that the US is an exceptional country

548. Lyombe S Eko. New Media, Old Regimes: Case Studies in Comparative Communication Law and Policy. (Lexington Books, 2012).
549. The Constitution of the United States of America. (1789).
550. Genelle Belmas & Wayne Overbeck. Major Principles of Media Law, 2015. Cengage Learning, 2014.
551. Ruthann Robson. First Amendment: Cases, Controversies, and Contexts. . CALI eLangdell Press, 2016.
552. Lyombe S Eko. *New Media, Old Regimes: Case Studies in Comparative Communication Law and Policy*. (Lexington Books, 2012).

where citizens are unified by an allegiance to a common set of ideals including individualism, anti-authoritarianism, and egalitarianism.[553]

315. In the "American way of life", the interests of the individual are valued above those of the community. As constitutional scholar Thomas Emerson summarized this point: "Society and the state are not ends in themselves; they exist to serve the individual."[554] The opening words of the First Amendment also echo the anti-authoritarian attitude of American political culture that was and remains highly skeptical of government authority. In matters that concern individual freedoms, including speech and expression, the state is not presumed to know best, and the government carries a heavy burden of proof before it can be constitutionally sanctioned to impose restrictions. In Eko's words, the First Amendment is "a libertarian charter of negative rights under which the government is barred from infringing on the rights of the people in matters of freedom of expression"[555].

316. A different, but historically influential, kind of exceptionalism characterizes France. Eko characterizes French exceptionalism as "culturalist", meaning that what this posture emphasizes is "the uniqueness and specificity of the French language, culture, and civilization"[556]. In terms of freedom of speech, this position translates into a positive free speech system where the government relies on affirmative steps to filter out the forms of speech it finds objectionable for shared national public discourse. The qualifying limitations on free speech are indicated in broad terms in Article 11 of the Declaration of the Rights of Man and Citizen[557] that was one of the fundamental texts included in the preamble to the French Constitution of 1958:

> The free communication of ideas and opinions is one of the most precious of the rights of man. Every citizen may, accordingly, speak, write, and print with freedom, but shall be responsible for such abuses of this freedom as shall be defined by law.

317. Under the French legal system, freedom of communication is thus a fundamental constitutional right, but it comes with qualifications built into the Constitution. The qualifications outlined in the Declaration draw the boundaries of liberty at the harm the exercising of freedoms may inflict on others or on society. In line with this position, a person has "the freedom to do everything which injures no one else," the law can "prohibit such actions as are hurtful to society," and opinions, including religious views, can be held freely "provided their manifestation does not disturb the public order established by law." In French democracy, governmental and

553. Seymour Martin Lipset,. American Exceptionalism: A Double-Edged Sword. New York: Norton, 1996.

554. Thomas Emerson. *Toward a General Theory of the First Amendment*. Faculty Scholarship Series 2017, no. May 17 (1963): 880. http://digitalcommons.law.yale.edu/fss_papers/2796.

555. Lyombe S Eko. *New Media, Old Regimes: Case Studies in Comparative Communication Law and Policy*. 59 (Lexington Books, 2012).

556. *Ibid., 60.*

557. *Declaration of the Rights of Man In The Avalon Project: Documents in Law, History and Diplomacy*. (Yale Law School, 1789, accessed May 31, 2017 at http://avalon.law.yale.edu/18th_century/rightsof.asp).

social interests that are safeguarded in law will be protected against "abuses" of free speech, resulting in a political culture characterized by "the supremacy of the law over rights."[558]

318. Less well-known or influential in international politics, nevertheless Kuwait too qualifies as exceptional in its region. As discussed in Chapter 1, among the sheikhdoms of the Persian Gulf, Kuwait is the only country with an indigenous tradition of political participation and democratic institutions.[559] These institutions may work imperfectly and offer only partial liberal democratic guarantees to citizens, but their existence makes Kuwait unique regionally. There are several explanations for the roots of this Kuwaiti exceptionalism, including external factors like threats from neighboring Iraq and internal ones such as the liberal leanings of the ruler at the time the country gained its independence.[560] But regardless of its origins, scholars are in agreement that the 1962 Constitution established a democratic socio-political order[561] "under which sovereignty resides in the people, the source of all powers."[562]

319. From a politico-cultural perspective, the Kuwaiti Constitution is another manifestation of the massive state modernization project that transformed Kuwait in the middle of the twentieth century. Oil-era modernization was state-led and built on urban development and social welfare.[563] The Constitution confirms the importance of the state and in Part II provides an extensive list of duties the state pledges to perform for its citizens, including national security, support for the family, protection of youth and the old, and provision of medical care and education. The built environment created in the 1960s and 1970s also served as a visible confirmation of the new state's autonomy, presenting to the world the new face of Kuwait as a "truly modern" country.[564] The decades of transformation were marked by popular support for modernization. While the state—under the patriarchal guidance by the ruler—led the process, society also subscribed enthusiastically to the idea of creating a new Kuwait. The disenchantment with the unintended social consequences of Kuwait's project modernity, or indeed the general postcolonial critiquing of development ideals as expressions of Western cultural hegemony were yet to emerge. Introducing constitutional law modelled on Western countries was accepted as one of "the traffic rules of the economic-social-political road to modernization" newly developing countries had to follow.[565]

320. An influential strand of constitutional theory argues that constitutions also serve as devices of precommitment, created by the constitution-makers as protection

558. Lyombe S Eko,. New Media, Old Regimes: Case Studies in Comparative Communication Law and Policy. 61. (Lexington Books, 2012).
559. Mary Ann Tétreault. *Stories of Democracy: Politics and Society in Contemporary Kuwait.* (Columbia University Press, 2000).
560. Michael Herb. *The Wages of Oil: Parliaments and Economic Development in Kuwait and the UAE.* (Cornell University Press, 2014).
561. *Ibid.*
562. Constitute. *Kuwait's Constitution of 1962 Reinstated in 1992.* https://www.constituteproject.org/constitution/Kuwait_1992.pdf?lang=en (accessed May 15, 2017).
563. Farah Al-Nakib. *Kuwait Transformed: A History of Oil and Urban Life.* (Stanford University Press, 2016).
564. *Ibid.*
565. Michel Rosenfeld & András Sajó. *The Oxford handbook of comparative constitutional law.* 22. (2012, Oxford University Press).

against their own predictable tendency to make unwise decisions, or as a way of binding others from making unwise choices in the future.[566] In light of the heavy political maneuvering that was needed to push through the liberal foundations of the Kuwaiti Constitution, particularly in the face of opposition within the ruling family,[567] it is possible to read parts of the Constitution as confirmation of the "precommitment device" theory. Article 175 puts explicit limits on amending the Constitution in a way that prohibits regression: "The provisions relating to (…) the principles of liberty and equality, provided for in this Constitution, may not be proposed for revision except (…) to increase the guarantees of liberty and equality."[568] The same article also declares inviolable the hereditary "Amiri system," confirming the predominance of the ruling family. Yet the democratic provisions of the Constitution lend popular legitimacy to the rule of the Al-Sabah and turn the Constitution into a contract between the Amir and Kuwaiti citizens about how the country should be governed.[569]

321. Similar to other modern constitutions, the founding document of the constitutional emirate also offers guarantees of freedom of speech. Articles 36 and 37 state:

> Freedom of opinion and of scientific research shall be guaranteed. Every person shall have the right to express and propagate his opinion verbally, in writing or otherwise, in accordance with the conditions and procedures specified by law.

> Freedom of the press, printing, and publishing shall be guaranteed in accordance with the conditions and manner specified by law.

322. This constitutional articulation of free speech rights resembles France's Declaration of the Rights of Man in placing qualifying limitations on free speech. In the Kuwaiti context, the provision that leaves it to legislation to define the contours of a key political freedom is identified as a source of potential problems.[570] The concerns raised by international watchdog organizations about the implementation of the 2015 cybercrimes law, or the domestic disputes generated by the electronic media law of 2016 (*see* Chapter 3, Section II, part k) appear to confirm that administrative law may not always be in dialogue with constitutional law. Or perhaps it is more accurate to say that for legislators (as well as for courts that interpret the laws), free speech is but one interest that needs to be weighed and balanced against other interests, and in Kuwait, freedom of speech does not take a preferred position over other interests, including communal values.

566. Jon Elster. *Ulysses Unbound: Studies in Rationality, Precommitment, and Constraints*. (Cambridge University Press, 2000).
567. Michael Herb. *The Wages of Oil: Parliaments and Economic Development in Kuwait and the UAE*. (Cornell University Press, 2014).
568. Constitute. Kuwait's Constitution of 1962 Reinstated in 1992. https://www.constituteproject.org/constitution/Kuwait_1992.pdf?lang=en (accessed May 15, 2017).
569. Nathan J Brown. *Constitutions in a Nonconstitutional World: Arab Basic Laws and the Prospects for Accountable Government*. (SUNY Press, 2002).
570. *Ibid., 56.*

323. In this regard, the approach of the Strasbourg-based European Court of Human Rights offers an illuminating example of the relationship between the letter and the spirit of free speech law. Article 10 of the European Convention on Human Rights[571] makes the following provisions for freedom of expression:

> 1. Everyone has the right to freedom of expression. This right shall include freedom to hold opinions and to receive and impart information and ideas without interference by public authority and regardless of frontiers. This Article shall not prevent States from requiring the licensing of broadcasting, television or cinema enterprises.
>
> 2. The exercise of these freedoms, since it carries with it duties and responsibilities, may be subject to such formalities, conditions, restrictions, or penalties as are prescribed by law and are necessary in a democratic society, in the interests of national security, territorial integrity or public safety, for the prevention of disorder or crime, for the protection of health or morals, for the protection of the reputation or rights of others, for preventing the disclosure of information received in confidence, or for maintaining the authority and impartiality of the judiciary.[572]

324. The list of circumstances under which limitations of free speech can be upheld seems sufficiently exhaustive to nearly emptying the first point of its substance. But the actual practice of the European Court has consistently favored freedom of speech by ruling that interference with it is necessary only if there is a "pressing social need" for it under particular circumstances. The restriction has to be proportionate to the aim pursued, and it must be supported with reasons that are relevant and sufficient. Additionally, the burden of proving that these requirements are met falls on the state pursuing the restriction, and the Court's decisions hinge on whether the state meets that burden.[573] In order to be ruled acceptable, state-imposed limitations on freedom of speech are subjected to careful scrutiny by the Court in whose hands rests the interpretation of the law.

325. Courts, of course, do not operate in a vacuum, and the decisions they make are reflections of national, regional, and international mentalities or logics. The next sections discuss particular cases that highlight freedom of speech issues in the politico-cultural contexts where they were raised and resolved.

571. Council Of Europe. European Convention on Human Rights. Rome: European Court of Human Rights, 1950.
572. *Ibid.*
573. Eric Barendt. Freedom of Speech. 64–65. (Oxford University Press, 2007).

Chapter 2. Legal Restraints on Freedom of Speech: Prior Restraint

326. Although legal scholarship rarely pays specific attention to underlying assumptions about media effects, lawmakers and courts appear to operate from a position that mass media have powerful effects on societies. These assumptions are implied in the general aversion toward restricting the free flow of information both between the government and the governed and among the members of the public. They can also be detected in court cases that deal with the harm, actual or potential, that messages may bring to individuals or to communities. New channels and forms of communication continue to bring about renewed discussions of what the relationship should be between them and the legal and regulatory regimes that shape freedom of speech. But the starting point in the US and British legal systems is a particular, special hostility reserved for censorship, or prior restraint as it is referred to in the Anglo-American practice.

327. Prior restraint, or pre-publication censorship, occurs when messages and ideas are suppressed before publication. A clear example would be a system where media products such as books and films must be submitted for inspection and approval to government bodies before they can be released to the public. Pre-publication censorship is monitored closely and its instances are decried by international human rights watchdog organizations. It tends to be identified with the institution of strict systems for prior scrutiny of printed and audio-visual materials in authoritarian regimes, although prior restraint censorship is not exclusive to undemocratic, authoritarian regimes. But the scope and justifications for suppressing speech vary greatly across countries and cultures and undergo shifts over time.

328. In England, licensing of the press was abolished in 1694, and the press has remained generally uncensored since. The abolishing of pre-publication censorship, however, did not concern the possibility of subsequent punishment for publication of matters considered illegal according to law. Such publications were considered abuses of liberty and objects of legal punishment in England and its colonies, including America—until the revolution that placed liberty at the heart of its achievements. However, historians also highlight a crucial phenomenon that characterized the relationship between the practice of free speech and the right of free speech preceding the American revolution: practice outpaced the legal framework and free speech was exercised on an extraordinarily diverse range of topics both in England and even more so in America. During colonial times, American popular tradition showed a capacity to liberalize legal doctrine, a dynamic which made a return in the second half of the twentieth century.[574]

329. In this context, it is worth noting Kuwait's institution of the diwaniyya, a traditional meeting place where men hold regular, small, informal gatherings to exchange news and discuss affairs of family and community. As a space, the diwaniyya is located in the home of its owner and enjoys strong protection from intrusion: Article

574. Keith Werhan. *Freedom of Speech: A Reference Guide to the United States Constitution.* (Praeger, 2004).

38 of the Kuwaiti Constitution states that places of residence are inviolable and "may not be entered without the permission of their occupants except in the circumstances and manner specified by law." As diwaniyyas by law cannot be regulated,[575] they ensure considerable freedom for the discussions taking place in their protected semi-public spaces. They can and have historically also served as a forum for political participation, particularly at times when state regulation of political life takes a turn toward repression.[576] For the purposes of this book, the most important aspect of the informal political discussions in the diwaniyya is that they provide an opportunity for citizens to exercise free speech outside and often beyond the legal framework that regulates speech in the country. Although, as discussed below, these practices of free speech translate haltingly at best into a liberalization of legal doctrine in Kuwait where pre-publication censorship and post-publication punishment remain widespread (cf. also Chapter 3, Section II, part c).

330. The historical experiences of colonial America with England's licensing and censorship laws inspired the American desire to build a constitutional system based on extended liberties after the revolution. As Madison said, "[the] security of the freedom of the press requires that it should be exempt not only from previous restraint by the Executive, as in Great Britain, but from legislative restraint also" (quoted in *Near v. Minnesota* 1931[577]). In the USA, the First Amendment has offered strong protection against government suppression of speech, but even these protections are not absolute in the sense of applying to every kind of expression. Certain categories of speech, including obscenity, incitement to violence, false commercial speech, and defamation with actual malice are excluded from constitutional protection. However, the preferred way of dealing with these unprotected forms of speech is to make them punishable after publication, instead of censoring them before publication.

331. Eric Barendt[578] argues that in assessing the operation of prior restraint, the most important factor to consider is the character and procedure of the censoring body. Administrative censorship, where control over publication is in the hands of an administrative official or committee, is less tolerable than judicial restraints because of several disturbing features of such systems. First, the administrative censors have a professional interest in maintaining censorship as it is the continuation of that practice that keeps them in their jobs. This is likely to induce an "unsympathetic attitude" to the publications they have to inspect.[579] Concerns over retribution from their employers or public outcry if they let something offensive pass through the system are further incentives to suppress publication. Second, administrative censors may lack precise standards according to which publications are to be assessed. Vague and unclear criteria invite the danger of the censor also banning constitutionally protected speech, if only because of a motivation to err on the side of caution. Additionally, censorship is comparatively easy to enforce and may not provide opportunities for the publisher to represent his views and defend his position. In summary of the vices of administrative

575. Shafeeq Ghabra. *Voluntary Associations in Kuwait: The Foundation of a New System?*. 45 Middle East Journal. 199,215 (1991).
576. Hesham Al-Awadi. *Kuwait.* In The Middle East, edited by Ellen Lust. (CQ Press, 2017).
577. 283 U.S. 697 (1931), accessed at http://caselaw.findlaw.com/us-supreme-court/283/697.html.
578. Eric Barendt,. *Freedom of Speech.* (Oxford University Press, 2007).
579. *Ibid., 122.*

prior restraint systems, they "contain within themselves forces which drive irresistibly toward unintelligent, overzealous, and usually absurd administration."[580]

332. Judicial prior restraint, where courts issue injunctions or other orders to block publication, are in principle free of the vices of administrative censorship and are more acceptable as the body determining whether an individual has a right to speak. Injunctions are usually granted after full hearings where both parties were able to present their case, and the decision is made on clearly established legal standards. The motivations of courts are also different from those of administrative censors, as their role is to apply legal principles impartially, without a predisposition to granting injunctions.[581] Nevertheless, the US Supreme Court has rarely chosen to uphold a judicial prior restraint, even in cases where national security or a defendant's right to a fair trial was argued to be at stake. In contrast, English courts frequently grant injunctions in cases where the prevention of publication is likely to protect commercial confidentiality, personal privacy, state secrets, or the fairness of trials. If a news media outlet chooses publication despite the injunction, it may be found guilty of contempt of court, and because such conduct interferes with the administration of justice, it is punishable by fine or imprisonment. Contempt of court is indeed said by American scholars to be, "without doubt, one of the most serious prior restraint problems facing journalists in the 21st century."[582]

333. In the twenty-first century's global media operations where the Internet is an increasingly dominant force, the differences in national press law regimes create new challenges for freedom of speech. A 2006 British terror plot case brought these challenges into sharp focus. In summer 2006, a group of British Muslim suspects was arrested in the UK on charges of plotting terrorist acts. The arrests occurred after months of surveillance of the group that had allegedly been plotting to use liquid explosives to blow up airplanes from Heathrow airport to the United States. During the months of the trial, the judge instructed the members of the jury to discount all outside influences.[583] Simultaneously, in accordance with British law, the media were prohibited from publishing prejudicial information about the defendants in order to protect the suspects' right to a fair trial. Such stringent reporting restrictions for criminal cases are alien to the US where reporting details of suspects in a criminal trial is protected by the Constitution. Consequently, the *New York Times* published an article about the details that were emerging about the case. The details were incriminating to the suspects and included the facts that British police found jihadist materials, martyrdom videos, and components for making a liquid explosive during raids of an apartment linked to the suspects. The *New York Times* story left readers with a clear impression that the suspects were guilty, a kind of reporting could not have been published in a British newspaper. The *Times* took the unprecedented step of not distributing the day's issue in the UK and blocking the online version of the article from British audiences with the help of technology originally developed for targeted Internet advertising. As

580. Thomas Emerson. *The Doctrine of Prior Restraint*. Yale Law School. 658. (1958, http://digitalcommons.law.yale.edu/fss_papers/2804/).
581. Eric Barendt. *Freedom of Speech*. (Oxford University Press, 2007).
582. Roy L Moore & Michael D Murray. *Media Law and Ethics*. 4th ed. 148. (Routledge, 2012).
583. Details of the trial are listed on the Department of Homeland Security's website at https://www.tsa.gov/news/releases/2008/09/08/uk-2006-liquid-explosives-plot-trial-overview.

the paper has staff, offices and assets in Britain, the UK courts have jurisdiction for contempt of court cases over it, and on balance the American newspaper chose not to risk a lawsuit.[584]

334. Despite enjoying extensive domestic protections under the First and Fourteenth Amendment, the *New York Times* opted for submitting its standards to another country's judicial prior restraint rules. The case highlighted the dilemmas faced by the media when publishing in countries with different press standards as well as the difficulties faced by nations in maintaining their press law systems in a global network of information flow. The latter issue poses particular challenges for countries with less free media systems, such as Kuwait, as will be discussed in more detail.

584. Catherine Spratt. *British Blockage*. The News Media & the Law 30, No. 4 (2006): 26.

Chapter 3. Censorship of Political Speech

335. Prior restraint as such may not be entirely incompatible with constitutional freedom of speech guarantees, but the hostility toward censorship calls for careful examination by the courts in each case. In the USA, First Amendment exceptionalism has inspired a heavy presumption against the constitutional validity of prior restraint, particularly for political speech. The landmark Supreme Court case that declared prior restraint unconstitutional in the twentieth century was *Near v. Minnesota* in 1931. Jay Near owned a muckraking newspaper, *The Saturday Press*, in the city of Minneapolis. Near was an "anti-Semite, anti-Catholic, anti-black, anti-labor, anti-Communist" yellow journalist[585] whose paper charged that the city's gambling, bootlegging, and racketeering were controlled by "a Jewish gangster" and that "Jew Gangsters [were] practically running Minneapolis," ordering corrupt and negligent city officials around. Near was brought to court for violating a Minnesota gag law, a statute that provided for the abatement, as a public nuisance, of a "malicious, scandalous and defamatory newspaper, magazine or other periodical." If found guilty of publishing a newspaper largely devoted to "malicious, scandalous and defamatory" articles, the publisher could under the statute be perpetually enjoined from publishing further. The law was intended as "protection of the public welfare," but the Supreme Court judged it to be an act of "effective censorship," thus an abridgement of the right to liberty of the press as guaranteed in the First and Fourteenth Amendments. As the majority opinion stated,

> [T]he operation and effect of the statute in substance is that public authorities may bring the owner or publisher of a newspaper or periodical before a judge upon a charge of conducting a business of publishing scandalous and defamatory matter—in particular that the matter consists of charges against public officers of official dereliction—and, unless the owner or publisher is able and disposed to bring competent evidence to satisfy the judge that the charges are true and are published with good motives and for justifiable ends, his newspaper or periodical is suppressed and further publication is made punishable as a contempt. This is of the essence of censorship.[586]

336. The Minnesota Gag Law was declared an unconstitutional restraint on the press, and Jay Near was allowed to continue publishing his newspaper. Although the decision was narrow, 5–4, it created a "potent instrument of modern constitutional law"[587] and set the pattern for subsequent cases where the constitutionality of pre-publication censorship acts or actions again became the issue.

337. In comparison, Kuwait's experience with pre-publication censorship of political speech shows a less clear trajectory. The ebb and flow of press freedom has followed the pattern of political struggles between the ruling family and parliament. The suspension of the Constitution by the ruler in 1976–1981 and 1986–1992 was

585. Fred W. Friendly. *Minnesota Rag*. 127. (Random House, 2013).
586. 283 U.S. 697 (1931), accessed at https://supreme.justia.com/cases/federal/us/283/697/case.html
587. Thomas Emerson,. *The Doctrine of Prior Restraint*. Yale Law School. 654. (1955, http://digitalcommons.law.yale.edu/fss_papers/2804/).

inevitably accompanied by tightening government control over the press, including the imposition of prior restraint censorship in Kuwaiti newsrooms. As Jurdi and Dashti[588] note, following the 1986 dissolution of parliament and suspension of the Constitution, the Ministry of Information appointed an individual censor to each of the newspapers to screen their contents for stories that may impact the government negatively. The fact that the government followed formal legal procedures in instituting the regime of prior restraint by modifying the press law to allow for the direct imposition of censorship underlines the pliability of law as a tool for regulating freedom of speech depending on the circumstances. The pliability of legal frameworks allows the press to "push at the imprecise boundaries laid down in vaguely worded prohibitions contained in press laws,"[589] while simultaneously allowing the government to invoke these laws to rein in the press.

338. These mechanisms can end up cementing the government's control over the press even after the lifting of explicit censorship. The boundaries of admissibility are given firmer tones under direct government intervention, and this induces self-censorship in the newsroom. Unwilling to risk legal action, the press becomes its own censor, a control system which is effective and pervasive without appearing to be so. Restored parliaments have not provided answers to the free speech dilemmas of the press either. Islamist MPs raise vocal objections to speech deemed incompatible with Islamic tradition, such as fashion shows and concerts, and may call government ministers to account over perceived lapses.

339. Throughout the ongoing power struggle over freedom of speech, the courts are in a position of arbiters in specific cases. Their judgments contribute to the interpretations of the law, albeit without necessarily achieving the clarification and precision of legal principles.

588. Nabeel A Jurdi. & Ali A Dashti. *Communication Policies in the State of Kuwait*. Annals of The Faculty of Arts XIV, No. 96 (1994).

589. Naomi Sakr. *Dynamics of GCC Press-Government Relations in the 1990s* S. 102–119 In Najem, Tom Pierre; Hetherington, Martin (Red) Good Governance in the Middle East Oil Monarchies. 110 (London: Routledge Curzon, 2003).

Chapter 4. Film Censorship

340. There tends to be a clear hierarchy assumed between different categories of speech based on their significance for and contribution to the political life of democratic societies. Traditionally, political speech has enjoyed the top position in the hierarchy of modes of expression, with other categories such as entertainment or commercial speech deemed less important and consequently given less constitutional protection. The hierarchical structuring of speech has been gradually changing over time, parallel with the extension of the concept of the "political" itself to speech not immediately related to affairs of the state or government. At the same time, the appearance of new media of communication, from film through video games to social media, has continued to necessitate rethinking their potential social and cultural significance in light of existing legal frameworks of communication. Depending on the national politico-cultural context, recognition of the significance of emerging forms of communication was made explicit either through granting constitutional protections to them, as demonstrated by American courts, or by extending governmental or social controls over them, as shown in Kuwaiti and British practices.

341. Discussions of regimes of governmental control of the press often give special emphasis to political speech, although censorship in other areas is equally indicative of the culture-specific logics underpinning laws and regulations. Film censorship demonstrates this issue well. In the US, the anti-prior restraint position developed in *Near v. Minnesota* was eventually extended to films in the 1952 Supreme Court case of *Burstyn v. Wilson*.[590]

342. Prior to the case, the exhibition of motion pictures was judged under a 1915 Supreme Court decision to be pure and simple business conducted for profit, and not worthy of regard as part of the press or as organs of public opinion.[591] *Burstyn v. Wilson* stated that films are "a significant medium for the communication of ideas" and important as an organ of public opinion even if they are designed to entertain as well as to inform, and even if their production and distribution constitutes big business conducted for private profit. First Amendment protection thus granted to motion pictures, the issue became whether a New York statute that permitted the banning of a film by government officers on the ground that it was "obscene, indecent, immoral, inhuman, sacrilegious," or "of such a character that its exhibition would tend to corrupt morals or incite to crime," was unconstitutional. The film in question was Roberto Rossellini's *The Miracle*, a story of an unbalanced, zealously religious peasant woman who is seduced by a stranger she believes to be her favorite saint, Joseph. She later remembers nothing of the seduction, and when it becomes evident that she is pregnant, she becomes convinced that her child was divinely conceived. The village ostracizes her and she retreats to a mountain-top church where she gives birth to a son, and motherhood appears to redeem her.

343. Although the film was initially approved for exhibition by the censors, and it premiered as scheduled, it provoked a public outcry that had not been anticipated. Rossellini himself said he intended the film as a story of man's inhumanity to man.

590. 343 US 495 (1952), accessed at https://supreme.justia.com/cases/federal/us/343/495/case.html.
591. *Mutual Film Corp. v. Industrial Commission of Ohio*, 236 U.S. 230 (1915).

Outraged Catholic cinemagoers in New York, however, saw the film as a blasphemous and sacrilegious work that makes a mockery of the virgin birth.[592] The film was banned, its case taken to New York courts that upheld the ban until the *Burstyn v. Wilson* decision where the Supreme Court declared unconstitutional the statute that allowed for denying a license for showing a film on a censor's conclusion that it was "sacrilegious". Citing *Near v. Minnesota*, the Court reiterated its position that "a previous restraint is a form of infringement upon freedom of expression to be especially condemned" and said that the state failed to meet the heavy burden of demonstrating that "sacrilege" presented the kind of exceptional case that would make the limitation of First Amendment freedom acceptable. The statute and the lower courts relied on a "broad and all-inclusive definition of 'sacrilegious'" that results in setting the censor "adrift upon a boundless sea amid a myriad of conflicting currents of religious views, with no charts but those provided by the most vocal and powerful orthodoxies." It is unacceptable that such an overbroad category could vest "unlimited restraining control over motion pictures in a censor."

344. A few years later, the Supreme Court effectively outlawed administrative prior restraint of films by imposing rigorous procedural restrictions on the prior submission of motion pictures to a censorship board. In *Freedman v. Maryland* (1965),[593] the Court held that motion picture censorship is not necessarily unconstitutional, but procedural safeguards to eliminate the dangers of censorship must be in place to avoid constitutional invalidity. As part of the procedure, the censor has the burden of proving that the film is unprotected by the Constitution and its distribution should not be allowed; a permanent ban could only be issued by a court order; and the court hearing determining the constitutionality of the ban must occur promptly following the temporary administrative ban. The decision added to making film censorship in the US in effect "a dead letter,"[594] leaving a voluntary film classification system run by the film industry itself as the only form of control. The rating system introduced in the 1960s was designed to achieve the goal of protecting unwilling people from exposure to offensive cinematic material, while allowing others to view more explicit movies if they so choose. Consistent with the American culture of free speech, achieving this goal through self-regulation of the film industry is preferred to government control.

345. Britain too employs a rating system for classifying films, but at the same time, it maintains a system of censorship that allows local authorities to legally make decisions about motion pictures, although in practice the decisions are made by the British Board of Film Classification (BBFC). In their own words, the BBFC is "an independent, self-financing and not-for-profit media content regulator" whose independence from the government is safeguarded by generating income only from the fees charged to the industry that submits works for classification.[595] The Board's mission includes protecting the public, especially children, from potentially harmful content, which is the classic supporting argument for censorship systems. Cuts can be and are frequently required for films that want a "15" certificate, but the Board's

592. Laura Wittern-Keller & Raymond J Haberski. *The Miracle Case: Film Censorship and the Supreme Court*. (University Press of Kansas, 2008).
593. 380 US 51 (1965), accessed at https://supreme.justia.com/cases/federal/us/380/51/.
594. Eric Barendt. *Freedom of Speech*. 133. (Oxford University Press, 2007).
595. *See* the BBFC's website at http://www.bbfc.co.uk/about-bbfc/our-mission.

guidelines operate with reasonably clearly defined and easily accessible contours of acceptability. The BBFC emphasizes that it is accountable to the public and revisits its age rating guidelines every four to five years following a major public consultation. This consultative mechanism is expected to ensure that classification standards and criteria can be adjusted in response to changing public attitudes. The net result is an efficient censorship system that allows distributors to enjoy its speed of decision and cost-effectiveness. Filmmakers and distributors seem to prefer this system that offers certainty against potential punishment for violations of statutes governing cinema.[596]

346. The Kuwaiti film censorship regime (whose relevant laws are discussed in Chapter 3, Section II, subsection n) offers a clear demonstration of how politico-cultural logics underpinning communication law lead to drastically different conclusions when societies need to balance freedom of speech with other values. The starting points for Kuwaiti censors are identical to some of the arguments used in the US and the UK where protecting the public, in particular children or the young, from harm is a recognized duty of the state. Unlike Britain, and in especially marked contrast to the US, Kuwait wishes to achieve this goal by maintaining a strict motion picture censorship system of the administrative kind. Censorship officers of the Ministry of Information are tasked with deciding the fate of licenses issued domestically for production of films, and for distribution and exhibition in the case of imported films. The system exhibits the deleterious effects of administrative censorship: administrators are left with excessive discretion in deciding what needs to be censored according to the law that relies on vague and elastic categories such as the protection of "spiritual values, Kuwaiti customs and traditions" and the prevention of "disruptions to public order or national unity" or offending "public morality" (see also §13. Censorship of Films) for judgment calls about creative works. The decisions are made in a closed process where filmmakers are not provided with opportunities to defend their artistic choices. Problems are further compounded by the practice that allows any member of the audience to make a complaint about a film that had been approved for release, and the censors lean toward revising their decisions in favor of appeasing the vocally complaining citizen or group regardless of how significant a portion of the population they represent.

347. The result for Kuwaiti filmmakers is stifled creative expression. As a filmmaker said, "Movies made under censorship are tasteless and colorless."[597] Important elements of public discourse, such as politics, sexuality, religion, and extreme violence are taboo subjects that creative talent can raise only in roundabout ways, by evoking symbols that do not allow the censors to know what the filmmakers are talking about. Acute awareness of the red lines that cannot be crossed also encourages self-censorship. A major problem of the existing administrative film censorship regime is the absence of a possibility of dialogue with writers and filmmakers. As a Kuwaiti scriptwriter complained about the censorship board, "I would like to negotiate with them and ask them why they cut certain passages. It is good that they preserve the rules, but we would want an explanation."[598]

596. Eric Barendt. *Freedom of Speech*. Oxford University Press, 2007.

597. Quentin Müller & Sebastian Castelier. *Made in Kuwait: Surviving Censorship in the Filmmaking Industry*. Middle East Eye http://www.middleeasteye.net/in-depth/features/censorship-kuwait-764920799

598. *Ibid.*

348. In the absence of dialogue that could help clarify matters, the rules of censorship remain vague and unexplained, compounding the problems of free artistic expression already posed by administrative censorship. The problem is even more acute for films imported from abroad, although foreign-made works make up the overwhelming majority of cinema offerings in Kuwait. It is unfeasible for foreign directors and producers to negotiate with Kuwaiti censors about their work, and the administratively issued cuts leave cinema-going audiences with truncated movies whose storyline is sometimes hard to follow.

Kuwait introduced a rating system, but anecdotal evidence suggests it remains inefficient.[599] Further measures, such as bleeping out swear words or airbrushing revealing outfits worn by characters[600] may leave the plot lines intelligible, but they clash with moviegoers' expectations. In short, the system of film censorship shows signs of inefficiency, and given the easy accessibility of movies online, audiences keen to watch tend to migrate to alternative platforms.

599. Danderma. *How Effective Is the Cinescape New Movie Rating?*, 2013.
600. Mark. *A New Kind of Cinema Censorship.* http://248am.com/mark/movies/a-new-kind-of-cinema-censorship/

Chapter 5. Protecting Individuals: Defamation

349. The right to dignity and good reputation has been recognized for millennia, far longer than freedom of speech. That, however, does not mean that when the right to reputation and the right of freedom of speech come into conflict, reputation is going to triumph. The past decades saw preference given increasingly to free speech and freedom of the press rights over the right to reputation, most markedly in the United States but also in Britain.

350. In the US, the seminal case that set the course for subsequent American defamation cases was decided in 1964. Fifty years later, on the anniversary of the announcement of the Supreme Court decision on *New York Times v. Sullivan* (1964), US media held commemorative celebrations, hailing the case as the "(re-)birth" of the First Amendment.[601] The case was brought by L.B. Sullivan, a commissioner in charge of the police in Montgomery, Alabama, who claimed that he was defamed in a full-page advertisement published in the New York Times.

351. The ad, under the title "Heed Their Rising Voices," was placed by supporters who wanted to call attention to the plight of people participating in the civil rights movement and raise funds to support them. The wording of the advertisement was filled with passionate political advocacy, but some of the details describing the atrocities were inaccurate. Although the newspaper had a fact-checking department for advertisements, on this occasion they did not check the accuracy of the claims in the ad because they saw no reason to question its contents.

352. The jury at the trial found the ad libelous and awarded Sullivan USD 500,000 in damages, which decision was affirmed by the Alabama Supreme Court. In a unanimous decision, the Supreme Court reversed and established the "actual malice" rule that states, "A State cannot under the First and Fourteenth Amendments award damages to a public official for defamatory falsehood relating to his official conduct unless he proves "actual malice"—that the statement was made with knowledge of its falsity or with reckless disregard of whether it was true or false."[602]

353. For the first time, the Court held that constitutional protections for speech and press could apply to libelous statements if they are made as criticism of the official conduct of a public official and they are made without actual malice. The court's reasoning held that libel suits could limit the "uninhibited, robust, and wide-open" debate on public issues the US is committed to, not only for the defendants in a case, but also by deterring others from speaking out of fear of legal action brought against them. Errors and misstatements inevitably occur in uninhibited public debates, but the imperfections of debate are preferable to stifling it with threats of libel. Some falsehood can be protected if the outcome is protection for speech that matters.

354. Actual malice raises the bar for proving defamation very high and gives strong protection to American media. The protection was further extended when the scope of the actual malice rule was widened to include not only public officials but

601. Andrew Cohen. *Today Is the 50th Anniversary of the (Re-)Birth of the First Amendment.* The Atlantic. (2014, accessed https://www.theatlantic.com/national/archive/2014/03/today-is-the-50th-anniversary-of-the-re-birth-of-the-first-amendment/284311/).

602. 376 U.S. 254 (1964), accessed at http://caselaw.findlaw.com/us-supreme-court/376/254.html.

also public figures, persons who command continuing public interest, such as army commanders, sports coaches, university athletic directors, or household-name celebrities.

355. The spread of the actual malice rule was halted ten years after it was introduced, with the Supreme Court decision in *Gertz v. Robert Welch, Inc.*[603] The case started in Chicago when a policeman called Nuccio was convicted of murder. The family of his victim hired Elmer Gertz, a reputable attorney, to represent them against Nuccio. Robert Welch, a wealthy candy manufacturer and founder of an ultra-conservative society, ran an article in his magazine attacking Gertz for his part in the trial. The article claimed that the murder trial was "part of a Communist conspiracy to discredit the local police" and alleged that Gertz was behind Nuccio's "frameup," implied that Gertz had a criminal record, and labeled him a "Communist-frontier."[604] None of the claims were true, and Gertz sued the magazine for libel.

356. In their decision, a 5-4 majority of the Supreme Court established that Gertz was neither a public official nor a public figure. As a private individual he would only need to prove negligence instead of actual malice on the magazine's part, and he could recover compensatory damages for the harm the magazine did to his reputation. The decision confirmed that the actual malice standard was not constitutionally required in all defamation cases, it is triggered by the public status of libel plaintiffs. According to the court's reasoning, the distinction is necessary because public officials and public figures expose themselves voluntarily to increased risks of injury from defamation, and they characteristically have greater opportunities to defend their reputation by having greater access to channels of public communication.

357. In US libel cases, categorizing the plaintiff as a public official or public figure is thus a decisive element. For private individuals, the courts must make further distinctions between claims that were made in speech that is of public concern and speech of only private concern. The fairly precise rules articulated for libel cases arguably have the advantage of making decisions more predictable and afford news media an easier way to decide whether the publication of particular stories poses a risk of a libel suit. However, critics point to a "dark side" of the heritage of *New York Times v. Sullivan.*[605]

358. Cass Sunstein[606] laments the impact the actual malice rule had on the state of public discourse where falsehoods about public officials and public figures can be widely circulated under constitutional protection. The new media landscape where bloggers and social media users create echo chambers for the instant sharing of harmful lies undermines civility of public discourse and contributes to "a climate of distrust and political polarization in the U.S.."[607] Other critics point out that the *New York Times v. Sullivan* ruling overprotects speech and under-protects reputation while also

603. 418 U.S. 323 (1974), accessed at https://supreme.justia.com/cases/federal/us/418/323/case.html.

604. *Ibid.*

605. Cass Sunstein. *The Dark Side of New York Times v. Sullivan.* (2014, accessed June 19, 2017, https://www.bloomberg.com/view/articles/2014-03-25/the-dark-side-of-new-york-times-v-sullivan).

606. *Ibid.*

607. *Ibid.*

making libel cases very expensive to fight.[608] Barron's[609] proposed solution to these problems is to promote a responsible press, partly through the adoption of legal approaches developed for defamation in Britain.

359. English law has disagreed with the US position that privileges free speech and press rights over the right to reputation. Prior to the enactment of the Defamation Act in 2013, tougher libel laws and a quirk of the British legal system enabled London to become the center of "libel tourism" where foreign nationals could sue for defamation. High-profile cases in this vein included Russian oligarch Boris Berezovsky suing *Forbes* magazine in London for a 1996 article that referred to him as the "Godfather of the Kremlin," even though the circulation of *Forbes* in England was negligible. Berezovsky chose England as the scene of his defamation battle because, as he explained, "In this country, if you say I am an elephant you have to prove it. In America I have to prove that I am not an elephant."[610] In other words, in England, the burden of proof falls on the defendant in libel cases, and publishers must prove that their information was truthful. That can sometimes be difficult to achieve, for example, if the journalists relied on confidential sources in getting the details of a story.

360. The differences between the English and American legal regimes concerning defamation were also brought into sharp focus in 2004 when a billionaire Saudi businessman, Khalid bin Mahfouz, successfully sued an American author, Rachel Ehrenfeld, about her allegations that the businessman funded al-Qaida through his charity organizations.[611] The allegations were published in the book *Funding Evil*, and although the book had no British publisher, bin Mahfouz was granted his suit because excerpts of the book were available online and 23 copies were sold through websites registered in the UK. Ehrenfeld refused to acknowledge the jurisdiction of the British court in the case, which enabled bin Mahfouz to obtain a judgment by default against her and win hundreds of thousands of pounds in damages and legal fees.[612] When Ehrenfeld filed a lawsuit against bin Mahfouz in New York to obtain a judgment barring the enforcement of the British verdict, the courts denied jurisdiction.

361. Five months later, however, the New York Legislature passed unanimously the Libel Terrorism Protection Act, dubbed "Rachel's Law" after Ehrenfeld's first name. The bill was designed to deter libel claimants from suing in foreign courts with the aim of inhibiting free speech in New York, and it soon inspired similar laws that were adopted in other states.[613] The need to protect American free speech rights against foreign defamation judgments was also incorporated into federal statute in 2010 with the Securing the Protection of our Enduring and Established Constitutional Heritage (SPEECH) Act. One of its tenets is that foreign libel judgments are unenforceable in

608. Benjamin Barron. *A Proposal to Rescue New York Times v. Sullivan by Promoting a Responsible Press*. 57 American University Law Review 73,127 (2007).

609. *Ibid.*

610. *Shuddup*. (2003, The Economist, accessed Jun. 19, 2017, http://www.economist.com/node/1632864).

611. Ehrenfeld v. Mahfouz, 518 F.3d 102 (2d Cir. 2008), accessed at http://caselaw.findlaw.com/us-2nd-circuit/1152735.html.

612. *Ibid.*

613. Sarah Staveley-O'Carroll. *Libel Tourism Laws: Spoiling the Holiday and Saving the First Amendment?* 4 New York University Journal of Law & Liberty 252,292 (2009).

the US unless the country that issued it offers at least as much protection for free speech as the First Amendment.

362. The 2013 Defamation Act[614] was introduced to reform defamation legislation in England partly as a response to the American backlash against libel tourism. In order to avoid trivial lawsuits, the law requires claimants to show they have suffered serious harm as a result of the defamation. To put an end to libel tourism, the act states that courts have jurisdiction only if England and Wales is "clearly the most appropriate place" in which to bring an action. The act also details the defenses that can be used in defamation cases.

363. Defenses include truth, honest opinion, privilege, and publication on matters of public interest. Defendants can use proof that the claims published are "substantially true" in their defense. Honest opinion works as a defense under the conditions that the statement complained of was a statement of opinion, not fact; the statement indicated, at least in general terms, the factual basis of the opinion, and the opinion could have been held by an honest person in possession of the facts. The honest opinion defense applies to opinions on any issue, not only to matters of public interest. Responsible publication on a matter of public interest was a new defense introduced in the act, expanding the older *Reynolds*[615] test that required defendants to show that they had acted responsibly, that is, they adhered to the standards of responsible journalism. Under the new requirement, defendants have to show that they "reasonably believed that publishing the statement complained of was in the public interest"[616].

Under the 2013 act, English law continues on a course where the importance of free speech is recognized and protected under defenses of privileges and responsible publication, but the right to reputation remains a right courts choose to protect even at the risk of having a "chilling effect" on the press. This shows the balancing between the two rights tilting toward reputation and dignity, although certainly not to the extent that is common across the Arab world, including Kuwait. Duffy and Alkazemi[617] conclude their survey of Arab defamation laws with the observation that "none of the libel and slander laws is in alignment with international norms."[618]

364. There are three factors that can be used to distinguish Arab defamation laws from the international norms.[619] These factors are that defamation is prosecuted as a criminal offense, there is no recognition of the privilege of commenting on matters of public concern involving public officials, and truth is not generally recognized as an absolute defense in defamation cases. Kuwait fares slightly better in the survey by virtue of the penal code containing provisions for recognizing truth as a defense in defamation cases if the claims made were based on facts and were directed at a public

614. The United Kingdom *Defamation Act 2013, Chapter 26.* (accessed at http://www.legislation.gov.uk/ukpga/2013/26/pdfs/ukpga_20130026_en.pdf).
615. *Reynolds v Times Newspapers.* 2 AC 127, (2001, accessed at https://publications.parliament.uk/pa/ld199899/ldjudgmt/jd991028/rey01.htm*).*
616. The United Kingdom *Defamation Act 2013, Chapter 26, S4(1)(b)..* (accessed at http://www.legislation.gov.uk/ukpga/2013/26/pdfs/ukpga_20130026_en.pdf).
617. Matt J. Duffy & Mariam Alkazemi. *Arab Defamation Laws: A Comparative Analysis of Libel and Slander in the Middle East.* 22 Communication Law and Policy 190. (2017).
618. *Ibid.*
619. *Ibid.*

official.[620] Nevertheless, the list of entities whose reputation must not be challenged is extensive and emphatically includes the judiciary.

365. The figure of the ruler is particularly strongly protected against defamation, as the Kuwaiti cases discussed in Part VII, Chapter 4 below illustrate. It is important to note, however, that the strict rules in place against defaming the Amir also enjoy broad support in those segments of the population that are of a traditional and religious mindset. This has been attributed to the "deeply rooted Islamic tradition and ideology that obeying and being respectful towards the ruler is an extension of your duty towards God."[621] The importance attached to the right to reputation can further be explained by anthropological research into honor-based collectivism.

366. As demonstrated in Peristiany,[622] Abu-Lughod[623] and elsewhere, social image and reputation are the bases of collectivism expressed in the concept of honor. Honor in Arab societies relies on compliance with traditional patterns of behavior and conforming to prevailing social norms. Self-worth is public in nature and relies on maintaining good reputation for oneself, one's family, and one's tribe. Challenges to good reputation therefore have far-reaching consequences; they involve social units far beyond the individual. Such considerations may get overlooked in assessments of the state of defamation law in Kuwait that focus on defamation as a legal tool for subduing political dissent.

---

620. *Ibid.*
621. Fatima Almatar. *Freedom of speech: A case of social media in Kuwait - Comparing the scope of freedom of expression in the Kuwaiti and the British Courts*. 4 International Journal of Educational Research and Development. 48. (2015).
622. Peristiany, J. G. 1965. *Honour and Shame: The Values of Mediterranean Society*. London: Weidenfeld and Nicolson.
623. Abu-Lughod, Lila. 1999. *Veiled Sentiments*. Berkeley: University of California Press.

Chapter 6. Protecting Communities: Hateful and Offensive Religious Speech and Blasphemy

367. The place of religion in a country's legal system is often used as a convenient shortcut to highlight the dichotomies of secular, tolerant, democratic, and free Western countries and the religious, intolerant, autocratic, and oppressed Islamic nations. The existence and application of blasphemy laws fit particularly well into well-rehearsed narratives of cultural or civilizational clashes. In the USA, blasphemy is defined by Black's Law Dictionary as "irreverence toward God, religion, a religious icon, or something else considered sacred." It is noted to be a crime at common law whose enforceability is undermined by its questionable constitutionality under the First Amendment. Other commentators go further by stating: designed to protect abstract ideas or religions, blasphemy laws are "inconsistent with universal human rights standards."[624]

368. Eko[625] articulates the issue as a clash of culture-specific logics behind the official, legal recognition of state religions and secular dogmas. There are wide divergences among countries based on their level of "entanglement" with religion. In the US, the "establishment clause" of the First Amendment bars the state from interfering with religious practice ("Congress shall make no law respecting an establishment of religion, or prohibiting the free exercise thereof"). As a result, the government has low political entanglement with religion as well as with the cultural aspects of religion and the normative requirements of religious doctrine.[626] Individuals are free to believe and organize around their faith as they will. Freedom of speech also means that people are protected in expressing their views about religion, even if such expressions come into conflict with the beliefs of others. In *Cantwell v. Connecticut*, a case brought about when a man belonging to Jehova's Witnesses was found guilty by the lower courts for breach of peace after he was evicted from a predominantly Catholic neighborhood where residents were displeased by his playing offensive sound recordings about Catholicism, the Supreme Court held that excesses of religious speech amounting to vilification or false statements about other creeds are constitutionally protected. First Amendment liberties provide a shield under which "enlightened opinion and right conduct on the part of the citizens (…) can develop unmolested and unobstructed,"[627] even if the process of development probably involves abuses. The rights of groups to not be offended or shocked are trumped by the individual's free speech rights, unless the exercising of liberties leads to incitement of violence intended to deprive others of their right to exercise their liberties.

---

624. Neil Hicks. *The Public Disorder of Blasphemy Laws: a Comparative Perspective*. 13. The Review of Faith & International Affairs. 51,58. (2015).
625. Lyombe S Eko. New Media, Old Regimes: Case Studies in Comparative Communication Law and Policy. (Lexington Books, 2012).
626. *Ibid., 68.*
627. 310 U.S. 296 (1940), accessed at https://supreme.justia.com/cases/federal/us/310/296/case.html.

369. In *Burstyn v. Wilson,*[628] the Court took the position that in a heterogeneous society like America that is composed by people of many races and many creeds, the state has no legitimate interest in imposing censorship on views that the followers of any religion would find distasteful. As the Court said, "It is not the business of government in our nation to suppress real or imagined attacks upon a particular religious doctrine, whether they appear in publications, speeches, or motion pictures."[629] Low state entanglement with religion is a constitutional principle that is observed in the US to the point where the legal category of blasphemy has become practically nonexistent.

370. Entanglement of church and state by itself is not an indicator of a democratic deficit, as the case of England demonstrates. England is an established democracy where there is no separation of the church and state in the sense that the state is "politically entangled with religion, as well as the cultural aspects of religion," although not the doctrinal aspects of the church.[630] The monarch is the head of the Church of England, carrying the title of Supreme Governor. The archbishops and senior bishops appointed by the monarch on the advice of the Prime Minister sit in the House of Lords, making the UK the only western democracy where the church is still represented in Parliament.

371. Blasphemy or blasphemous libel as a common law offense in England was given shape in the seventeenth century following the trial of yeoman John Taylor. Taylor made wild and inflammatory statements about the Christian religion, God, and Jesus Christ, and his sentence included a fine, imprisonment, and one hour in the pillory.[631] The judicial opinion provided on the case had a lasting influence, appearing to establish a tight link between religion and government. The opinion stated that the "wicked blasphemous words were not only an offense to God and religion, but a crime against the laws, State and Government" since "Christianity is parcel of the laws of England."[632] Subsequent blasphemy cases for two centuries quoted this opinion, confirming the widespread view that blasphemy was connected to sedition, an attack on the social order. Historically, blasphemy law in England served to preserve reverence for Anglican religious culture and widespread Christian belief. In blasphemy cases, the intention to blaspheme was not a requirement for proving the offense, it was sufficient for a conviction that the defendant vilified Christ and Christianity in an unseemly manner. Eventually, blasphemy law became secularized and was used to preserve public order, emphasizing the difference between reasoned arguments about religion and impassioned vilification, ridicule and insult.[633] For over fifty years after

628. 343 U.S. 495 (1952), accessed at https://supreme.justia.com/cases/federal/us/343/495/case.html.
629. Joseph Burstyn, Inc. v. Wilson. (1952). https://supreme.justia.com/cases/federal/us/343/495/case.html.
630. Lyombe S Eko. New Media, Old Regimes: Case Studies in Comparative Communication Law and Policy. 70. (Lexington Books, 2012).
631. Elliott Visconsi,. *The Invention of Criminal Blasphemy: Rex V. Taylor (1676).* 103 Representations. 30,52 (2008).
632. *Ibid., 31.*
633. Paul Kearns. *The end of blasphemy law.* 79 Amicus Curiae. 25, 27. (2008).

1921, the last time a person was given a prison sentence for blasphemy, no further cases were brought to the courts.

372. As British society became secularized, blasphemy law seemed to become a dead letter. Changing social and cultural norms expanded the boundaries of tolerance, and irreverent—but not coarse—literary treatments of Jesus no longer attracted legal consequences. Then in 1976, the June issue of *Gay News* published a poem titled "The Love that Dares to Speak its Name." The poem described in explicit detail the homosexual acts a Roman centurion engaged in with the body of Christ immediately after Christ's death. It also described promiscuous homosexual relationships between Jesus and the Apostles and other men in his lifetime. A religious conservative activist, Mary Whitehouse, brought a private prosecution against the paper and its editor, Denis Lemon, for blasphemous libel. The case eventually reached the House of Lords where the court upheld the lower courts' verdict that found Lemon and *Gay News* guilty of the offense[634]. The author of the poem, James Kirkup, insisted that his motives were pure, he did not intend to blaspheme, rather he wanted to create a work of art that would let readers see Christ in terms of modern sexual liberation.[635] But the intentions of the author and the publishers were not considered in judging blasphemy offenses, and in *Lemon* the court held that for a conviction it was sufficient to show that the publisher intended to publish material that could be found blasphemous objectively, by the jury.

373. The *Lemon* case highlighted the difficulties in reconciling blasphemy laws with freedom of speech. The root of the problem is finding rationales sufficiently convincing to make restrictions on free speech acceptable. Blasphemy laws are commonly justified on three grounds: the public order argument, the religious sensibilities argument, and the incitement argument.[636] According to the first argument, blasphemy can lead to breaches of peace if it provokes certain groups beyond endurance. The second argument would support banning blasphemy in order to protect a group's religious sensibilities against psychologically wounding, hateful speech that impairs the group's religious freedom. The third argument assumes that blasphemy can be used as a tool for stirring up hatred toward a group with the result that they become targets of violence.

It was the second argument, the idea that it was right to protect Christians against the shock and outrage provoked by the publication of the blasphemous material that was used in *Lemon*. But the common problem with these rationales for limiting freedom of speech is that there are no commonly shared standards for establishing what constitutes hate speech in the context of religion. In the absence of common standards, the courts may accept claims of outrage or hurt made by religious communities subjectively, with the result that speech would be proscribed although other communities would have easily tolerated it were similar remarks made about them.[637]

---

634. Lemon Whitehouse v. *Whitehouse -V- Lemon; Whitehouse -V- Gay News Ltd on Appeal from Regina -V- Lemon.* (1979). http://www.swarb.co.uk/c/hl/1979Whitehouse-GayNews.html.

635. Leonard Williams Levy. *Blasphemy: Verbal Offense against the Sacred, from Moses to Salman Rushdie.* (UNC Press Books, 1995).

636. Evelyn M. Aswad, Rashad Hussan, & M. Arsalan Suleman. *Why the United States Cannot Agree to Disagree on Blasphemy Laws.* BU Int'l LJ 32 (2014): 119.

637. Eric Barendt. *Freedom of Speech.* 122. 190–191. (Oxford University Press, 2007).

374. Following the *Lemon* case, no further private prosecutions on blasphemy charges succeeded. Salman Rushdie's *The Satanic Verses* was found not to fall under the scope of blasphemy law because the law protected only Anglican Christianity. The organization Christian Voice was equally unsuccessful in winning a case brought against *Jerry Springer: the Opera* for containing material contemptuous and reviling of Christianity and delivering such material in a scurrilous and ludicrous manner. Seeming increasingly anachronistic in the twenty-first century, England's blasphemy law was eventually abolished in 2008.[638] In recognition of the needs of the now religiously heterogeneous population of the UK, religiously motivated attacks on groups were recast as hate crimes. Protection from attacks on the basis of religion for all creeds was incorporated into the 2006 Racial and Religious Hatred Act[639] that defines religious hatred as an offense committed when a person uses threatening words or behavior, or displays any threatening written material, and intends to stir up religious hatred. In an attempt to avoid a "chilling effect" of the law, the Act also provides a free speech clause for religious hatred, according to which nothing in the Act "prohibits or restricts discussion, criticism or expressions of antipathy, dislike, ridicule, insult, or abuse of particular religions, or the beliefs or practices of its adherents."[640]

375. The standard case describing entanglement of religion and the state in Arab-Islamic countries states that the role of Islam in the life of the state and society is "maximal."[641] Religion enjoys supremacy over the state, and political, cultural, doctrinal entanglement with the local cultural interpretations of Islam is high. In some cases, such as in Saudi Arabia, the Quran and the Hadith have "constitutional authority,"[642] and all Islamic societies have the sacred intertwined with every aspect of social and political life and everyday culture. Islam is a whole way of life, like traditional Christianity was for pre-Enlightenment European societies. As a socio-political order, it is a communal phenomenon, thus the expressions of religious dissent threaten the foundations of the social consensus built on it.[643] In classic Sharia law, degrees of belief are a matter between a person and God, and there is no worldly punishment for disbelief. Apostasy and blasphemy become legal issues when the individual decides to make his views public in speech, writing, or behavior. The political and social consequences of publication provide the grounds for punishing apostasy and blasphemy, regardless of the intention of the speaker. This is so because what matters for the

638. Lucinda Maer. *The Abolition of the Blasphemy Offences*. Standard Note SN/PC/04597. Accessed June 6, 2017. (2008).
639. The United Kingdom. *Racial and Religion Hatred Act, Chapter 1.* (2013, accessed at http://www.legislation.gov.uk/ukpga/2006/1/pdfs/ukpga_20060001_en.pdf).
640. The United Kingdom. *Racial and Religion Hatred Act, Chapter 1.* 29J (2013, accessed at http://www.legislation.gov.uk/ukpga/2006/1/pdfs/ukpga_20060001_en.pdf).
641. Lyombe S Eko. *New Media, Old Regimes: Case Studies in Comparative Communication Law and Policy*. 71. (Lexington Books, 2012).
642. *Ibid.*
643. Christopher J van der Krogt. . *Why Is Freedom of Speech a Problem for So Many Muslims?*. In Freedom of Speech and Islam, edited by Erich Kolig, 42. (Ashgate, 2014).

community is the Muslim individual's social practices, which in blasphemy cases amount to an open rejection of "a solemn social relationship."[644]

376. The Western conclusion drawn on the Islamic position on blasphemy is that the Sharia "does not provide a basis for genuinely free expression on matters of religion."[645] The assessment is repeatedly supported by instances of "sanctimonious demagogy" in Islamic societies, such as the time the company that produces 7Up was accused in a Saudi local newspaper of blasphemy because of the allegation that, when seen from the back, the 7Up logo looks similar to the word Allah written in Arabic.[646] The State of Kuwait occupies a more ambivalent position, due to the constitutional provision that makes Sharia a main source, not the main source of legislation. Nonetheless, the gradual Islamicization of Kuwaiti law discussed in Chapter 1 is also reflected in the country's laws on blasphemy and apostasy. Blasphemy is illegal, as confirmed in the 2006 Press Law that prohibits "meddling, defamation, slander, or mocking in any forms of expression" in matters concerning God, the Quran, Prophets, or the companions, wives, and family of Prophet Muhammad. Compared to the now defunct English law, Kuwait's legal provisions are more inclusive in the sense that they protect all monotheistic religions. But unlike the UK's Racial and Religious Hatred Act, Kuwaiti law is not fashioned after strict hate speech legislation and does not allow expressions of harsh criticism in the field of religion. The elasticity of the articulation of what constitutes blasphemy in Kuwait, together with the possibility that any individual can bring such charges, leaves the door wide open to prosecutions.

377. The 2016 case of Sheikha Al-Jassem highlighted the potential tensions between Kuwait's liberal constitutional provisions and some Islamicized legislations. Al-Jassem is professor of philosophy at Kuwait University. Discussing religiously motivated extremist conduct in a television interview with Al-Shahed satellite channel in March 2016, she stressed that politics and religion should be kept apart. She contrasted the country as it was in the 1960s and 1970s with the current state of society where the external markers of religious conduct, including longer beards, the niqab and gender segregation at universities, have become increasingly dominant in public life. In response to the interviewer's question about voices that claim the Quran, Sharia, and religion are more important than the Constitution, Al-Jassem said, "This is the undoing of our democratic regime." She elaborated further by saying, "Anyone who believes that the Quran, or the Sharia, or the interpretations of these religious texts are above the Constitution is betraying the state of Kuwait."[647]

378. A barrage of attacks followed the broadcasting of the interview, including legal complaints filed with the public prosecutor on allegations of blasphemy in

644. Talal Asad. *Free Speech, Blasphemy, and Secular Criticism.* In Is Critique Secular? Blasphemy, Injury, and Free Speech, edited by Talal Asad, Wendy Brown, Judith Butler and Saba Mahmood, 43. (University of California, 2009).

645. Christopher J van der Krogt. *Why Is Freedom of Speech a Problem for So Many Muslims?.* In Freedom of Speech and Islam, edited by Erich Kolig, 22,43. (Ashgate, 2014).

646. Trevor Mostyn. *Censorship in Islamic Societies.* 22. (Saqi Books, 2002).

647. *Kuwaiti Professor of Philosophy Sheikha Al-Jassem: People Who Believe That the Quran Is above the Constitution Are Betraying Kuwait.* (The Middle East Media Research Institute, 2016, https://www.memri.org/tv/kuwaiti-professor-philosophy-sheikha-al-jassem-people-who-believe-quran-above-constitution-are/transcript).

accordance with Article 29 of Law No. 31 of 1970, Amending the Penal Code, and Article 11 of the 2007 Audio-Visual Crimes Law.[648] Al-Jassem was summoned for questioning by public prosecutors on two separate occasions, during the first of which she learned that the complainant said he had been "psychologically damaged" by her remarks.[649] In June, the Public Prosecutor of Kuwait decided not to charge Al-Jassem with blasphemy. The prosecutor dismissed the complaints against Al-Jassem with the words that "freedom of speech cannot be curtailed and not every discussion on religious matters is blasphemy."[650] While in this case the constitutionally safeguarded values of freedom of speech won, the complaints lodged against Al-Jassem with the public prosecutor reveal the uncertainties resulting from laws that are not articulated with sufficient precision.

379. The psychological hurt reported by the complainant would obviously not have been suffered by Al-Jassem had similar remarks been made about her. In fact, some of the responses she received were abusive, including epithets of apostasy hurled at her, without inducing Al-Jassem to lodge complaints of her own. As the case demonstrates, in the absence of common standards across groups on matters concerning religion, the tendency is toward proscribing speech that may well have been tolerated. The threat of prosecution can serve as a deterrent, and Al-Jassem herself indicated in the original television interview that she was exercising self-censorship when discussing the sensitive topics she was asked about.

380. The prosecutor's observation that not every discussion on religious matters is blasphemy was accurate also in the sense that Al-Jassem's comments were political, directed at Islamist political forces, including MPs in parliament. The entanglement of state and religion, however, can make it quite difficult to distinguish between political and religious categories of speech. Blasphemy allegations inevitably involve political allegations too, particularly in a country like Kuwait where stirring up sectarian divisions is seen as a potential threat to national security. As a result, blasphemy offenses are inextricably linked with threats of sedition.

381. The complex mechanisms through which intertwined political and religious forces and discourses shape the communication sphere in Kuwait were revealed in the 2012 case of Hamad Al-Naqi. Social media by this point was increasingly serving as an echo chamber of sectarian infighting, and prior to this case, several Sunni social media users had been sentenced for vitriolic anti-Shia messages posted online. Al-Naqi was a Shia blogger who was arrested for a series of posts on Twitter that allegedly insulted the Prophet, the Prophet's wife and companions, mocked Islam, provoked sectarian tensions, insulted the rulers of Saudi Arabia and Bahrain, and tarnished the image of Kuwait abroad. The blogger was also charged with misusing his mobile phone to spread the comments. Although Al-Naqi claimed that the offending messages were posted by someone else who had hacked his account, he was found guilty of

648. Amnesty International. *Kuwait*. (2016, https://www.amnesty.org/download/Documents/MDE1741452016ENGLISH.PDF).

649. Sebastian Usher. *Kuwait academic charged with blasphemy over TV interview*. (2016, BBC, accessed Jan. 24, 2018, http://www.bbc.com/news/world-middle-east-36046706).

650. Front Line Defenders. *Blasphemy Charges Dropped against Shaikha Binjasim*. (2016). https://www.frontlinedefenders.org/en/case/case-history-shaikha-binjasim.

several offenses and sentenced to ten years in prison with hard labor.[651] The precise contents of the Twitter messages that were judged blasphemous were as a rule not reported in media accounts of the unfolding case, making it more difficult to initiate reasoned public discussions about the offending claims internationally. At least one source describes them as provocative statements with sectarian implications which started with, "the Prophet Muhammad feared one of his Companions," as well as more sacrilegious comments relating to the Prophet's (PBUH) marital affairs.[652]

382. The mockery stipulated by Kuwait's anti-blasphemy statutes is evident in the tweets, and legally they appear to satisfy the statutory conditions established for a conviction. Yet, especially the second one is also grotesque to the point of raising the possibility of reading it as rhetorical hyperbole incapable of vilifying the revered figure of the Prophet, though well suited for stirring up sectarian tensions already brewing in the wake of the Arab uprisings elsewhere and the Syrian situation. Stirred to retaliative action by the Al-Naqi case, Kuwait's Sunni-dominated parliament of 2012 endorsed a legal amendment that was to introduce the death penalty for blasphemy for Muslims who refused to repent for their crime.[653] Continuing to balance between competing political factions, the Amir refused to enact the bill. What the story highlights is the difficulties of separating religious speech and political speech in Kuwait where, despite the liberal provisions of the Constitution, the mosque and the state are still entangled in an at least partially Islamic fashion.

651. Amnesty International. *Kuwaiti Man Sentenced to 10 Years' Imprisonment for 'Insulting' Tweets.* (2012). https://www.amnesty.org/en/latest/news/2012/06/kuwait-faces-prison-sentence-over-blasphemous-tweet/

652. Frederic M. Wehrey. *Sectarian Politics in the Gulf: From the Iraq War to the Arab Uprisings.* (Columbia University Press, 2014).

653. *Kuwait close to death penalty law for blasphemy.* (2012, Reuters, accessed Jan. 24, 2018 http://www.reuters.com/article/us-kuwait-blasphemy-idUSBRE8420SG20120503).

Part VII. Selected Cases in Kuwaiti Media Law

383. The final chapter includes case studies in which laws described in this book have been applied. The compiled cases include varying types of offenses, ranging from blasphemy to indecency and beyond. The offending speech was often not published in English-language newspapers partially due to the possible repercussions of repeating offensive speech; however, some details were available in the Arabic language, such as in Wahid.[654] International watchdog agencies from around the world kept some records of the offensive speech, which was sometimes used to exemplify its nature. Since academic works are constitutionally protected, the authors felt it was a disservice to the reader not to include explicit examples from Kuwaiti media law because of the learning potential it provides for Kuwaitis, and those interested in the Kuwaiti media, to build upon and advance the legal system in which the Kuwaiti media operates. Sensitive readers should take the necessary precautions when proceeding with this chapter, as it includes various explicit examples of offensive speech.

654. Taleeq Wahid. *Haythiyat Walmantooq Hokm Sara Al-Drees Bitohmat Almasas Bithat Alamiriyah Fe Mawqi' Twitter*. (2013, accessed Jun. 19, 2017, http://alziadiq8.com/33260.html).

Chapter 1. Blasphemy

384. In 1999, Dr. Ahmad Al-Baghdadi, faculty member of the Department of Political Science at Kuwait University, was interrogated and given a suspended six-month sentence for blasphemy. Dr. Al-Baghdadi was an expert in Islamic law and history.[655] He was indicted for using the word "failure" in an article he had written in 1996 for the university's student magazine *al-Sho`ula* entitled "An Opportunity to Solve the Oppression of Backwardness." The article described Prophet Mohammad's early failure to convert Mecca to Islam for a period of thirteen years. In the article, Dr. Al-Baghdadi wrote:

> The Prophet (PBUH) failed in forcing Islam upon the society of Mecca for a period of thirteen years, whereas Islam entered the hearts of the Companions from the people of Yathrib or Medina before the arrival of the Prophet (PBUH) in Yathrib.[656]

385. Dr. Al-Baghdadi's writing also encouraged students to oppose the new Islamic trend that he viewed as a danger in society. His remarks angered students and some faculty, and Dr. Al-Baghdadi received anonymous death threats. When a former minister of education published a newspaper article supporting him, both men were denounced as atheists by media, clergy, lawyers, and students. Other lecturers from the university called for tolerance, and the government issued a statement lamenting the decline of political tolerance and the hasty accusations of apostasy.

386. The courts agreed with those who regarded the article's association of "failure" with Prophet Mohammad as an insult and great defamation of the Prophet and considered the statement blaspheming Islam in violation of Kuwait's 1961 Press and Publications Law. As the Misdemeanors Appeals Court stated in their opinion on the case, "The writer of the article was disrespectful to the Prophet, peace be upon him. He also regarded religion as a cause for corruption of mankind, which would necessarily imply discrediting the basic tenets of the Islamic creed."[657] The appellate court then reduced the sentence to one month but ordered his incarceration and denied the possibility of appeal.

387. The Human Rights Committee expressed concern regarding the vagueness of Chapter III of Law No. 3 of 1961 on Printing and Publication, stating that the vagueness of the wording gave the judges a wide space to interpret it and apply restrictive standards that go against the right of free expression, as well as violating Article 19 of the International Covenant on Civil and Political Rights (ICCPR) which Kuwait acceded in May 1996.

---

655. Jonathan F. Fanton. *Imprisoned Kuwaiti Scholar.* Human Rights Watch. (accessed Jun. 7, 2017, https://www.hrw.org/news/1999/10/12/imprisoned-kuwaiti-scholar).
656. Human Rights Watch. *2000 country report on Kuwait.* (accessed Jun. 14, 2017, https://www.hrw.org/reports/2000/kuwait/kuwait-06.htm).
657. Human Rights Watch. *Kuwait: Promises Betrayed - Restrictions on Freedom of Expression.* (accessed Jan. 31, 2018, https://www.hrw.org/reports/2000/kuwait/kuwait-06.htm).

388. The Academic Freedom Committee and other human rights organizations appealed to the Amir of Kuwait to suspend Dr. Al-Baghdadi's sentence, and after spending fourteen days in prison, he was pardoned by the Amir Sheikh Jaber. Sheikh Jaber ruled Kuwait between 1977 until 2006, and Kuwaitis supported their beloved monarch's return to ruling after Kuwait's liberation from the Iraqi invasion.[658]

389. Dr. Al-Baghdadi remained an outspoken critic of what he perceived as the growing influence of Islamist politics in Kuwait. He continued to energetically advocate his views for secularism, especially in the context of education. In a 2004 article titled "Music and Developing Artistic Taste Are More Important than Rote Quran Learning and Religious Studies," he reacted to reports that the Ministry of Education intended to push private schools towards increasing the Islamic components of their curriculum. He was sued for "contempt of Islam" for the contents of his article. The lower court acquitted him, ruling that the article only expressed his personal opinion. The appeals court, however, ruled that Dr. Al-Baghdadi went beyond the limits of expressing opinion and legitimate criticism when his comments suggested a link between Islamist education and intellectual backwardness and terrorism. The court sentenced the author for slandering the Holy Quran and Islam to a one-year suspended jail term. He was ordered to pay KWD 2,000 to suspend his prison sentence, and he was put on a three-year probation. Dr. Al-Baghdadi conceded defeat and described the ruling as a game of "Russian roulette" with the law where he can only lose.[659] He announced that he was going to apply for political asylum in the West and declared that he would not write in Kuwait again.

---

658. *8 Sanawat Montho Raheel Ameer Alkhayr Walwafaa.* (2014, Alanbaa, accessed June 23, 2017, http://alanba.com.kw/437554).
659. Ali Taqi. *Kuwaiti Academic Quits Writing after Court Verdict.* (Gulf News, Mar. 27, 2005).

Chapter 2. Indecency

390. In 2000, the Misdemeanors Appeals Court found the writer Laila Al-Othman and the publisher Yahiya al-Rubay'an guilty of violating Article 204 of the Penal Code.[660] The 1960 Kuwait Penal Code provides harsher punishment for indecency than the Printing and Publishing Law. Article 204 of the Penal Code states that anyone who "prints or sells or distributes or exhibits pictures or drawings or forms or anything immoral" will face up to three years in prison or a KWD 3,000 (USD 9,839) fine. The writer and the publisher were first sentenced to two months in prison, but the appeals court changed the sentence to a fine of KWD 1,000 for distributing Al-Othman's novel *al-Rahiil* which was considered to be blasphemous and obscene. The court found the book "included expressions that violate God, and indecent and shameless expressions." Even though the ruling didn't specify which expressions were indecent and shameless, during pretrial questioning, the prosecutors focused on a description of the "lustful" coming together of sea waves in the novel as well as a passage where a male character, in an expression of the depths of his despair, tells his roommates they can rape him. Al-Othman's novel was published in 1984 and was distributed legally in Kuwait until it was banned in the wake of the court case.[661]

391. The liberal daily *Alqabas* denounced the sentencing as a setback for freedom of expression, saying on its front page, "Kuwait and culture pay the price once more." On the other hand, Islamists welcomed the ruling as a boost to their campaign against "immorality."

392. A statement handed to the court by the lawyers, and published by the newspaper *Al-Siyassah*, said Arabic and Islamic literature is full of such writings. The statement asked, "Do people now have a different definition of decency?" The lawyers were calling for an explanation because the judges did not say what they found offensive in the books.

393. Al-Othman remains a celebrated writer, and in 2004, she founded the Laila Al-Othman prize for young literary talent. Six of her books continue to be banned in Kuwait till date.[662]

660. Amnesty International. *Freedom of expression in Kuwait remains under threat*. (2000, accessed Jun. 14, 2017, https://www.amnesty.org.uk/press-releases/freedom-expression-kuwait-remains-under-threat).

661. *...Bemoan a Wound" Kuwaiti Writers Convicted*. (1999, Al Jadid, accessed Jun. 14, 2017, http://www.aljadid.com/content/bemoan-wound-kuwaiti-writers-convicted-0).

662. Amnesty International. *Freedom of expression in Kuwait remains under threat*. (2000, accessed Jun. 14, 2017, https://www.amnesty.org.uk/press-releases/freedom-expression-kuwait-remains-under-threat).

Chapter 3. Sectarian Sedition

394. In 2016, the Misdemeanors Court acquitted former MP and former Kuwait University faculty Dr. Abdullah Al-Nafisi of violating the National Unity Law and inciting sectarian sedition in an interview he gave on satellite TV channel Wisal. In the interview, Dr. Al-Nafisi spoke about Iran's interference in the affairs of Arab countries, including Kuwait and discussed the possibilities of military aggression by Iran. In court, his lawyer claimed that his client's statements were not offensive, they were merely part of a general analysis of the situation in the Gulf.

395. This was not the first time Dr. Al-Nafisi was accused of threatening national unity by stirring up sectarian strife. In 2015, he was charged with undermining national unity for a talk he gave at a seminar held under the title "Safavid intervention and the threat to the Gulf" in Fahaheel. He was acquitted in the lower courts, but the Court of Appeals overturned those verdicts and fined him KD 10,000. The Cassation Court ruled in favor of Dr. Al-Nafisi and freed him. His defense lawyer explained that his client did talk about the Shiite sect, but he was talking about the Iranian Safavid intervention, since the Safavid neither belongs to the Sunni nor the Shiite faith, but it was a sect or a political party.

396. Previously, in 2013, Dr. Al-Nafisi was interrogated by the public prosecution for a speech he gave at a diwaniya meeting held to highlight the dangers posed by Iran to the Gulf and Kuwait.[663] In his speech, Dr. Al-Nafisi said that some Shiite MPs have links with Iran, and he claimed a Shiite MP took part in the assassination attempt on the life of then-Amir Sheikh Jaber Al-Sabah in 1985, while another one was involved in the 1988 hijacking of a Kuwaiti passenger plane. On this occasion, Dr. Al-Nafisi was released on a KWD 5,000 bail following the questioning.[664]

Similarly in 2017, the Court of Cassation upheld the not guilty decision of the Appeals Court regarding famous Kuwaiti cleric Dr. Othman Al-Khamis' indictment for disdaining Shiite citizens and inciting sectarian strife in a television program on Wisal channel.[665] The first degree court found him guilty and fined him KWD 20,000 (USD 65,746), while the Appeals Court found him not guilty.

397. Regardless of using severe phrases in his speech, the court believed these phrases were part of Islamic history and still under study and research. As his expressions are part of freedom of opinion and thought, he cannot be prosecuted for them. The phrases did not include statements to disdain Shiite citizens, did not challenge their faith, and did not include stirring sectarian strife either. Dr. Al-Khamis denied all charges leveled at him.[666]

---

663. B. Izzak. *Media Draft Law under Fire for Stiff Penalties.* http://www.pressreader.com/kuwait/kuwait-times/20130411/281479273888485. Jun. 14, 2017.

664. *Ex-MP Nafisi acquitted in 'sedition' charges— 'Royal' sued for abusing ruling family.* (2015, Arab Times, Dec. 24, 2017, http://www.arabtimesonline.com/news/ex-mp-nafi-si-acquitted-in-sedition-charges-royal-sued-for-abusing-ruling-family/).

665. Jaber El-Hamoud. *Court Acquits Dr Nafisi of Inciting 'Sectarian' Sedition.* Arab Times, Jul. 2, 2016.

666. *Alistinaf Fe Bara'at Alkhamees: La Yajooz Muhakamat Huriyat Alrai.* (Media Court, 2017, http://mediacourt.net/3142).

Chapter 4. Challenging and Insulting the Ruler

398. Unlike the previous examples, the cases here distinguish themselves because they are committed on social media. Also, the cases here are not committed by academics but by common individuals and even a member of the ruling family. Although cases presented in this chapter range several decades, many of the cases in this section took place in the mid-2010s.The laws applied are not always the main media laws one would expect to be utilized and the responses to the cases also differ. The development of the 2016 electronic media law influences how future cases would be examined; however, it is important to remember that precedent is less important in Kuwait's legal environment due to its incorporation of the civil legal system.

399. In January 2014, human rights activist Abdullah Fairouz Abd al-Kareem was convicted on the basis of Article 25 of the State Security Crimes Act and was sentenced to five years in prison and permanent exile after his release for posting on Twitter remarks that were viewed as insults to the Amir.[667] Article 25 of the penal code sets prison sentences of up to five years for anyone who publicly objects to the rights and authorities of the Amir or faults him. Al-Kareem was also indicted for misusing his mobile phone to disseminate objectionable comments.

400. The conviction was based on several tweets, which indirectly referenced someone who resides at Dar Salwa. Dar Salwa is the residence of Amir Sheikh Sabah al-Ahmad Al-Sabah. In an impolite demeanor, Al-Kareem accused a Twitter user by the name of Goutier of verbal abuse and made references that suggest that this individual resides in Dar Salwa.

401. The sentence for exile was based on the fact that Al-Kareem, although he has a Kuwaiti national ID and passport, was not issued a citizenship certificate by the Ministry of Interior. Consequently, he is treated as a foreigner and the penalty of deportation is mandatory for his case as stipulated in Kuwaiti legislation.[668]

402. Another example took place in 2016 when a grandnephew of the Amir, Sheikh Abdullah Salem Al-Sabah, was sentenced to three years in jail and a KWD 5,000 fine for making malicious statements criticizing the Amir and the ruling family in video messages he posted on Snapchat.[669] He was detained after petitions were filed against him by another member of the ruling family and the Diwan Amiri.

403. Also in 2016, pro-democracy activist Sara Al-Drees was detained for twenty-one days for posting tweets considered as an insult to the Amir.[670] Al-Drees is a 29-year-old Kuwaiti citizen, and identifies as a human rights activist and blogger, in

667. Human Rights Watch. *Kuwait: Jail, Exile for Insulting Emir.* (2014, accessed Jun. 14, 2017, https://www.hrw.org/news/2014/01/26/kuwait-jail-exile-insulting-emir).

668. UnitedNations. *Opinions Adopted by the Working Group on Arbitrary Detention at Its Seventy-Third Session, 31 August—4 September 2015* Human Rights Council, https://documents-dds-ny.un.org/doc/UNDOC/GEN/G15/263/87/PDF/G1526387.pdf?OpenElement.

669. *Royal' released on bail.* (2015, Arab Times, http://www.arabtimesonline.com/news/royal-released-on-bail/).

670. Human Rights Watch. "*Kuwait: Teacher Faces Jail over Twitter Comments.*" (2013, accessed Jun. 13, 2017, https://www.hrw.org/news/2013/07/20/kuwait-teacher-faces-jail-over-twitter-comments).

addition to being a teacher. Al-Drees had a significant following on social media, including 185,000 Twitter followers and 57,000 Instagram followers. She received a sentence of twenty months for insulting the Amir, after she was first prosecuted by the authorities in 2013.[671] On that occasion, four of her tweets made reference to repressions of Kuwait's political opposition movements, including a tweet where she said about the ruling family, "We loved you as a part of Kuwait's history, rejecting violations by some of you, but we now feel that you are spongers imposed on us by our Constitution." The Appeals Court upheld the sentence but Al-Drees subsequently received an Amiri pardon.

404. The 2016 case was brought on by a string of tweets Al-Drees wrote in response to her critics as part of a longer debate. Upon discussing her pardon of 2013, she wrote insulting terms in one of tweets; in the tweet that utilized offensive terms, she spoke of her "affection for Musallam Al-Barrak." Under Article 25 of Law No. 1970/31, Articles 20, 2-1/27 of Law No. 3 of 2006 relating to Printing and Publications, Articles 15/1 and 1/70 of Law No. 37 of 2014 relating to Communications and Information Technology, and Articles 1/6, 8, 9-10, 11 of the Cyber Crimes Law No. 2015 Al-Drees was charged with publicly challenging the rights of the Amir and his authority, insulting the office of the Amir, deliberately misusing phone communications by writing the texts on her Twitter account, and publishing through the Internet texts that included criticism of the Amir's person. Al-Drees was acquitted in January 2017.

405. In 2016, 13 people known as the "Fintas group" were arrested on accusations that they spread false news and rumors by faking and publishing a video clip on social media that could shake confidence in the judicial system by insulting it, as well as insulting the Amir. The video clip showed the head of the constitutional court receiving bribes.

406. The Fintas Group was discovered after security forces detained a demonstrator at Erada Square and found slanderous and false information and provocations against the security forces on his mobile phone that was confiscated. The defendant's phone revealed a WhatsApp discussion group under the name "Fintas," and the messages shared in the group were seen as an attempt to overthrow the regime in Kuwait, insulting the Amir and the judges.[672] Members of the group included lawyers, journalists, and members of the ruling family. The Appeal Court upheld the ruling of the First Court sentencing members of the group to ten years, five years and one year in jail.[673]

407. In February 2017, the Court of Cassation clarified that the law requires the offense of insulting the Amir or encroaching on his mandate to be committed in a public place with public access.[674] The court explained that everyone has the right to freedom of opinion and expression, and there is no punishment for privately held thoughts or opinions. But, there are punishments for publicizing opinions that violate

671. RefWorld. *Kuwait: Sarah Al-Drees Trial Observation Report.* (2016, World Organisation Against Torture, accessed Jun. 13, 2017, http://www.refworld.org/docid/584e806d4.html).

672. Hussein Alabdullah. *Alistinaf Toayed Habs Athaa Group Finas 5 Sanawat Libathhom Maqata'a Muse'a Lria'ees Alqadha.* (Aljarida, Jan. 20, 2017).

673. Mirza Al-Khuwaylidi. *Kuwait: Appeal Court Refuses to Set Free "Fintas Group."* (Asharq Al Awsat Jul. 14, 2016).

674. Hassan Abdullah. *Altamyeez: Alisa'a Lilameer Jareema Alniyah Fa'in Tawafaret Bi'ay Wasila Haq Iqab Martabha.* (Aljarida, Feb. 21, 2017).

the law through any means of public communications. Freedoms can be limited in such cases because the outcomes go further to influence others. Therefore, managing this kind of freedom is permissible to prevent strife and chaos, insecurity and fragmentation in the country.

Chapter 5. License Violations

408. In 2015, The Commerce and Information Ministries by administrative decision No. 79 for the year of 2015 revoked the license and closed down the premises of the "Dar Al Watan Journalism Printing and Publishing Company," which published the *Al-Watan* Newspaper[675]. The decision was made in accordance with Law No. (3) of 2006 regarding Print and Publications and the decision of the Minister of Commerce and Industry No. (38) for the year 2015 on the dissolution of Dar Al Watan Press, Printing and Publishing Company (KSC). Later, the TV channel belonging to the same company was also shut down. The ministries justified their action by stating that the parent company of the newspaper and the TV channel had "accumulated losses exceeding 75 percent of its capital," thereby failing to meet the financial and commercial requirements to keep its license to publish and broadcast.[676]

409. Many believed the revocation of the licenses was politically motivated rather than purely administrative. Previously, the *Al-Watan* newspaper—which was owned by Sheikh Ali Al-Khalifa Al-Sabah, a former minister and a member of the ruling family—and the *Alam Al-Youm* newspaper that was close to the political opposition were suspended for two weeks for violating a media blackout placed on reports about the ongoing investigation into the "conspiracy videotape" case.[677] The case involved leaked recordings of an alleged plot to topple the government.[678]

The company challenged the decision in court, but lost in the appeals court. *Al-Watan* was first issued in 1962 as a weekly paper and became a daily in 1974. Alwatan TV (Kuwait Media Group) started in 2006, the year in which the Kuwaiti media was deregulated.

410. In July 2015, the government also revoked the license of the *Alam Al-Youm* newspaper and Al-Youm TV for violating license regulations. The owner, Jaber Al-Shammari was stripped of his Kuwaiti citizenship, which made him ineligible to own media under the 2006 press law that restricts media ownership to Kuwaiti nationals. He successfully challenged the government on the revoking of his citizenship, winning rulings in his favor from both the lower and appeals courts. Acting on news of an Amiri promise to reinstate the citizenship of those from whom it was revoked in 2014, Al-Shammari withdrew his lawsuit before the Court of Cassation, Kuwait's Supreme Court, could issue a decisive verdict on his case.

---

675. CPJ. *Kuwaiti Court Upholds Government Shutdown of Al-Watan Newspaper*. (2015, accessed Jan. 31, 2018, https://cpj.org/2015/02/kuwaiti-court-upholds-government-shutdown-of-al-wa.php).
676. *Al Watan TV closed*. (2015, Kuwait Times, accessed Jun. 14, 2017, http://news.kuwaittimes.net/al-watan-tv-closed/).
677. Ahmed Hagagy & Sylvia Westall. *Kuwaiti Newspapers Suspended over 'Plot' Tape Stories*. (2014, Reuters, https://www.reuters.com/article/us-kuwait-media/kuwaiti-newspapers-suspended-over-plot-tape-stories-idUSBREA3J0H920140420).
678. Altamyeez: Tonawel Ba'ad Man Alsha'an Alsahafa Liqadeyat Alshereet Al'am Lemasasiha Bimasalih Hayawi. (Aljareeda, 2017, accessed Dec. 10, 2017 http://storage.googleapis.com/jarida-cdn/pdfs/1509993468372103200/1509993485000/file.pdf).

Chapter 6. State Security

411. In December 2013, rumors of a "conspiracy" for a coup against Kuwait's ruling structure surfaced on social media. Details of the conspiracy were shared through a Twitter account, alleging that in a secretly taped conversation former Speaker of Parliament Jassem Al-Kharafi and former Prime Minister Sheikh Nasser Al-Mohammad Al-Sabah were plotting the details of the coup. Rumors also claimed that the recordings, both audio and video, were in the possession of former energy minister Sheikh Ahmad Al-Fahad Al-Sabah who had been locked in bitter political rivalry with Sheikh Nasser. In response to the allegations he categorically denied, Kharafi filed a lawsuit and demanded that authorities obtained the tapes with the recordings from Sheikh Ahmad Al-Fahad.

412. The case was referred to the public prosecution for investigation. The public prosecutor had the man behind the Twitter account that first broke the story arrested. After interrogations and several days' detention, the man was released on bail. The prosecutor also summoned Sheikh Ahmad Al-Fahad as a witness. After his questioning, Sheikh Ahmad provided reporters with no details about the contents of the recordings except to say they concerned "local, parliamentary, (ruling) family, financial and regional issues." However, further information from the public prosecution's interrogation of Sheikh Ahmad was soon leaked to the press. Several Members of Parliament, especially opposition politicians, seized the opportunity provided by the leaks to call for an urgent, transparent investigation of the case and demanding answers from the current prime minister to a host of questions, including ones inquiring whether the recordings contained "a plot to overthrow the regime in Kuwait" and "any future arrangements for the future Amir," or "a plot to dissolve the National Assembly."[679]

413. The escalation of the situation prompted the public prosecutor to order the investigation into the tape recordings to be conducted in secret, issuing a media blackout according to which the press, the audio-visual media, the Internet, and electronic networks (social media) were banned from "broadcasting" any news about the ongoing investigation. The prosecutor said he would inform the media about the results of the investigation "immediately" after it was completed, but in the meantime he made this decision "for sake of preserving public interests"[680] and to benefit the investigation. The gag order could be issued based on the Press and Publication Law and the Audio-Visual Media Law that give the Public Prosecutor or the Director of Investigations the right to order a ban.

414. The press initially observed the ban. However, while the investigation was still in progress, the National Assembly held a debate about the case in a closed session, during which the prime minister told MPs that according to the report by experts who examined the tapes, the videotapes were "tampered with" and "do not represent genuine

679. Kuwait Times. *Conspiracy' video sends shockwaves in Kuwait—MPs, opposition demand full truth or PM's resignation."* (2014).

680. Kuwait News Agency. *Prosecutor orders investigation into tape case be secret* (2014, accessed May 17, 2017, https://www.kuna.net.kw/ArticleDetails.aspx?id=2371672&Language=en).

and reliable copies."[681] These developments were shared with the public in a statement issued by the speaker of the National Assembly after the closed session. In response, Sheikh Ahmad Al-Fahad also issued a statement, and two newspapers decided to run it. The two papers, *Al-Watan* and *Alam Al-Youm*, were suspended by the Ministry of Information for two weeks for violating the media blackout after a court order was issued on a request by the public prosecution for their temporary closure based on Article 15 of the 2006 Press and Publications Law. The suspensions were repeated two months later, this time for five days, for a repeat violation of the news blackout.[682]

415. A third newspaper, *Al-Jarida*, was also caught up in controversy after defying the gag order and publishing an article related to the videotapes. While the inquiry into the "conspiracy" videotapes was dropped by the public prosecutor in March 2015 due to a lack of evidence for criminal acts as the tape was ruled "bogus,"[683] and Sheikh Ahmad Al-Fahad ended up apologizing profusely in a statement he personally read out on Kuwait Television for his "recent prejudice, abuse and slander, intentional and unintentional" that was rooted in information the "competent judicial authorities affirmed were not valid or correct,"[684] the case against *Al-Jarida* took another two years to settle. In June 2017, the Court of Cassation ruled in favor of the newspaper, acquitting it from the charges of violating the public prosecutor's gag order.

The Court said the paper published political news related to an issue that was considered of public interest. The Court also explained that the press is the backbone of democratic freedom, and the case was covered with the intent of enlightening society by providing updated information regarding the issue in a timely manner. The case was a public interest case prior to the news coverage of it, as information had spread on social media. The Kuwaiti News Agency (KUNA) published a response from the Prime Minister regarding the videotape after a warning was already issued. *Al-Jarida* did not maliciously publish news about the case, but felt the need to do so since information was spreading through other means.[685]

681. Al-Jazeera *Kuwait says coup-plot clip 'tampered with'.* (2014, accessed May 17, 2017, http://www.aljazeera.com/news/middleeast/2014/04/kuwait-says-coup-plot-clip-tampered-with-201441516464646785.html).
682. *Kuwait orders temporary closure of newspapers over defiance of gag order.*" (2014, Middle East Eye, accessed at http://www.middleeasteye.net/news/kuwait-orders-temporary-closure-newspapers-over-defiance-gag-order-1223929265).
683. *Kuwait drops court case over 'plot' tape.* (Reuters, 2015).
684. *Shaikh Ahmad offers public apologies to Emir, foes.* (Gulf News, 2015, accessed at http://gulfnews.com/news/gulf/kuwait/shaikh-ahmad-offers-public-apologies-to-emir-foes-1.1480072).
685. Altamyeez: Tonawel Alsahafa Liqadeyat Alshereet Yaed Min Alshaan Al'am Lemasasiha Bimasalih Hayawi. (Aljareeda, 2017, accessed Dec. 10, 2017 http://storage.googleapis.com/jarida-cdn/pdfs/1509993468372103200/1509993485000/file.pdf).

Selected Bibliography

8 Sanawat Montho Raheel Ameer Alkhayr Walwafaa. (2014, January 15). *Alanbaa*. Retrieved from ttp://alanba.com.kw/437554

Abdullah, H. (2017, January 31). Alqimlas Liljareeda: 3143 Qadia Talaqatha Niyabat Alelam Alam Almadi Minhal 2865 Jarima Elektroniya Retrieved from http://www.mohamoon-kw.com/default.aspx?action=DisplayNews&type=2&id=37783&Year=20170131

Abdullah, H. (2017, February 21). Altamyeez: Alisa'a Lilameer Jareema Alniyah Fa'in Tawafaret Bi'ay Wasila Haq Iqab Martabha. *Aljarida*. Retrieved from http://www.aljarida.com/articles/1487605918156217900/

Abdullah, M. (2015). Mashroo Alelam Alelektroni. *Aljarida*. Retrieved from http://www.aljarida.com/articles/1468435509747917700/

Abu-Lughod, L. (1999). *Veiled Sentiments*. Berkeley: University of California Press.

Al-Awadi, H. (2017). Kuwait. In E. Lust (Ed.), *The Middle East*. Thousand Oaks, CA: CQ Press.

Al-Kandari, A., Melkote, S. R., & Sharif, A. (2016). Needs and Motives of Instagram Users that Predict Self-disclosure Use: A Case Study of Young Adults in Kuwait. *Journal of Creative Communications, 11*(2), 85–101.

Al-Kandari, A. A., Al-Sumait, F. Y., & Al-Hunaiyyan, A. (2017). Looking perfect: Instagram use in a Kuwaiti cultural context. *Journal of International and Intercultural Communication*, 1–18.

Al-Khuwaylidi, M. (2016, July 14). Kuwait: Appeal Court Refuses to Set Free "Fintas" Group. *Asharq Al Awsat* Retrieved from https://english.aawsat.com/m-alkhuawlidi/news-middle-east/kuwait-appeal-court-refuses-set-free-fintas-group

Al-Moqatei, M. (1989). Introducting Islamic Law in the Arab Gulf States: A Case Study of Kuwait. *Arab LQ, 4*, 138.

Al-Murshidi, A. (2016). مناقشة قانونية للمسؤولية الجنائية في جرائم الصحافة. *mohamah.net*. Retrieved from http://www.mohamah.net/law/مناقشة-قانونية-للمسؤولية-الجنائية-في

Al-Nakib, F. (2016). *Kuwait Transformed: A History of Oil and Urban Life*: Stanford University Press.

Al-Nakib, R. (2012). Human Rights, Education for Democratic Citizenship and International Organisations: Findings from a Kuwaiti UNESCO ASPnet School. *Cambridge Journal of Education, 42*(1), 97–112.

Al-Remaidhi, A., & Watt, B. (2012). Electoral Constituencies and Political Parties in Kuwait: An Assessment. *Election Law Journal, 11*(4), 518–528.

Al-Sabah, M. (2013). *Gender and Politics in Kuwait: Women and Political Participation in the Gulf* (Vol. 130): Ib tauris.

Al-Saoudi, A., & Taher, A. (2011). الديمقراطية الكويتية: التاريخ، الواقع، المستقبل. Cairo, Egypt: Al-Arabi Publishing and Distribution.

Al Nashmi, E., Cleary, J., Molleda, J.-C., & McAdams, M. (2010). Internet political discussions in the Arab world: A look at online forums from Kuwait, Saudi Arabia, Egypt and Jordan. *International Communication Gazette, 72*(8), 719–738.

Al Watan TV closed (2015, April 6). *Kuwait Times* Retrieved from http://news.kuwaittimes.net/al-watan-tv-closed/

Alabdullah, H. (2017, January 20). Alistinaf Toayed Habs Athaa Group Finas 5 Sanawat Libathhom Maqata'a Muse'a Lria'ees Alqadha. *Aljarida*. Retrieved from http://www.aljarida.com/articles/1484844738558911200/

Aladwani, A. M. (2015). Facilitators, characteristics, and impacts of Twitter use: Theoretical analysis and empirical illustration. *International Journal of Information Management, 35*(1), 15–25.

Albaidan, F. (2010). Derasa fe Akhlaqiyat Mihnat Alsahafa, May 9. *Alaan*. Retrieved from http://www.alaan.cc/pagedetails.asp?nid=52034&cid=92#.WRwxSoVOIhd

Albloshi, H., & Alfahad, F. (2009). The Orange Movement of Kuwait: civic pressure transforms a political system *Civilian Jihad* (pp. 219–232): Springer.

AldiwanAlamiri. (2017). The Initials in Kuwait History. Retrieved from http://www.da.gov.kw/eng/picsandevents/first_time_in_kuwaits_history.php

Alelam Alelectroni Muhalafat Wa Eyoob.. Walhikooma Tueed Alnathar Feh. (2015). *Aljarida*. Retrieved from http://www.aljarida.com/articles/1462436984316940600/

Alelam Alkuwaitiya: Qanun Alelam Alelekroni La Yashmal Alhisabat Alshakhsiya. Retrieved from http://www.kuna.net.kw/ArticleDetails.aspx?id=2579769&language=ar

Alelectrony, M. A. (2016, December 29). Hajat alhikomatayn alothmaniya walberitaniya wara insha'a albarq fe alkhaleej: 100 'am ala iftitah maktab altelegraph fe alkuwait. *Alqabas*. Retrieved from http://alqabas.com/339447/

Alhajri, T. (2014). Tortious liability of mass media for the invasion of personal rights: A comparative study between English law and Kuwaiti law. *International Review of Law*, 8.

Alihsa'at alsikaniya: taqderat alsikan fe montasaf al'am. (2013). Retrieved from https://www.csb.gov.kw/Socan_Statistic.aspx?ID=67

Alistinaf fe bara'at alkhamees: La yajooz muhakamat huriyat alrai. (2017, January 16). *Media Court*. Retrieved from http://mediacourt.net/3142

Selected Bibliography

Aljassem, S. (2016, June 24). *Alqabas*. Retrieved from https://alqabas.com/author/sheikhaal-jassem/

Almashiki, M. (2008). *The Media in the Arab Gulf.* State of Kuwait: Alfalah Publishing.

Almatar, F. (2015). Freedom of speech: A case of social media in Kuwait–Comparing the scope of freedom of expression in the Kuwaiti and the British Courts. *International Journal of Educational Research and Development, 4*(4).

Almukhtasoon Walqanuniyun Min Halaqat Niqash Elelam Alelektroni: Yuharem Alhuriyat Walshabab Bishaklah Alhali. (2015). *Alerada*. Retrieved from http://alerada.net/2015/04/27/26717

Alqabas Tansher Nas Qanun Almatbuat Walnashr Almotamad Min Alhikooma Altathalem fe Hal Rafth Altarkhees Khilal 60 Yawman Amam Alqadaa Aledara. (2005, December 12, 2005). *Alqabas*. Retrieved from http://alqabas.com/81373/

Alqaseer, J. (2013). *Political Advertising in Kuwait A Functional Discourse Analysis.* University of South Carolina.

Alrushaid, A. M. (2003, July 19). Mashroo Mithaq Sharaf Sahaji: Wajhat Nathar Kuwaitiyah. *Akwasat News*. Retrieved from http://www.alwasatnews.com/news/321297.html

Alrushaid Yadu Litafeel Alraqabah Althatiyah Wawadaa Mithaq Sharaf Sahafi. (2007, May 22). Retrieved from http://beta.www.skedaddle.co.uk/Articles.aspx?ArticleID=277536&CatID=102

Alrushaid Yuqadim Mashru Mithaq Sharaf Lilamilin fe Asahafah Alkuwaitiyah. (2003, June 9). Retrieved from http://www.kuna.net.kw/ArticlePrintPage.aspx?id=1352495&language=ar

AlSaudi, A., & Taher, A. (2011). الديمقراطية الكويتية: التاريخ - الواقع - المستقبل: Al- Arabi For Publishing.

Alshanoofi, M. (1999). *Tareekh Ale'elam Fi Alkuwait Wal Khaleej*. Kuwait: Department of Mass Communication

Altantheem Alqadhaey fe Nitaq Alqanun Alaam. (2012). Ministry of Justice.

Qanun Raqam 21 Lisanat 2015 Fe Shaan Riayat Altifil, (2015).

Amnesty International. (2012). Kuwaiti man sentenced to 10 years' imprisonment for "insulting" tweets. Retrieved from https://www.amnesty.org/en/latest/news/2012/06/kuwait-faces-prison-sentence-over-blasphemous-tweet/

Amnesty International. (2016). KUWAIT. Retrieved from https://www.amnesty.org/download/Documents/MDE1741452016ENGLISH.PDF

AmnestyInternational. (2015). The "Iron Fist" Policy: Criminalization of Peaceful Dissent in Kuwait

Asad, T. (2009). Free speech, blasphemy, and secular criticism. In T. Asad, W. Brown, J. Butler, & S. Mahmood (Eds.), *Is Critique Secular? Blasphemy, Injury, and Free Speech* (pp. 20–63). Berkeley: The Townsend Center for the Humanities, University of California.

Selected Bibliography

Asiri, A. P. S. i. K. (2007). *Alnitham Asiyasi Fel Kuwait* (9th ed.). Kuwait: Alwatan Press.

Association, K. J. About Us. Retrieved from http://www.kja-kw.com/show_page_en.aspx?pid=1

Aswad, E. M., Hussan, R., & Suleman, M. A. (2014). Why the United States Cannot Agree to Disagree on Blasphemy Laws. *BU Int'l LJ, 32*, 119.

Ayish, M. (2011). Radio Broadcasting in the Arab World. *N. Mellor, M. Aysih, N. Dajani, y K. Rinnawi, Arab Media. Globalization and Emerging Media Industries*, 67–84.

Ayish, M. (2011). Television Broadcasting in the Arab World: Political Democratization and Cultural Revivalism. In M. A. Noha Mellor, Nabil Dajani, Khalil Rinawi (Ed.), *Arab Media: Globalization and Emerging Media Industries* (pp. 85–102). Cambridge, UK: Polity Press.

Ayish, M., & Sakr, N. (2010). Dynamics of development in Arab broadcasting. *Middle East Journal of Culture and Communication, 3*(1), 3–7.

Ayish, M. I. (2010). Arab state broadcasting systems in transition the promise of the public service broadcasting model. *Middle East Journal of Culture and Communication, 3*(1), 9–25.

Barendt, E. (2007). *Freedom of speech*: Oxford University Press.

Barron, B. (2007). A Proposal to Rescue New York Times v. Sullivan by Promoting a Responsible Press. *American University Law Review, 57*(1), 73–127.

Beauty and the Beast pulled from cinemas in Kuwait. (2017). Retrieved from http://www.bbc.com/news/entertainment-arts-39337844

Becker, L. B., Vlad, T., & Nusser, N. (2007). An evaluation of press freedom indicators. *International Communication Gazette, 69*(1), 5–28.

Belmas, G., & Overbeck, W. (2014). *Major Principles of Media Law, 2015*: Cengage Learning.

". . . Bemoan a Wound" Kuwaiti Writers Convicted. (1999). Retrieved from http://www.aljadid.com/content/bemoan-wound-kuwaiti-writers-convicted-0

Biersdorfer, J. D. (2012). Q&A: The Difference between 4G and 4G LTE. *The New York Times*. Retrieved from https://gadgetwise.blogs.nytimes.com/2012/03/26/qa-the-need-for-speed/?_r=1

Blueprint for Free Speech. (2016). Kuwait: Whistleblowing protection, overview. Retrieved from https://blueprintforfreespeech.net/document/kuwait-overview#footnote012

Brown, N. (2007). Pushing toward Party Politics? Kuwait's Islamic Constitutional Movement. *Middle East Series*. Retrieved from http://carnegieendowment.org/files/cp79_brown_kuwait_final.pdf

Brown, N. J. (2002). *Constitutions in a nonconstitutional world: Arab basic laws and the prospects for accountable government*: Suny Press.

Selected Bibliography

Cagaptay, S. (2010). Muslims vs. Islamists Retrieved from http://www.washingtoninstitute.org/policy-analysis/view/muslims-vs.-islamists

CAIT. (2016). Consolidated Kuwait National ICT Indicators Report. Retrieved from https://www.e.gov.kw/sites/kgoarabic/Forms/FinalConsolidatedEnglishReportSinglePages.pdf

Cantwell v. Connecticut. (1940). *632*. Retrieved from https://supreme.justia.com/cases/federal/us/310/296/case.html

Case against gender segregation rejected—"Part of domestic workers law unconstitutional". (2015, December 17, 2015). *Arab Times*. Retrieved from http://www.arabtimesonline.com/news/case-against-gender-segregation-rejected-part-of-domestic-workers-law-unconstitutional/

Castellano, D. J. (2009). Common Law and Civil Jurisprudence. Retrieved from http://www.arcaneknowledge.org/histpoli/commoncivil.htm

Clooney, A., & Webb, P. (2016). The Right to Insult in International Law. *Colum. Hum. Rts. L. Rev., 48*, 1.

Cohen, A. (2014, March 9). "Today Is the 50th Anniversary of the (Re-)Birth of the First Amendment." *The Atlantic*. Retrieved from https://www.theatlantic.com/national/archive/2014/03/today-is-the-50th-anniversary-of-the-re-birth-of-the-first-amendment/284311/

The Constitution of the United States of America, Amendment 1 C.F.R. (1789).

Cougar: Mithaq Alsharaf Alelami Takbeel Lilhuriyat Watanaqudan Lildemoqratiyah. (2008, July 9). *Alrai*. Retrieved from http://s1.alraimedia.com/CMS/PDFs/2008/7/9/10600/P14.pdf

European Convention on Human Rights, (1950).

Crystal, J. (1995). *Oil and politics in the Gulf: Rulers and merchants in Kuwait and Qatar* (Vol. 24): Cambridge University Press.

Danderma. (2013). How effective is the Cinescape new movie rating? (Vol. 2017).

Dashti, A. A. (2008). *The Effect of Online Journalism on the Freedom of the Press: The Case of Kuwait*: University of Stirling

Dashti, A. A. (2009). The role of online journalism in political disputes in Kuwait. *Journal of Arab & Muslim Media Research, 2*(1–2), 91–112.

Dashti, A. A., Al-Abdullah, H. H., & Johar, H. A. (2015). Social media and the spiral of silence: the case of Kuwaiti female students' political discourse on Twitter. *Journal of International Women's Studies, 16*(3), 42.

Dashti, A. A., & Mesbah, H. (2016). The perceptions of female media professionals in Kuwait about their job: an empowerment perspective. *Feminist Media Studies, 16*(2), 276–292.

DawlatAlkuwait. (2017). Qanun Raqam 3 Lesanat 2006 Fe Shaan Almatboat Walnashr.

Declaration of the Rights of Man (1789). from Yale Law School http://avalon.law.yale.edu/18th_century/rightsof.asp

DemocracyReportingInternational&KuwaitTransparencySociety. (2008, November). Assessment of the Electoral Framework. Retrieved from http://democracy-reporting.org/newdri/wp-content/uploads/2016/02/dri_kuwait_report_08.pdf

DLAPiper. (2016a, October 5). Key telecommunications laws, regulations and policies. *Telecommunications Laws of the World.* Retrieved from https://www.dlapiperintelligence.com/telecoms/index.html?t=laws&c=KW

DLAPiper. (2016b, October 5). Overview of Legal Landscape. *Telecommunications Laws of the World.* Retrieved from https://www.dlapiperintelligence.com/telecoms/index.html?t=overview&c=KW

Doha Centre for Media Freedom. (2006). Law No (3) for the Year 2006 on Press and Publications: Kuwait. Retrieved from http://www.dc4mf.org/sites/default/files/press_law_kuwait.pdf

DohaCentreforMediaFreedom. (n.d.). Law No (3) for the Year 2006 on Press and Publications- Kuwait. Retrieved from http://www.dc4mf.org/sites/default/files/press_law_kuwait.pdf

Duffy, M. J. (2013). GCC Media Regulations Lead to Timid Press (Vol. 24/7/2017).

Duffy, M. J. (n.d.). Media laws and regulations of the GCC countries: Summary, analysis and recommendations. Retrieved from http://www.dc4mf.org/sites/default/files/gcc_media_law_en_0.pdf

Duffy, M. J., & Alkazemi, M. (2017). Arab Defamation Laws: A Comparative Analysis of Libel and Slander in the Middle East. *Communication Law and Policy, 22*(2), 189–211.

Ehrenfeld, R. (2009, June 9). The chill of libel tourism. *The Guardian* Retrieved from https://www.theguardian.com/commentisfree/libertycentral/2009/jun/09/libel-tourism-rogues-gallery

Eko, L. S. (2012). *New media, old regimes: case studies in comparative communication law and policy*: Lexington Books.

El-Hamoud, J. (2016, July 2). Court acquits Dr Nafisi of inciting "sectarian" sedition. *Arab Times*. Retrieved from http://www.arabtimesonline.com/wp-content/uploads/pdf/2016/jul/02/06.pdf

Elareshi, M., Ziani, A.-K., & Gunter, B. (2014). How GCC University Students Get Local News and Information. *Studies in Media and Communication, 2*(2), 1–12.

Ellerbeck, A. (2016, December 9). Security risk for sources as U.S. border agents stop and search journalists. Retrieved from https://cpj.org/blog/2016/12/security-risk-for-sources-as-us-border-agents-stop.php

Elster, J. (2000). *Ulysses unbound: Studies in rationality, precommitment, and constraints*: Cambridge University Press.

Selected Bibliography

Emerson, T. (1955). The Doctrine of Prior Restraint. *Faculty Scholarship Series*. Retrieved from http://digitalcommons.law.yale.edu/fss_papers/2804/

Emerson, T. (1963). Toward a General Theory of the First Amendment. *Faculty Scholarship Series, 2017*(May 17), 2796. Retrieved from http://digitalcommons.law.yale.edu/fss_papers/2796

Ex-MP Nafisi acquitted in "sedition" charges—"Royal" sued for abusing ruling family. (2015, December 24). *Arab Times*. Retrieved from http://www.arabtimesonline.com/news/ex-mp-nafi-si-acquitted-in-sedition-charges-royal-sued-for-abusing-ruling-family/

Expanded surveillance powers could threaten work of journalists in UK. (2917, May 5). Retrieved from https://cpj.org/2017/05/expanded-surveillance-powers-could-threaten-work-o.php

Fahmy, S., Wanta, W., & Nisbet, E. C. (2012). Mediated public diplomacy: Satellite TV news in the Arab world and perception effects. *International Communication Gazette, 74*(8), 728–749.

Failaka Island contender for UNESCO recognition. (2013, June 23). *Kuwait Times*. Retrieved from http://news.kuwaittimes.net/failaka-island-contender-for-unesco-recognition/

Fanton, J. F. (1999, October 12). Imprisoned Kuwaiti Scholar. Retrieved from https://www.hrw.org/news/1999/10/12/imprisoned-kuwaiti-scholar

Fixed Line Service. (2015). Retrieved from https://www.v4telecom.co.uk/fixed-line-service

Freedom House. (2016). Kuwait. Retrieved from https://freedomhouse.org/report/freedom-press/2016/kuwait

Freedom of the Press 2016 Methodology. (2016). Retrieved from https://freedomhouse.org/report/freedom-press-2016-methodology

Friendly, F. W. (2013). *Minnesota Rag*: Random House.

Front Line Defenders. (2016). Blasphemy charges dropped against Shaikha Binjasim. Retrieved from https://www.frontlinedefenders.org/en/case/case-history-shaikha-binjasim

Gelvanovska, N., Rogy, M., & Rossotto, C. M. (2014). Infrastructure Deployment and Developing Competition *Directions in Development-Information and Communication Technologies* (pp. 59–99).

Ghabra, S. (1991). Voluntary associations in Kuwait: the foundation of a new system? *Middle East Journal, 45*(2), 199–215.

Graham, M., Stephens, M., & Hale, S. (2013). Featured graphic. Mapping the geoweb: a geography of Twitter. *Environment and Planning A, 45*(1), 100–102.

Greenhouse, C. J. (1998). Legal pluralism and cultural difference: What is the difference? A response to Professor Woodman. *The Journal of Legal Pluralism and Unofficial Law, 30*(42), 61–72.

Hafez, K. (2002). Journalism ethics revisited: A comparison of ethics codes in Europe, North Africa, the Middle East, and Muslim Asia. *Political Communication, 19*(2), 225–250.

Hagagy, A., & Westall, S. (2014, April 20). Kuwaiti newspapers suspended over "plot" tape stories. *Reuters*. Retrieved from http://www.reuters.com/article/us-kuwait-media-idUSBREA3J0H920140420

Hamza, W. (2016, December 17). Abul: Awda'a alalameen fe almowasalat lan tataghayer. *Alqabas*. Retrieved from http://alqabas.com/334474/

Herb, M. (2002). Emirs and Parliaments in the Gulf. *Journal of Democracy, 13*(4), 41–47.

Herb, M. (2014). *The wages of oil: Parliaments and economic development in Kuwait and the UAE*: Cornell University Press.

Herb, M. (2016). The origins of Kuwait's national assembly. *London School of Economics and Political Science*.

Hicks, N. (2015). The Public Disorder of Blasphemy Laws: a Comparative Perspective. *The Review of Faith & International Affairs, 13*(1), 51–58.

The History of Ministry. (2017). Retrieved from http://moc.gov.kw/English/history.html

Human Rights Watch 2000 country report on Kuwait. Retrieved from https://www.hrw.org/reports/2000/kuwait/kuwait-06.htm

Innovating in the Digital Economy. (2016). *The Global Information Technology Report 2016*. Retrieved from http://www3.weforum.org/docs/GITR2016/GITR_2016_full%20report_final.pdf

International, A. (2000, March 27). Freedom of expression in Kuwait remains under threat. Retrieved from https://www.amnesty.org.uk/press-releases/freedom-expression-kuwait-remains-under-threat

International Labor Organization. (2014). Kuwait (311). *NATLEX: Database of national labour, social security and related human rights legislation*. Retrieved from http://www.ilo.org/dyn/natlex/natlex4.detail?p_lang=en&p_isn=99822&p_country=KWT&p_count=311

IREX. (2017). Media Sustainability Index 2017. Retrieved from https://www.irex.org/sites/default/files/pdf/media-sustainability-index-europe-eurasia-2017-full.pdf

Izzak, B. (2013, April 10). Media draft law under fire for stiff penalties. *Kuwait Times*. Retrieved from http://www.pressreader.com/kuwait/kuwait-times/20130411/281479273888485

Izzak, B. (2016). MP Fadhl demands holiday on Christmas, erect large ree on Safat Square; 200 Kuwaiti Christians living in Kuwait. Retrieved from http://news.kuwaittimes.net/website/mp-fadhl-demands-holiday-christmas-erect-large-tree-safat-square-200-kuwaiti-christians-living-kuwait

Johar, H. A. (2017). [Personal Interview].

Selected Bibliography

Joseph Burstyn, I. v. W. (1952). Retrieved from https://supreme.justia.com/cases/federal/us/343/495/case.html

Jurdi, N. A., & Dashti, A. A. (1994). Communication Policies in the State of Kuwait. *Annals of The Faculty of Arts, XIV*(96).

Kaposi, I. (2015). The culture and politics of Internet use among young people in Kuwait. *Cyberpsychology: Journal of Psychosocial Research on Cyberspace, 8*(3).

Kazan, F. (1994). Kuwait. In K. Yahya & H. Mowlana (Eds.), *Mass Media in the Middle East*. Connecticut: Greenwood Press.

Kearns, P. (2008). The end of blasphemy law. *Amicus Curiae, 2008*(76), 25–27.

Khedr, A. A. (2010, February 2010). Kuwait's Legal System and Legal Research. Retrieved from http://www.nyulawglobal.org/globalex/Kuwait.html

Kramer, M. (1980). The Ideals of an Islamic Order. *The Washington Quarterly, 3*(1), 3–13.

Kuwait. Retrieved from http://www.pressreference.com/Gu-Ku/Kuwait.html

Kuwait. (2014). *A project of the American Bar Association-Section of International Law.* Retrieved from http://www.impowr.org/country/Kuwait

Kuwait. (2016a). Retrieved from https://freedomhouse.org/report/freedom-press/2016/kuwait

Kuwait. (2016b). *ITU Development Index* Retrieved from http://www.itu.int/net4/ITU-D/idi/2016/#idi2016countrycard-tab&KWT

Kuwait. (2017). Retrieved from https://rsf.org/en/taxonomy/term/163

Kuwait's Constitution of 1962 Reinstated in 1992. (2017, March 28). *Comparative Constitutions Project.* Retrieved from https://www.constituteproject.org/constitution/Kuwait_1992.pdf?lang=en

Kuwait's new cybercrimes law restricts free expression and targets online activists. (2016). Retrieved from https://www.ifex.org/kuwait/2016/01/22/cybercrimes_law/

Kuwait: Electronic Crimes law threatens to further stifle freedom of expression. (2016, January 21). Retrieved from https://www.amnesty.org/en/latest/news/2016/01/kuwait-electronic-crimes-law-threatens-to-further-stifle-freedom-of-expression/

Kuwait: Jail, Exile for Insulting Emir. (2014, January 26). Retrieved from https://www.hrw.org/news/2014/01/26/kuwait-jail-exile-insulting-emir

Kuwait: Teacher Faces Jail over Twitter Comments. (2013, July 20). Retrieved from https://www.hrw.org/news/2013/07/20/kuwait-teacher-faces-jail-over-twitter-comments

Kuwaiti court upholds government shutdown of Al-Watan newspaper. (2015). Committee to Protect Journalists. New York. Retrieved from https://cpj.org/2015/02/kuwaiti-court-upholds-government-shutdown-of-al-wa.php

Kuwaiti women win right to obtain passport without husband's approval (2009, October 22). *The Telegraph*. Retrieved from http://www.telegraph.co.uk/news/worldnews/middleeast/kuwait/6402047/Kuwaiti-women-win-right-to-obtain-passport-without-husbands-approval.html

Law No. 8 of 2016 Regarding the Regulation of Electronic Media. (2016, February 14). *The Kuwait Times*. Retrieved from http://news.kuwaittimes.net/website/law-no-8-of-2016-regarding-the-regulation-of-electronic-media/

LeVine, M. (2008). *Heavy metal Islam: rock, resistance, and the struggle for the soul of Islam*: Crown.

Levy, L. W. (1995). *Blasphemy: Verbal offense against the sacred, from Moses to Salman Rushdie*: UNC Press Books.

Lipset, S. M. (1996). *American Exceptionalism: A Double-Edged Sword*. New York: Norton.

Locksley, G. (2009). *The media and development: what's the story?*: World Bank.

Maer, L. (2008). The Abolition of the Blasphemy Offences. *Standard Note SN/PC/04597*. Retrieved from http://researchbriefings.parliament.uk/ResearchBriefing/Summary/SN04597

Mallat, C. (2007). *Introduction to Middle Eastern Law*: Oxford University Press on Demand.

Mansell, R., Ang, P. H., Steinfield, C., Ballon, P., Graaf, S. v. d., & Grimshaw, D. J. (2015). *The International Encyclopedia of Digital Communication and Society* (Vol. 1). West Sussex, UK: John Wiley & Sons.

Mark. (2015, May 15). A new kind of cinema censorship. Retrieved from http://248am.com/mark/movies/a-new-kind-of-cinema-censorship/

Mark. (2017). Disney Pulled Beauty and the Beast from Kuwait Cinema *UPDATED*. Retrieved from http://248am.com/mark/movies/disney-pulled-beauty-and-the-beast-from-kuwait-cinema/

McPhail, T. L. (2010). *Global communication: Theories, stakeholders, and trends*: John Wiley & Sons.

Middle East. (2016). Retrieved from http://www.internetworldstats.com/middle.htm

Middle East and North Africa. (2017). Retrieved from https://cpj.org/mideast/

Ministry of Communications. (2017). Law Organizing Postal Works

MoC Kuwait's fixed infrastructure to be privatised. (2016). Retrieved from https://www.telegeography.com/products/commsupdate/articles/2016/03/22/moc-kuwaits-fixed-infrastructure-to-be-privatised/

Monteith, S., Glenn, T., & Bauer, M. (2013). Searching the internet for health information about bipolar disorder: some cautionary issues. *International journal of bipolar disorders, 1*(1), 22.

Selected Bibliography

Moore, R. L., & Murray, M. D. (2012). *Media law and ethics* (4th ed ed.). New York: Routledge.

Mostyn, T. (2002). *Censorship in Islamic societies*: Saqi Books.

Mourtada, R., & Salem, F. (2012). Social media in the Arab world: influencing societal and cultural change. *Arab social media report, 2*(1), 1–28.

Mourtada, R., Salem, F., Al-Dabbagh, M., & Gargani, G. (2011). The role of social media in Arab Women's empowerment. *Dubai, Dubai School of Government, 1*, 26.

Müller, Q., & Castelier, S. (2017). Made in Kuwait: Surviving censorship in the filmmaking industry. Retrieved from http://www.middleeasteye.net/in-depth/features/censorship-kuwait-764920799

NationalAssembly. (2015a). Dirasat Wabihooth: Tajreem Alentikhabat Alfariyah. Retrieved from http://www.kna.kw/clt-html5/run.asp?id=1183

NationalAssembly. (2015b). Distour Dawlat Alkuwait: Almothakara Altafseriyah. Retrieved from http://www.kna.kw/clt-html5/run.asp?id=51#

Neal, R. W. (2014). Underwater Internet Cables: "Submarine Cable Map" Shows How The World Gets Online. *International Business Times*. Retrieved from http://www.ibtimes.com/underwater-internet-cables-submarine-cable-map-shows-how-world-gets-online-1559604

New Cyber Crimes Law restricts free expression and targets online activists. (2016, March 8, 2016). Retrieved from https://rsf.org/en/news/new-cyber-crimes-law-restricts-free-expression-and-targets-online-activists

Nod to Electronic Media Law-Shias Boycott. (2016, January 13). *Arab Times*. Retrieved from http://www.arabtimesonline.com/news/nod-to-electronic-media-law-shias-boycott/

Noose left at U.S. newspaper's office door. (2017, April 28). Retrieved from https://cpj.org/2017/04/noose-left-at-us-newspapers-office-door.php

Odine, M. (2011). Middle East media: Press freedom in Kuwait. *Journal of Advanced Social Research, 1*, 177–190.

Olimat, M. S. (2013). Women and the Kuwaiti National Assembly. *Journal of International Women's Studies, 12*(3), 76–95.

Onyebadi, U., & Alajmi, F. (2016). Gift solicitation and acceptance in journalism practice: An assessment of Kuwaiti journalists' perspective. *Journalism, 17*(3), 348–365.

Ostroff, D. (2010). Engines of Content Diversity: A Brief Chronicle of Communication Satellite Policies. In S. Van Bauwel & E. Van Damme (Eds.), *Diverse mediawerelden: hedendaagse reflecties gebaseerd op het onderzoek van Frieda Saeys* (pp. 161–175): Academia Press.

Ottaway, M. (2011, April 4, 2011). Bahrain: Between the United States and Saudi Arabia. Retrieved from http://carnegieendowment.org/2011/04/04/bahrain-between-united-states-and-saudi-arabia-pub-43416.

Peristiany, J. G. (1965). *Honour and Shame: The Values of Mediterranean Society*. London: Weidenfeld and Nicolson.

Pintak, L., & Ginges, J. (2012). Arab journalists. In D. H. Weaver & L. Willnat (Eds.), *The global journalist in the 21st century* (pp. 429–442). New York: Routledge.

PR, D. (2016, August 24). GatesAir Completes Phase Two Rollout of DVB-T2 Digital TV Network in Kuwait. Retrieved from http://www.tvtechnology.com/thewire/gatesair-completes-phase-two-rollout-of-dvbt2-digital-tv-network-in-kuwait/6784/view.

Qutb, S. (2000). Social Justice in Islam, trans. John B. Hardie and Hamid Algar, rev. ed: Islamic Publications International.

Raghavan, S. (2017). Disney's hit 'Beauty and the Beast' is banned in Kuwait for its "gay moment". *The Washington Post*. Retrieved from https://www.washingtonpost.com/news/worldviews/wp/2017/03/22/disneys-hit-beauty-and-the-beast-is-banned-in-kuwait-for-its-gay-moment/?utm_term=.a49a85735b1f.

RefWorld. (2016). Kuwait: Sarah Al-Drees Trial Observation Report. Retrieved from http://www.refworld.org/docid/584e806d4.html.

Restrictions on Freedom of Expression. Retrieved from https://www.hrw.org/reports/2000/kuwait/kuwait-06.htm.

Robson, R. (2016). *First Amendment: Cases, Controversies, and Contexts.*: CALI eLangdell Press.

Rosenfeld, M., & Sajó, A. (2012). *The Oxford handbook of comparative constitutional law*: Oxford University Press.

'Royal' released on bail. (2015, December 30). *Arab Times*. Retrieved from http://www.arabtimesonline.com/news/royal-released-on-bail/.

Rugh, W. A. (2004). *Arab mass media: Newspapers, radio, and television in Arab politics*: Greenwood publishing group.

Sadek, D. A., Crystal, J. A., Anthony, J. D., & Ochsenwald, W. L. (2016). Kuwait *Encyclopædia Britannica*: Encyclopædia Britannica, inc.

Sakr, N. (2003). Dynamics of GCC Press-government Relations in the 1990s, s. 102–119 i Najem, Tom Pierre; Hetherington, Martin (red) Good Governance in the Middle East Oil Monarchies: London: Routledge Curzon.

Sakr, N. (2006). Media Policy as a Litmus Test of Political Change in the GCC1. *"Constitutional Reform and Political Participation in the Gulf" first*, 132.

Sakr, N. (2017). Provision, protection or participation? Approaches to regulating children's television in Arab countries. *Media International Australia, 163*(1), 31–41.

Salih, K. O. (1991). Kuwait: Political consequences of modernization, 1750–1986. *Middle Eastern Studies, 27*(1), 46–66.

Selvik, K. (2011). Elite rivalry in a semi-democracy: The Kuwaiti Press scene. *Middle Eastern Studies, 47*(3), 477–496.

Selvik, K., Nordenson, J., & Kebede, T. A. (2015). Print Media Liberalization and Electoral Coverage Bias in Kuwait. *The Middle East Journal, 69*(2), 255–276.

Shaikh, T. (2016, July 23, 2016). Kuwait swelters in 54C heat—what could be the highest temperature ever recorded on earth. *The Independent*. Retrieved from http://www.independent.co.uk/news/world/middle-east/kuwait-swelters-record-breaking-54c-heatwave-weather-7152911.html.

Sharif, A. A., & Al-Kandari, A. A. (2010). The use of online bulletin boards by females in the Gulf Cooperation Council Countries. *Telematics and Informatics, 27*(1), 42–50.

Shilad, J. (2017, June 8). Amid Gulf tensions, press is used as a political pawn. Retrieved from https://cpj.org/blog/2017/06/amid-gulf-tensions-press-is-used-as-a-political-pa.php.

Shuddup. (2003, March 13). Retrieved from http://www.economist.com/node/1632864

Siems, M. M. (2007). Legal origins: reconciling law & finance and comparative law. *McGill Law Journal, 52*(1).

Smith, M. (2012). Kuwait Internet firm blasts price cuts, infrastructure. Retrieved from http://www.reuters.com/article/net-us-kuwait-internet-idUSBRE88Q11U20120927.

Spratt, C. (2006). British Blockage. *The News Media & the Law, 30*(4), 26.

StateDepartment. (2013). Kuwait. *2012 Report on International Religious Freedom*. Retrieved from http://www.state.gov/j/drl/rls/irf/religiousfreedom/index.htm?year=2012&dlid=208398.

Qanun Raqam 16 Lianat 1960 Bi Isdar Qanun Aljazaa, 16 C.F.R. (1960).

StateOfKuwait. (1962, November 11). Aldistour Alkuwaiti. Retrieved from http://www.kna.kw/clt-html5/run.asp?id=2024

Qanun Raqam 15 Lisanat 1995 Fe Shaan Mokafahat Altadkheen, 15 C.F.R. (1995).

Qanun Raqam 10 Lisanat 2007 Fe Shaan Himayat Almonafasa, 10 C.F.R. (2007a).

Qanun Raqam 62 Lisanat 2007 Fe Shaan Qama' Alqash Fe Almoamalat Altejariyah, 62 C.F.R. (2007b).

Law 10 (2011).

Qarar Wizaree Raqam 134 Lisanat 2014, 134 C.F.R. (2014).

Qarar Wizaree Raqam 361 Le'am 2015 Ministerial Decree 361 C.F.R. (2015).

Law No. 8 (2016).

Marsoom raqam 5 l'sanat 2017 fee sha'an ikhtisas wazir aldawlah l'sho'on alkhidmat, 5 C.F.R. (2017a).

StateofKuwait. (2017b). Radio Live Broadcast. Retrieved from http://www.media.gov.kw/LiveRadio1.aspx.

Staveley-O'Carroll, S. (2009). Libel Tourism Laws: Spoiling the Holiday and Saving the First Amendment? *New York University Journal of Law & Liberty, 4*, 252–292.

Straumann, R. (2015). Changing Internet Access. *Investigating the Changing Connectivities and Potentials of Sub-Saharan Africa's Knowledge Economy.* Retrieved from http://geonet.oii.ox.ac.uk/blog/changing-internet-access/.

Sunstein, C. (2014, March 25). The Dark Side of New York Times v. Sullivan. Retrieved from https://www.bloomberg.com/view/articles/2014-03-25/the-dark-side-of-new-york-times-v-sullivan.

Szymanski, D. M., Gupta, A., Carr, E. R., & Stewart, D. (2009). Internalized misogyny as a moderator of the link between sexist events and women's psychological distress. *Sex Roles, 61*(1–2), 101–109.

Tamanaha, B. Z. (2008). Understanding legal pluralism: past to present, local to global. *Sydney L. Rev., 30*, 375.

Tamanha, B. Z. (2000). A Non□Essentialist Version of Legal Pluralism. *Journal of Law and Society, 27*(2), 296–321.

Taqi, A. (2005, March 27). Kuwaiti academic quits writing after court verdict. *Gulf News*. Retrieved from http://gulfnews.com/news/gulf/kuwait/kuwaiti-academic-quits-writing-after-court-verdict-1.282286.

Taqi, T. (2017). Advertising and Promotion in the State of Kuwait. Retrieved from http://www.hg.org/article.asp?id=32357.

Taqrir Alkuwait Liltanafisiya 2014–2015. Retrieved from http://www.kuwaitncc.org/reports/KNCC201415.pdf.

Tétreault, M.A. (2000). *Stories of democracy: Politics and society in contemporary Kuwait*: Columbia University Press.

The Middle East Media Research Institute. (2016). Kuwaiti professor of philosophy Sheikha Al-Jassem: People who believe that the Quran is above the constitution are betraying Kuwait. Retrieved from https://www.memri.org/tv/kuwaiti-professor-philosophy-sheikha-al-jassem-people-who-believe-quran-above-constitution-are/transcript.

Thuroczy, F. A. (2010). Kuwait: Democratization in Process: Five factors of democratization and their state in Kuwait. Bachelor Thesis: Lund University. Retrieved from https://lup.lub.lu.se/luur/download?func=downloadFile&recordOId=1627007&fileOId=1627008?.

Tosone, C. (2009). Sotto Voce: Internalized misogyny and the politics of gender in corporate America. *Psychoanalytic Social Work, 16*(1), 1–11.

Toumi, H. (2013, June 3, 2013). Kuwaiti MPs push for reinstating co-education. *Gulf News*. Retrieved from http://gulfnews.com/news/gulf/kuwait/kuwaiti-mps-push-for-reinstating-co-education-1.1191933.

Tunisia. (2017). Retrieved from https://freedomhouse.org/report/freedom-press/2012/tunisia.

UNESCO. (2009). Kuwait. *World Anti Piracy Observatory.* Retrieved from http://www.unesco.org/culture/pdf/kuwait_cp_en.

United Nations. (1948). Universal Declaration of Human Rights Retrieved from http://www.ohchr.org/EN/UDHR/Documents/UDHR_Translations/eng.pdf.

United Nations. (2015, November 18). Opinions adopted by the Working Group on Arbitrary Detention at its seventy-third session, 31 August—4 September 2015. Retrieved from https://documents-dds-ny.un.org/doc/UNDOC/GEN/G15/263/87/PDF/G1526387.pdf?OpenElement

Valenti, P.C., & Slot, B. (2007). Mubarak al-Sabah: Founder of Modern Kuwait, 1896–1915: JSTOR.

van der Krogt, C.J. (2014). Why Is Freedom of Speech a Problem for So Many Muslims? In E. Kolig (Ed.), *Freedom of Speech and Islam* (pp. 22–43). Farnham: Ashgate.

Visconsi, E. (2008). The Invention of Criminal Blasphemy: Rex v. Taylor (1676). *Representations, 103*(1), 30–52.

Wahid, T. (2013, July 8). Haythiyat Walmantooq Hokm Sara Al-Drees Bitohmat Almasas Bithat Alamiriyah Fe Mawqi' Twitter. Retrieved from http://alziadiq8.com/33260.html

Wehrey, F. M. (2014). *Sectarian politics in the Gulf: from the Iraq war to the Arab uprisings*: Columbia University Press.

Werhan, K. (2004). *Freedom of speech: a reference guide to the United States Constitution.* Westport: Praeger.

Wheeler, D. (2000). New media, globalization and Kuwaiti national identity. *The Middle East Journal*, 54. 432–444.

Wheeler, D. L. (2006). *The Internet in the Middle East: Global expectations and local imaginations in Kuwait*: SUNY Press.

Whitehouse v. Lemon. (1979). Whitehouse -v- Lemon; Whitehouse -v- Gay News Ltd On Appeal From Regina -v- Lemon. Retrieved from http://www.swarb.co.uk/c/hl/1979Whitehouse-GayNews.html.

Wittern-Keller, L., & Haberski, R. J. (2008). *The Miracle case: film censorship and the Supreme Court*: Univ Pr of Kansas.

WorldFactbook. Legal Systems. Retrieved from https://www.cia.gov/library/publications/the-world-factbook/fields/2100.html#ku.

WorldFactbook. (2017, May 9). Kuwait. Retrieved from https://www.cia.gov/library/publications/the-world-factbook/geos/ku.html

WorldRadioMaps. (2017). Radio Stations in Kuwait City. Retrieved from http://worldradiomap.com/kw/kuwait.

Yetiv, S. (2002). Kuwait's democratic experiment in its broader international context. *The Middle East Journal*, 56. 257–271.

Index

The numbers here refer to paragraph numbers.

Index

Made in the USA
Monee, IL
18 October 2026

66041380R10103